AF844911

Social Class and the Helping Professions

Social Class and the Helping Professions

A Clinician's Guide to Navigating the Landscape of Class in America

Debbie C. Sturm
Donna M. Gibson
EDITORS

Routledge
Taylor & Francis Group
NEW YORK AND LONDON

Routledge
Taylor & Francis Group
711 Third Avenue
New York, NY 10017

Routledge
Taylor & Francis Group
2 Park Square, Milton Park,
Abingdon, Oxon OX14 4RN

First issued in paperback 2017

© 2012 by Taylor & Francis Group, LLC
Routledge is an imprint of the Taylor & Francis Group, an informa business

ISBN 13: 978-1-138-11057-1 (pbk)
ISBN 13: 978-0-415-89365-7 (hbk)

For permission to photocopy or use material electronically from this work, please access www.copyright.com (http://www.copyright.com/) or contact the Copyright Clearance Center, Inc. (CCC), 222 Rosewood Drive, Danvers, MA 01923, 978-750-8400. CCC is a not-for-profit organization that provides licenses and registration for a variety of users. For organizations that have been granted a photocopy license by the CCC, a separate system of payment has been arranged.

Trademark Notice: Product or corporate names may be trademarks or registered trademarks, and are used only for identification and explanation without intent to infringe.

Visit the Taylor & Francis Web site at
http://www.taylorandfrancis.com

and the Routledge Web site at
http://www.routledgementalhealth.com

Contents

Preface

Estimates from the 2008 Annual Social and Economic Supplement (ASEC, 2008) produced by the U.S. Census Bureau show 39.8 million people were living in poverty, up from 37.3 million one year earlier, and just prior to the recent economic collapse in our country. Millions more Americans continue to live just above the poverty line, a vulnerable position where a minor inconvenience to most—a car repair, brief illness, child care disruption—can threaten their ability to stay employed, to keep the power on, or to eat. Statistics reveal that at some point in their lives, most Americans will have experienced at least minimum situational poverty (i.e., job loss or temporary financial hardship) or, for a lower but significant number, chronic poverty spanning years or generations. According to Rank and Hirschl (1999), nearly one-third of the American population will spend one year living below the poverty line by the age of 35. More than half of Americans will spend a year below the poverty line by the age of 65. And by the time they reach age 85, two-thirds of Americans will have experienced poverty. People of color face an even greater risk.

For those who are interested in understanding experiences of social class personally or professionally, the literature offers a significantly larger emphasis on poverty than on other aspects of social class. And while large numbers of people experience at least periods of poverty during their lifetime, it is important to remember that every person experiences social class and nearly half experience fluctuations in social class at some point in their lives. Few studies have addressed the role of individuals' experiences of social class; however, those studies that do exist suggest that early social class experiences may be as significant as more obvious, or visible, demographic factors, such as race and gender (Hunt, 1996; Lane, 1962; M. Lewis, 1978; Liu, Ali, et al., 2004; Liu, Soleck, Hopps, Dunston, & Pickett, 2004; Nelson, Englar-Carson, Tierney, & Hau, 2006; Stacey & Singer, 1985). Essentially, we know that experiences of social class impact multiple aspects of the individual's view of self and the world. As counselors and other helping practitioners, examining experiences of social class is a pathway to better understanding our clients' lived experiences.

The intent of this book is to provide a comprehensive look at the intersection of social class and the helping professions from not only a sociological perspective, but also a practical clinical perspective. Each chapter includes case studies and reflections that offer readers opportunities to apply the specific content of the chapter through a lens of their own values and experiences. Helping professionals can utilize these as they challenge themselves in their own personal growth and development. Additionally, educators and trainers will find these exercises helpful in classrooms, workshops, and supervision sessions in order for their students and supervisees to develop an awareness of social class issues in their practices. It is our hope that each reader will walk away from this experience with a clearer understanding of social class as it relates to self, as well as the tools and confidence to open a meaningful conversation with your clients.

We begin this book with an introduction to the global, historical, and sociological aspects of class as well as an in-depth look at urban and rural poverty, the middle class, and upper class and economic privilege. Section I not only provides an examination of the social constructs, but also creates an opportunity for readers to examine their own experience with social class and engage in the self-examination that is necessary as therapists prior to working with diverse groups. Chapter 1 includes an introduction to the concepts of social class and classism from an international or global perspective and a brief historical overview of the evolution and influence of class structures. As the chapter progresses, the focus becomes more defined to social class and classism as it is perceived in the United States, with a rationale given for this narrower focus to be explored in the following chapters.

In Chapter 2, the overarching concept of social class in the United States is discussed and readers are invited to look at the multiple ways in which social class is defined in our culture, as well as how it defines our culture. Through narratives, self-reflection exercises, and opportunities for additional learning, the role of social class in the American culture is examined and used as a foundation for the following three chapters. Chapters 3 through 5 look specifically at poverty, both urban and rural, middle-class America, and wealth and economic privilege. Through a similar use of narratives and self-reflection exercises, it is our hope that readers will take a personal walk through each of these chapters and give thought to their own story as well as the stories and experiences of our clients.

In Section II, our focus shifts from the sociological constructs and personal examination to a closer examination of the experiences of our clients. Chapter 6 examines the intersection of class and race and not only allows the reader to debate this internally, but also provides tools to open this discussion with one's clients. In addition to race and class comes the notion of opportunity and the American dream. The American dream, a belief deeply embedded in American culture, promotes the idea that hard work and educational commitment will result in success and higher class status (Bullock & Limbert, 2003). And although the American dream serves as an inspiration for many, others argue it simplifies issues of opportunity, social class, and equality, reducing the complexities to a matter of hard work or desire, and may inhibit clients of lower socioeconomic status. In addition, individuals in the helping profession who hold strong beliefs about the American dream may harbor negative attitudes and attributions about the cause, blame, and responsibility toward those who fail to achieve middle- or upper-class definitions of success. In Chapter 7, the role of class and opportunity as they relate to clients' views of career, success, and opportunity is examined, and tools are provided through which helpers can empower their clients and value their pursuit of their own dream.

The remaining three chapters in Section II examine the role social class plays in mental health and mental health counseling, in the family structure and in counseling families, and in the experiences people have throughout the educational process and in the schools. Chapter 8 not only examines the role of social class on mental health and well-being, but also looks closely at how counselors can address those issues when working with clients in various settings and from diverse socioeconomic backgrounds. In addition to the individual's experience with social class and well-being, we will examine the experience of families and their relationship with social class. Family health and well-being are influenced by countless factors, among them the economic stability or employment status within the family, housing, security, the type of neighborhood, the interaction with those nearby, and available resources. Chapter 9 assists the reader in walking with families as they examine the impact of past and present social class experiences as well as visions or hopes as they move forward. Finally, Chapter 10 invites the reader into our schools. Since the mid-1990s, one of the most significant names associated with poverty, social class, and schools is Dr. Ruby K. Payne. For many in the helping professions, the work of Ruby Payne is seen as just the beginning of the examination, discourse, and action we need to take. In this chapter, the complex interplay of social class, education, achievement, empowerment of children and families, and advocacy/action come together. In the mix of this complex interplay emerge discussion tools, reflection exercises, and a foundation for better assisting children and families within the framework of our school systems.

We organized this book into three sections with a progression in mind. While Section I examines the sociological aspects of class and provides the reader a personal opportunity to examine self in relation to experiences and beliefs about social class, Section II invites the reader into the world of the client in some more specific ways. As we transition into Section III, our goal is to provide specific techniques or models to use within your own clinical practice. We begin with how to assess clients' experiences of class and classism and how those experiences have shaped their current worldview and view of self. We also talk about the ways in which experiences of social class are internalized at various points across the life span. For example, early experiences of poverty or socioeconomic differences influence the development of beliefs about self, about family, about justice and fairness, and about opportunity and means, essentially forming a worldview that influences people throughout their lives. How these views are internalized, how they can be challenged to create healthier alternatives for our clients, and specific interventions related to social justice and advocacy are the specific approach to Chapter 11.

In Chapter 12, a model for working with people in poverty is presented. The CARE model focuses on examining personal strengths and resources, connecting people to the things that provide an avenue for empowerment, and a unique approach for helpers to assess progress and remain focused on strength and resiliency. Chapter 13 provides practitioners with an important discussion on the role of social class in our assessment, diagnosis, and treatment process, as well as case studies and tools for assisting with fair and accurate progression through each of these processes. The manifestation of social class, be it through difficulty accessing resources, inconsistency with treatment, or through access to top-of-the-line and abundant resources, undoubtedly impacts all aspects of diagnosis, assessment, and treatment planning. Finally, while the American Counseling Association's ethical guidelines clearly invite counselors into the realms of advocacy as a professional imperative, we discovered that our own journey exploring the effects of social class personally as well as the multitude of layers experienced by our clients elicited an internal call to some type of action. Social class means something unique to every single person and defines your place in this world in a personally significant way. Chapter 14 is the outcome of wrestling with the question.

So now what do we do? This encompasses not only an examination of social class through the lens of social justice and advocacy models, but also the wonderings that emerged among all our writers through this process.

One last wondering we had while envisioning this book was the experience you, our readers, will have as you explore the many aspects of social class in your own life and in the stories of your clients. In order to begin that process, we asked each of our contributing writers to journal their experience during this process. We offer an epilogue as a means not only to share some summaries and conclusions, but also to bring together the experiences of those who walked through this experience so that you can follow in their footsteps.

About the Editors

Debbie C. Sturm, PhD, is an assistant professor in the Department of Graduate Psychology at James Madison University. She is a licensed professional counselor in the state of South Carolina and has been practicing since 2004. Her primary research interests directly parallel her clinical experiences, which focus on trauma, poverty and community violence, immersion or volunteer experiences of counselor trainees with diverse populations, and mindfulness-based approaches to improving mental health and well-being. Sturm has experience working with children and families impacted by violence and children in the foster care system.

Donna M. Gibson, PhD, is an associate professor of counselor education at the University of South Carolina. She has practiced as a psychologist in public schools, mental health agencies, hospitals, and private practice; she is currently practicing as a licensed professional counselor/intern in South Carolina. Her primary research interests focus on leadership and professional identity development in professional counselors and counselors-in-training. Gibson's own identity is a result of extended family issues related to social class and classism.

About the Contributors

Lyndon Abrams, PhD, is an associate professor in the Department of Counseling in the College of Education at the University of North Carolina at Charlotte. Abrams earned a BS in criminal justice from Charleston Southern University, a master's of education in counseling and guidance from Clemson University, and a PhD in counselor education from Texas A&M University–Commerce. Currently, Abrams teaches counseling theory, multicultural counseling, and supervises counseling students in their clinical training. He has formerly worked in a university counseling center and as a unit coordinator and counselor with emotionally and behaviorally challenged adolescents. His research interests include racial identity development, social desirability responding, and efforts to increase the participation of underrepresented groups in STEM career fields.

Kathy Biles, PhD, is the school counselor program coordinator at Oregon State University–Cascades. Biles earned a BS in psychology from Charleston Southern University and her MS degree in counseling is from Oregon State University, Corvallis. While working as a school counselor, Biles earned her PhD in counseling, with an emphasis in counselor education, from Oregon State University. Biles' research interests include addictions and adolescent substance abuse, school counselor leadership, student motivation and academic achievement, and social justice and advocacy. She has worked as an addictions counselor while serving in the Navy, as a counselor for an Upward Bound program, and as a middle school and high school counselor. She has presented workshops on student motivation and academic achievement at national and state conferences. One of Biles' favorite subjects to teach is social and cultural perspectives. Her passion is to develop her graduate students' awareness and knowledge of social justice and the skills to advocate on different levels. Her own advocacy has been at the local, state, and national levels, including meeting with state congressional leaders in Washington, DC.

Wanda Briggs, PhD, completed her doctoral study at the University of North Carolina at Charlotte and is currently an assistant professor and counseling and development program coordinator at Winthrop University. Her primary teaching responsibilities include counseling theories, psychopathology and diagnosis courses, as well as practicums and internships in clinical mental health and school counseling. Her clinical and research interests include counselor preparation and supervision, promotion of empathy development in counselor trainees, community mental health, and issues of diversity in counseling. She has worked as a counselor in private practice with adult women, adolescents, and children.

Peggy L. Ceballos, PhD, is an assistant professor at the University of North Carolina at Charlotte. She graduated from the University of North Texas with a specialization in play therapy. Ceballos has worked in elementary schools and as a mental health professional in community settings in New Orleans. Most of her clinical experience has been with at-risk minority children, including preadolescents and adolescents. Ceballos has presented at the state, national, and international levels regarding play therapy and expressive arts.

Colette T. Dollarhide, EdD, is a licensed professional counselor and counselor educator (senior lecturer) at The Ohio State University. As a practitioner, she has experience as a career counselor and university administrator as well as a school counselor and consultant, which has given her a unique perspective on the ways that class issues influence career counseling. At Ohio State, she teaches career counseling, multicultural counseling, and school counseling; she has published numerous articles and two textbooks, and is currently the editor of a national journal.

William Evans, PhD, is a professor of counselor education at Westminster College. He has conducted research ranging from an exploration of local child and adolescent assessment practices and training with internationally recognized therapists to examining faculty, student, and institutional characteristics related to national accreditation decisions made by counselor education programs. Evans, who is the coordinator of the school counseling program in Westminster's graduate program, joined the Westminster faculty in 2001. He earned an undergraduate degree from the Pennsylvania State University, a master's from Youngstown State University, and his PhD from Kent State University. Evans is a licensed professional counselor and a nationally certified counselor.

Louisa L. Foss, PhD, is an assistant professor and program coordinator of the clinical mental health counseling program at Southern Connecticut State University in New Haven. Foss received her PhD in counselor education and supervision from Kent State University. She is a nationally certified counselor and has been a licensed professional counselor since 1999. Foss has worked with people living in poverty throughout her counseling career. She was employed as a counselor in a maximum security facility for adolescent males, an outpatient partner violence treatment program, an urban child guidance clinic, and a community mental health agency for both adults and children. In her current position, Foss maintains a strong commitment to advocating for the needs of people living in poverty and has provided numerous lectures and presentations on her approach to counseling this unique population.

Susan Furr, PhD, is a professor in the Department of Counseling at the University of North Carolina at Charlotte. She began her career as a middle school counselor and then worked for 16 years as a psychologist at a university counseling center. During this time, she developed a clinical interest in crisis intervention, particularly in the area of suicide. She also developed a line of research in this area. Another area of clinical interest was developed in the area of grief and loss counseling. For the past 14 years, Furr has taught courses in counseling theories, ethics, career counseling, the design and leadership of psychoeducational groups, grief counseling, crisis intervention, and practicum in the Department of Counseling.

Margaret M. Generali, PhD, is currently an assistant professor in the Counseling and School Psychology Department at Southern Connecticut State University, and the program coordinator and the coordinator of field placement and supervision of the school counseling program. She received her PhD in counseling psychology at the University of Connecticut. She is a certified school counselor in the state of Connecticut. Generali has been a full-time faculty member for 4 years. She brings to the classroom over 8 years of full-time clinical experience in both school and university settings. Throughout her career, she has worked with people living in poverty in a variety of settings, including social service agencies, judicial courts, and public schools. Generali's research interests include counselor education and supervision, multicultural and equity issues in counseling, and empirical counseling techniques.

Tanesha Jones, MA, is a doctoral candidate of counselor education and supervision in the Department of Educational Studies in the College of Education at the University of South Carolina. She has a master's degree in rehabilitation counseling and has worked as a rehabilitation counselor, specifically on career-related issues.

Christopher Lucey, PhD, is interested in research involving adolescent suicide and crisis intervention. His other research interests include assessment and diagnosis, family therapy, and adolescent counseling. Lucey teaches diagnosis and psychopathology, child and adolescent therapy, and field placement and practicum classes in marriage and family therapy. He is a licensed professional clinical counselor in Ohio and a marriage and family therapist in California. He has worked in a variety of clinical settings that include inpatient adolescent psychiatric facilities in New Castle, Delaware, an outpatient child and adolescent mental health clinic in Akron, Ohio, and emergency rooms in Maryland and Ohio. Lucey has worked as a crisis intervention counselor and coordinator of the admissions assessment program at the Akron Child Guidance Center.

Virginia Magnus, PhD, completed her doctoral study at the University of North Carolina at Charlotte and is currently a UC Foundation assistant professor and school counseling coordinator at the University of Tennessee at Chattanooga. Her primary teaching responsibilities include multicultural counseling, grief and loss, crisis, addictions counseling, professional school counselor courses, as well as mental health and school counseling internships. Magnus' research interests include counselor development, locus of control in middle school students, school counselor supervision, substance abuse and the aging population, and multicultural counseling. Her clinical experience includes working with adolescents in substance abuse treatment and adult female offenders, and as a school counselor.

Julie M. L. Martin, EdS, is a PhD candidate in counselor education at the University of South Carolina. She is a licensed marriage and family therapist who maintains a private practice, specializing in couples and families. Martin has years of experience counseling families in her local school district, enhancing her skills with adolescents and parents.

Sara McKeown, EdS, NCC, LPC/I, graduated from the University of South Carolina, where she received her education specialist degree in marriage, couples, and family counseling. She is a nationally certified counselor and a licensed professional counselor–intern. Her clinical experience has focused on working with adolescents and families. McKeown's areas of interest include trauma, art, yoga, and wellness in counseling.

Joyce Mphande-Finn, EdD, LCPC, is the clinical coordinator of the master of science in counseling program at Oregon State University–Cascades. She has a BA in education from the University of Malawi, a BSc in business administration from Berea College, an MA in counseling, and a doctor of education degree with an emphasis on counselor education and supervision from the University of Montana. Her other research interests include looking at the impact of HIV/AIDS on the social support structure (extended family systems), especially in developing countries; perspectives on multicultural issues in higher education; gender and women issues; and effects of trauma in women/children exposed to domestic violence.

Chanta Pressley, BS, received her educational specialist degree in the School of Counseling at the University of South Carolina and is a school counselor in the state of South Carolina. She has worked for the university as an academic coach, serves the program through her role on the board of Chi Sigma Iota, and is working with multifamily groups within the school system. Pressley's interests include LGBT issues in the schools, preventing teen pregnancy, raising awareness among students and families of issues of sexuality, and creating effective and creative opportunities for diversity training.

Clarrice A. Rapisarda, PhD, is an assistant professor in the Department of Counseling at the University of North Carolina at Charlotte. Rapisarda has been a practicing counselor for over 11 years. Her clinical experience working with clients has covered settings from inpatient mental health, intensive outpatient mental health, to community and school-based counseling. During this time, Rapisarda provided counseling services in English and Spanish to culturally diverse clients from early childhood to later adulthood in the form of individual, family, couples, and group counseling. In addition to her clinical experience, Rapisarda has taught numerous sections of the Assessment and Evaluation Methods research course for master's students in the Department of Counseling over the last 5 years. Rapisarda has also taught a psychopathology course for master's counseling students. Diagnosis, assessment, and treatment planning have been integral parts of her clinical experience.

Carl Sheperis, PhD, has over 20 years of clinical experience in the assessment and treatment of behavioral disorders and psychopathology in infancy and childhood. Sheperis has over 50 publications and presentations, including his most recent textbook for Prentice Hall, *Research in Counseling: Quantitative, Qualitative, and Mixed Methods,* coauthored with M. Harry Daniels and J. Scott Young. Sheperis has received numerous awards for his work as a counselor educator, including the 2010 ACA Counselor Education Advocacy Award, the 2005 Outstanding Counselor Educator Award from the Southern Association for Counselor Education and Supervision, and the Donald Hood Research Award from the Association for Assessment in Counseling and Education.

Donna Sheperis, PhD, earned her doctorate in counselor education from the University of Mississippi. A core faculty member in the MS Counseling Program of Walden University, Sheperis is a licensed professional counselor, national certified counselor, and approved clinical supervisor with 20 years of experience in community counseling settings. She has served as cochair of the ACA Ethics Committee and has authored nine articles in peer-reviewed journals, nine book chapters, an instructor's manual to a research text, and has a foundational textbook in clinical mental health counseling in press. Sheperis presents regularly on a variety of topics and has received numerous awards for her teaching, scholarship, and research. Her primary areas of interest include counselor development, assessment of mental health and coping, counseling ethics, and supervision.

Amy Sifford, PhD, LPC, is an outpatient therapist with over 20 years experience in the human services field. She specializes in treating individuals and families involved with the Department of Social Services or Juvenile Court Services. She also serves as mental health consultant for Head Start centers in Gaston County, North Carolina. In addition, Sifford facilitates support groups for women and child victims of domestic violence at the local women's shelter. She also serves as the founder and president of the local PFLAG chapter and advocate for the LGBT community both professionally and personally.

Elease Slaughter, BA, is a candidate for an educational specialist degree in school counseling at the University of South Carolina. She currently works as a graduate assistant in the African American studies program and is a recipient of the School Counseling Special Education Grant. She has previous experience working with educational outreach programs at the College of Charleston. Slaughter's interests include social justice in K–12 education and school–family partnerships.

Shawn L. Spurgeon, PhD, is an assistant professor in the Educational Psychology and Counseling Department at the University of Tennessee at Knoxville. He currently teaches courses in the mental health counseling program, including professional ethics, formal measurement and evaluation, theories, substance abuse, and psychopathology. His research interests include African American males and their development throughout the lifespan, clinical skills with adolescents, and identity development among professional counselors. He has previous clinical work experience as a crisis assessment counselor, an intake/assessment counselor, a family counselor, and a mental health counselor. His work experience includes private practice, family service agencies, and community mental health agencies. The majority of his clinical experiences focused on troubled adolescents and their families, using a rational emotive behavior therapy orientation from a family systems perspective.

A. Renee Staton, PhD, is professor and director of the counseling psychology program at James Madison University. She is a licensed professional counselor with over 10 years of experience providing counseling and consultation for a diverse clientele, including children, adults, and groups. Her clinical interests include women's concerns, specifically healthy development and wellness of girls and young women, and working with families. Her consultation work includes social justice concerns and multicultural competence.

Daniel Stroud, PhD, is the coordinator for the clinical mental health MS in counseling program at Oregon State University–Cascades. He has a BS degree in physical education and health. His MS, from Clemson University, and PhD, from the University of New Mexico, are in counselor education. Stroud's research interests primarily focus on corrective feedback exchange, addressing problematic behavior, and applying group work principles across the counseling curriculum.

Cirecie West-Olatunji, PhD, currently serves as an assistant professor of counselor education at the University of Florida. Nationally, West-Olatunji has initiated several clinically based research projects as codirector and cofounder of the University of New Orleans–Xavier University Joint Research Centers for Multiculturalism and Counseling. She is the coauthor of *Future Vision, Present Work*, a book focusing on diversity in early childhood, as well as several journal articles and book chapters related to multicultural counseling and education. Internationally, West-Olatunji has provided consultation and training to the Buraku Liberation Movement in Osaka, Hiroshima, Tottori, and Fukuoka in the area of culturally relevant antibias education for young children. She has also provided consultation in Singapore in the area of multicultural pediatric counseling. West-Olatunji has served as an educational consultant for the Public Broadcasting Service (PBS) in the creation of a children's television show (*Puzzle Place*) focusing on diversity through KCET-TV in Los Angeles. West-Olatunji is a licensed professional counselor as well as marriage and family therapist. She is also a state-approved (LA) domestic and family mediator.

I

1

A Global and Historical Introduction to Social Class

Cirecie West-Olatunji and Donna M. Gibson

A global understanding of social class in the literature specific to certain forms of helping through counseling has yet to be reached. This is due to several issues. The first is that counseling as a professional concept has yet to be embraced uniformly in an international context. While the counseling profession has some standing in the United States and Europe, more traditional mental health professions, such as psychology, psychiatry, and social work, are more evident in other regions of the globe (Portal, Suck, & Hinkle, 2010). Due to this reason, integrating social class issues into counseling has not been a priority for countries with emergent counseling programs. Rather, these programs typically focus on establishing themselves as legitimate degree programs with viable job placement opportunities for their graduates. A second issue that explains why a globalized conceptualization of social class has not surfaced is related to the complexity of the concept (Hutchison, 2011). In a meta-analysis of the concept of social class in mental health literature, Lin, Ao, and Song (2009) found that there were 89 different terms being used for this construct. This lack of a streamlined view of social class may, in part, be due to the fact that the term *class* is culturally situated and therefore relative. Finally, social class issues are enshrouded with socialized beliefs about self and other, thus making it difficult to separate our attitudes about social class from our ability to objectively define and employ our understanding in meaningful ways in our clinical practices (Balmforth, 2009; L. Smith, 2010).

With that being said, a useful definition of social class can be borrowed from the work of Kraus, Cote, and Keltner (2010), who suggested that, as a construct, "social class arises from the social and monetary resources that an individual possesses. Thus, social class is measured by indicators of material wealth, including a person's educational attainment, income, or occupational prestige" (p. 1716). Why is an understanding of social class so important? Primarily, social class often defines one's positioning in society—to what degree an individual receives privileges or is marginalized. In Western societies, such as the Americas and Europe, there is a perception that Western countries have moved to classless societies. However, social marginalization in health care, education, the workforce, and housing are evident. For instance, disproportionality in mental health diagnoses persists among lower-class individuals in the United States (Liu, Soleck, Hopps, Dunston, & Pickett, 2004). In other words, if you are poor, you are more likely to be diagnosed with a mental health condition than if you were middle class or above. This disproportionality in diagnoses, for example, has been linked to counselor misperceptions about individuals from lower classes (L. Smith, 2010). Yet, very little has been written about this phenomenon. What has been written has been conceptual or theoretical in nature rather than empirical.

SOCIAL CLASS AS A CONSTRUCT

Three areas shape the discussion of social class within mental health literature: (1) conceptualization of clients, (2) self-perception as clinician, and (3) intersectionality of identity for both clients and clinicians. Accurate conceptualization of client issues and needs is the hallmark of effective counseling (West-Olatunji, 2008). Clinician encapsulation has been discussed as a barrier to effective counseling in relation to issues of race, ethnicity, culture, religion, sexual orientation, and gender. However, very little attention has been paid to clinician bias in relation to social class. One such study conducted in Britain (Balmforth, 2009) focused on social class and counselor bias by interviewing seven counselors about their experiences as clients. The researcher found that power dynamics played a significant role in the clients' perceptions of their counseling experiences when the counselor was perceived to be of higher social standing than the client. In the one case where the client perceived the counselor as of the same social standing, class identity did not seem to be as salient. Further, participants in the study did not perceive their counselors as being aware of their feelings and perceptions about the clinical interactions. For clinicians, the ability to accurately conceptualize the client's needs is imperative to effective service delivery (West-Olatunji, 2008). This becomes more significant as a correlate to clinician efficacy when considering work with diverse clients. Another study that explored counselor conceptualization skills in relation to social class investigated the relationship between social class and empathy (Kraus et al., 2010). In a sequenced set of three nested studies in which they solicited the responses from university personnel and students, the researchers found that participants from lower-class backgrounds displayed more empathy toward others and incorporated more of an ecological approach to their perceptions of others. Their findings suggest that one's social positioning may have a significant impact on counselors' ability to accurately and effectively conceptualize clients' concerns.

HELPING PROFESSIONALS AND SOCIAL CLASS

Helping professionals' self-perception as a member of a social class is another area of interest. One of the major tenets of multicultural counseling is the ability to self-reflect about one's own biases (Arredondo et al., 1996). This assumption about clinician efficacy is based upon the belief that our own lived experiences serve as barriers to first recognizing and then understanding the experiences of others. In the clinical setting, this is paramount given our task of interpreting clients' histories and hypothesizing about what can transform their current situations into self-actualizing experiences. Over the past 3 decades, the counseling profession, specifically, has made great strides in assisting counselor trainees to become more culturally competent when working with clients who are diverse based upon ethnocultural, religious, ability, gender, and sexual orientation differences. Moreover, counselors have facilitated similar growth in other mental health disciplines with the adoption of the multicultural counseling competencies in psychology, social work, and education, for example. Recently, other competencies have been developed to provide specificity with particular client populations, such as the advocacy competencies (Toporek, Lewis, & Crethar, 2009) and the LGBTQ counseling competencies (Association for Lesbian, Gay, Bisexual, and Transgender Issues in Counseling [ALGBTIC], 2010). However, little discussion has focused on self-awareness and social class.

Perhaps helping professionals have been slow in developing discourse around clinicians and social class because of our implicit beliefs about this construct. In the United States, in particular, race and gender are more dominant in our discourse than social class. Part of this is due to socially embedded beliefs about diversity in U.S. society, that any individuals can achieve and advance as far as their talents and industriousness will take them. This is the bootstraps concept wherein hard work and the myth of meritocracy prevail (Sue & Sue, 2008). In other countries, the concept of social class is more visible and accepted in societies. In India, for example, the country continues to struggle with discrimination against Dalits (formerly known as "untouchables") and has instituted several constitutional provisions to address this social issue (Waughray, 2010). Japan also wrestles with the challenge of confronting socialized beliefs about the *barakumin*, who are considered to have hereditary underclass status (Yoshino & Murakoshi, 1977). However, it has been suggested that the social silence around social stratification globally is linked to issues of social identity construction (L. Smith, 2010). Thus, there may be some reflexivity between clinicians' own constructed identities, the issues of systemic oppression, and their inclination to openly discuss their own social identity, social class, and social positioning among peers.

MULTICULTURAL CONCERNS AND SOCIAL CLASS

As clinicians begin to open up the discourse on social class, a major task is to begin framing the discussion beyond the roots of sociological theories to counseling pedagogy. At present, theorizing about social class requires an understanding of complex, multilayered theoretical constructs embedded in 18th-century sociological literature (West-Olatunji, 2010b). Further, what is available in the literature about lower-class individuals for practitioners is often pejorative in nature. Additionally, discussion about social class is still framed within the experiences of mainstream values and does not take into consideration the concerns of women and people of color. More importantly, existing literature on social class is disjointed. Hence, social class scholarship with a focus on women, LGBTQ, disability, and cultural hegemony has been disconnected from the social class discussion. For example, the literature on traumatic stress is used to frame the emotional and psychological effects of systemic oppression and cultural hegemony on historically marginalized groups in the United States. Additionally, much of the foundational discussion on social class has used the intellectualism of European philosophers to the exclusion of female and culturally diverse scholars (Belgrave & Allison, 2006). Finally, womanist scholars have advanced the discussion of intersectionality to highlight the confluence of culture, gender, and class for women of color.

SELF-REFLECTION OPPORTUNITY 1.1

Borrowing from the multicultural counseling competencies (Arredondo et al., 1996), enhancing awareness, knowledge, and skills are useful tools for increasing clinical competence when working with clients of varying social class. Increasing awareness means to focus on one's own biases in order to: (1) identify and shelve any barriers to the therapeutic alliance and (2) effectively conceptualize the client's concerns (West-Olatunji, 2008). Table 1.1 reflects four socially embedded messages about social class with examples from the first author's experiences about these messages.

Now, use Table 1.2 to reflect on your own internalized views about social class. What messages were socially constructed for you? From what institutional sources did these messages emerge? What messages did you receive about these beliefs from your familial system?

Knowledge

Our socially embedded perceptions of others often create single stories that lack depth and context. Altering these single stories requires the creation of multiple realities to move beyond our culturally encapsulated beliefs. New knowledge

Table 1.1 My Socially Embedded Messages About Social Class

Socially Embedded Message	Source From Social Environment (media, institution, etc.)	Messages From Early Experiences
Poor people are lazy	Commercial advertising (television, magazines, Internet)	Explicit and implicit messages from parents that provided a rationale for why other people in our neighborhood were not as successful as our family
Lower-class people are not as intelligent as middle- and upper-class individuals	Reports on educational attainment that highlighted the underachievement of poor students	Most of the students in the advanced courses at my schools were from middle- and upper-class families; the implicit message was that the students not in the classes were not as intelligent
Middle- and upper-class people are more trustworthy	Crime reports that highlight lower-class people as the majority of the criminals	Not seeing poor people in positions of authority or major responsibility
Wealthy people are snobs	Social media: movies, television, Internet	An absence of upper-class people in my working class neighborhood

Table 1.2 Socially Embedded Messages Exercise

Socially Embedded Message	Source From Social Environment (media, institution, etc.)	Messages From Early Experiences

Table 1.3 My Single Stories: Knowledge Acquisition Exercise

	Socially Embedded Messages	Contact	Reflection
1			
2			
3			
4			

construction is needed to assist the counselor in rescripting old (ineffective) perceptions of the client's reality. Thus, it becomes important to acquire accurate information about the client's environmental influences. To begin your investigation to increase knowledge about a particular social class group, watch a movie/film or read a book, and then seek out an opportunity to interact with members. As follow up, reinsert your socially embedded messages from Table 1.2 in the first column of Table 1.3 to document your experiences, then document your experiences in the second column ("Contact"). Provide a brief reflection narrative for each experience.

Skill

Having awareness about one's biases and then learning about the lived experiences of others is insufficient alone to significantly impact clinical effectiveness. Increasing clinical skills is the ultimate goal in cultural competence. Thus, it becomes imperative that clinicians change the way in which they practice counseling with clients of varying social classes. Noted below is a self-reflection exercise that focuses on four key phases of clinical activity: assessment, conceptualization, evaluation, and intervention. First, reflect on your experiences with a client in your practice, particularly one who represents a social class group with which you would like to increase your skill level. In each box, document your clinical activity and note how it incorporates your awareness of social class. First,

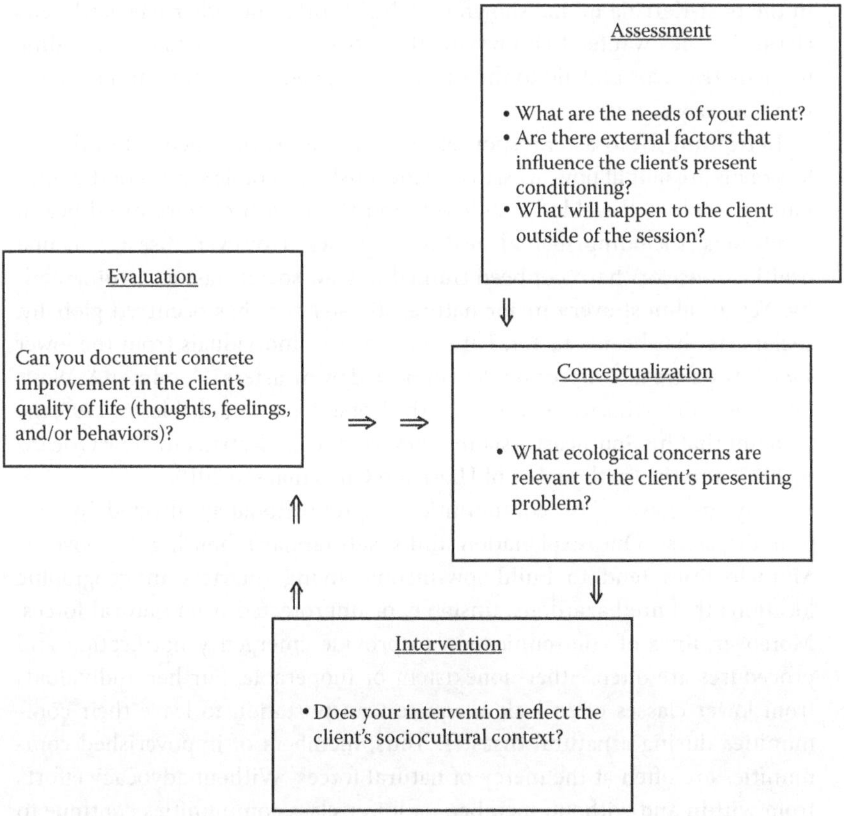

Figure 1.1 Four phases of clinical activity.

assess the status of your client, then *conceptualize* the client's needs, next provide an appropriate *intervention*, and finally, *evaluate* the effectiveness of the intervention (Figure 1.1).

Case Study 1.1: Disasters and Social Class

Nowhere have the issues of disasters and social class been more evident with worldwide implications than during the aftermath of Hurricane Katrina in the Gulf Coast area, and more particularly, in New Orleans. Shortly after the devastation of the hurricane, the levees broke, causing the massive flooding that forever changed the city of New Orleans. Around the time that Hurricane Katrina hit New Orleans, I was out of the country providing consultation in Asia. While I had prepared an elaborate training program on multicultural counseling, the participants were far more interested in the post-Katrina events shown on CNN World and other televised news channels. They wanted to know why the U.S. government was not providing immediate rescue and aid to the survivors trapped on rooftops and in attics. I had no easy answers.

In training for disaster response, counselors and other mental health professionals are taught how to assess for the most vulnerable sectors of the community, such as the elderly, children, and those with compromised health conditions, including mental health diagnoses. However, disaster mental health counselors have not been trained to view social class as a vulnerability. Yet, in almost every major natural disaster that has occurred globally, social class has been a factor. Large numbers of individuals from the lower social strata are disproportionately impacted by disasters (Goodman & West-Olatunji, 2009). This was true during the Kobe (Japan) mudslides in 1995, the tsunami that hit Southeast Asia in 2004, Hurricane Katrina in New Orleans in 2005, and the earthquakes of Haiti and Guatemala in 2010.

Why are lower-class communities disproportionately affected by natural disasters? One explanation links substandard housing to poverty. Municipalities tend to build low-income living quarters in geographic locations that are hazardous, unstable, or unprotected from natural forces. Moreover, lines of communication to provide emergency notification and procedures are often either nonexistent or inoperable. Further, individuals from lower classes often lack adequate transportation to leave their communities during a natural disaster. Thus, members of impoverished communities are often at the mercy of natural forces. Without advocacy efforts from within and without, members of lower-class communities continue to experience systemic marginalization and suffer disproportionately during disasters.

RECOMMENDATIONS

In order to change the way in which we practice counseling to address socially embedded norms about social class, it is important that we emphasize the concept of humanism that is a core element of our profession. To be more fully human, we must: (1) move away from our single stories about social class, (2) expand our circle of influence by seeking interactions with those individuals who are outside of our social class group, and (3) challenge false assumptions made by others.

Moving away from the single story requires reflection and critical discourse to challenge our belief systems. This is not an easy task, as we have seen from the previous work of multicultural counseling scholars. Students being trained in helping professions as well as professionals alike struggle with adopting new attitudes and beliefs about diverse groups of people. Restorying about social class will be no different, and perhaps even more difficult. However, what we have learned from the historiography of multicultural counseling is that we can (and do) rescript, relearn, and retool to more effectively serve culturally diverse clients. With the advancement of counseling in a global context, the 21st century allows the profession to learn from developing counseling programs in Asia, Eastern Europe, and southern Africa (Portal et al., 2010). Counselors and counselor educators in the global arena show promise as potential leaders of the discussion on counselors and social class, given the salience of social class outside of the United States. The American Counseling Association and other international counseling organizations, such as the International Association for Counselling, need to develop an international agenda that actively promotes international dialogue about social class. The venue could be both face-to-face and digital to allow for greater participation worldwide. Additionally, international organizations need to augment publishing opportunities for international scholars to disseminate their constructed knowledge with wide distribution globally.

Expanding your circle of influence involves making contact with members of various social classes where familiarity is lacking. Contact can include varying levels of interaction. To get started, counselors may wish to identify community activities where intimate contact is not required. Many communities hold seasonal or ritual events that are open to the public and advertised widely. This is an excellent opportunity to observe and acquire context about different social class groups. For more intimate contact, counselors can engage in extended dialogue with diverse community members to seek deeper understanding about their lived experiences.

Another way in which clinicians are extending their circles of influence is by engaging in immersion activities (Tomlinson-Clarke & Clarke, 2010). Various divisions within the American Counseling Association have sponsored trips to disaster-impacted areas of the United States and other countries, thus allowing counselors and counselor trainees to challenge their beliefs about diverse populations. Helping professionals are also encouraged to join international counseling groups or participate in international counseling conferences held outside of the United States to engage in cross-national dialogues about social class. Finally, counselors can participate in social networking groups for clinicians to exchange information with other clinicians, particularly those with divergent experiences and opinions, to aid in critical analysis of our socially constructed beliefs.

Once we begin the journey of self-awareness, reflection, and critical analysis, it is important that counselors take action to address the external factors that limit the self-actualization of individuals. Hence, advocacy becomes an essential tool for counselors to counter the cultural and social hegemony that plays a key role in social class dynamics (West-Olatunji, 2010a). One way in which helping professionals can take action is to raise awareness among our peer group about social class–related inequities that impact our clients' well-being. Raising awareness can be in the form of conference presentations, peer-reviewed journal articles, professional newsletters, social media announcements, or community seminars. Educators of helping professionals can seek out community representatives to visit their classrooms to provide guest lectures to educate counselor trainees about current issues. Another way in which clinicians can take action is to partner with community stakeholders to minimize or eliminate outside forces that are negatively impacting a community. Clinical educators can develop service learning opportunities for students to integrate real-world experiences about social class with the conceptual knowledge within the curriculum (Goodman & West-Olatunji, 2009; Hagan, 2004; Masucci & Renner, 2000). This reciprocal relationship can mutually benefit the community as well as the clinical trainees in that the community receives much-needed resources and the clinical trainees learn more about the community's needs.

In sum, the helping professionals need to augment the discussion about social class and create safe places for counselors to disclose issues of class-based identity and its relationship to the counseling process. Such a discussion about social class in counseling needs to incorporate a theoretical foundation beyond the early works of 18th-century European intellectuals, to include contemporary theorists from international, culturally diverse, and engendered perspectives. Finally, advancement of a discussion on social class and counseling needs to incorporate issues of advocacy and social justice in order to include action-oriented, contextual responses to clients' problems.

A GLOBAL PERSPECTIVE ON THE UNITED STATES

Just as it as difficult to define *social class* in a global sense, it is difficult to define it in the United States. However, a global perspective of social class issues can provide perspective on the social class issues prevalent in the United States. With the current emphasis in training helping professionals to recognize and confront their own cultural biases and behaviors, helping professionals are learning to comprehend and respect the uniqueness of culture (Gerstein & Ægisdóttir, 2007). This is applicable to both international and U.S. populations. It reminds helping professionals that modifying cultural assumptions, values, biases, and behaviors (Ægisdóttir & Gerstein, 2005; Gerstein & Ægisdóttir, 2005; Gerstein, Rountree, & Ordonez, 2007) is necessary to advocate for clients who are coping with issues related to social class (Pedersen, 2003). This form of social justice counseling integrates an assumption of multiculturalism that integrates using techniques that fit the presumed characteristics of clients (Freire, Koller, Piason, & Silva, 2005). Hence, utilizing recommendations for training helping professionals to work with international clients may be appropriate for working with clients in the United States.

One recommendation for working with international clients is for helping professionals to learn more about issues that are relevant to clients in specific countries (Gerstein & Ægisdóttir, 2007). If this recommendation is extrapolated to issues of social class, the sociopolitical context of specific countries is highly relevant to clients. Additionally, helping professionals in the United States should learn more about the sociopolitical context of social class in this country and how it affects their clients. Many times objectivity in counseling relationships is sought by remaining ignorant of the sociopolitical forces that affect clients' lives, positively and negatively. In regard to social class issues, helping professionals can learn more about classism and how class is perceived and experienced in the United States in order to help clients in their awareness of these issues and begin the empowerment and advocacy process with them to combat the barriers resulting from social class issues affecting their lives.

In addition to adapting international counseling training recommendations in working with U.S. clients experiencing issues related to social class, infusing knowledge gained from working with other countries provides for a clearer understanding of how culture influences behavior (Gerstein & Ægisdóttir, 2005). This new understanding may lead to professionals evaluating the appropriateness and applicability of existing counseling theories and models in working with clients on social class issues. Clinicians may discover a need to learn different counseling approaches and models to help their clients. Therefore, applying a globalized form of learning about social class issues in the United States is a reflexive form of learning that is beneficial to both helping professionals and their clients.

CONCLUSION

It is clearly a challenge to grasp the meaning of *social class* across different groups representing different countries. Although complex, it is an exercise that can be rich in experience. As helping professionals, there is much to learn in gaining a global perspective of social class issues that affect individuals and groups. Additionally, there is much to offer in return at an international level as well as within the United States.

The United States was created without any "set" class boundaries and continues in this framework today, meaning that the interpretation of class and social status is left up to the individual person. However, issues related to class and social status are very evident in American society. Access to adequate medical care, educational opportunities, and bullying are some of the issues presenting in a counseling setting that may be related to social class. Did you consider the possibility of social class influence on these issues? Instead of being "color-blind," are you blind to class? By taking a slice of an issue that is being presented in counseling, helping professionals can examine the possible sociopolitical influences related to the issue. Is it difficult to examine social class issues in your own society of the United States? If so, it is time to develop an awareness of social class within your own life. This is the first step in helping others who are affected negatively by barriers constructed by social class. By deconstructing your own social class issues, you begin the process of helping clients construct new narratives of social class in their own lives.

RESOURCES

Books/Journal Articles

Amatea, E., & West-Olatunji, C. (2007). Joining the conversation about educating our poorest children: Emerging leadership roles for school counselors in high-poverty schools. *Professional School Counseling, 11*, 81–89.

Schwartz, J. L., Donovan, J., Guido-DiBrito, F. (2009). Stories of social class: Self-identified Mexican male college students crack the silence. *Journal of College Student Development, 50*(1), 50–66.

Smith, L. (2010). *Psychology, poverty, and the end of social exclusion: Putting our practice to work.* New York: Teachers College Press.

Organizations

Center for Community Change: Helps poor people to improve their communities, and change policies and institutions that affect their lives.

Goal Irish relief and development agency dedicated to providing aid to street children and refugees and the poorest of the poor in the third world.

Synergos Institute: Dedicated to developing effective, sustainable, and locally based solutions to global poverty, particularly in Africa, Asia, and Latin America.

Center for Impact Research (CIR): Seeks to improve the social and economic conditions of the poor through grassroots research aimed at identifying innovative policy strategies that address the needs of low-income women, men, and children.

The Urban Institute: A nonpartisan economic and social policy research organization.

National Center for Children in Poverty (NCCP): A research and policy organization at Columbia University that identifies and promotes strategies that prevent child poverty in the United States and that improve the lives of low-income children and families.

MDRC: A social policy research organization dedicated to learning what works to improve the well-being of low-income people.

Poverty and Race Research Action Council (PRRAC): Generates, gathers, and disseminates information regarding the relationship between race and poverty, and promotes the development and implementation of policies and practices that alleviate conditions caused by the interaction of race and poverty.

Videos/Films

The Education of Little Tree: This is a touching story that takes place during the Great Depression about a young Indian boy who was orphaned at five years old and raised by his Cherokee grandparents, who named him Little Tree.

Smile Pinki: This documentary follows the organization SmileTrain through the impoverished areas of India. The film focuses on a girl named Pinki, who has a cleft lip, and includes footage of her family and community.

Bastard Out of Alabama: Difficult tale of poor, struggling South Carolinian mother and daughter, who each face painful choices with their resolve and pride. Bone, the eldest daughter, and Anney, her tired mother, grow both closer and farther apart.

City of God: Filmed with mostly residents of Rio de Janeiro (Brazil), City of God paints a gritty and violent portrait of the birth of the gang wars in the impoverished areas of Rio de Janeiro.

Gifted Hands: The Ben Carson Story: Ben Carson, a gifted neurosurgeon who accepts any challenge to save a child's life, tells his story with humility and honesty, constantly giving credit for his remarkable achievements to his mother, brother, and God.

Homeless to Harvard: The Liz Murray Story: Liz is a young girl who is taken care of by her loving but drug-addicted parents. Liz becomes homeless at 15, and after her mother dies of HIV, she begins her work to finish high school. Then she becomes a star student and earns a scholarship to Harvard University through an essay contest sponsored by the *New York Times.*

2

Understanding Social Class in the United States

A. Renee Staton, William Evans, and Christopher Lucey

The United States has long been considered distinct from other nations, in part because of the belief that it is the land of opportunity, a meritocracy in which all people have a chance to achieve the American dream (Levine, 2006). Expanding the claim in the Declaration of Independence that all "men" are created equal, the grand narrative of the United States tells the story of a country that offers opportunity and the potential for social mobility unrealized anywhere else in the world. Indeed, the "rags to riches" narrative made popular in Horatio Alger novels characterized the zeitgeist of 20th-century America. The message was clear: If a person works hard enough and is "of good character," nothing should stop his or her socioeconomic ascent. Conversely, if people are not willing to work hard or are not "of good character," they and only they are responsible for their lot in life. The country's promise seemed so expansive that in the early days of the 20th century some sociologists argued that class had little to do with daily life and would likely continue to have little to no effect on people in general (Aronowitz, 2003). At that time, many continued to believe that one of the characteristics that defined the United States as a truly great nation was the absence of a feudal system, resulting in a potential heretofore unrecognized around the globe for people to transcend class-related proscriptions and limitations. This notion, despite its obvious denial of the reality of slavery in our past, has been inculcated into prevailing beliefs about the character of the United States to such a degree that "class denial" (Aronowitz, 2003, p. 15) has become an artifact of U.S. culture. Thus, along with the often accepted tenet that anyone who tries hard enough can succeed, the sometimes unspoken corollary in the United States is that those who do not succeed have only themselves to blame.

A truly classless society, one in which barriers are impediments that can be overcome with hard work, is inherently appealing to many. The myth of a classless society evens the playing field, alleviating the guilt of those who have privilege and giving hope to those who experience poverty and need. The notion of classlessness is also reinforced by many politicians, who, regardless of party affiliation, feel obligated to mollify constituents who are uncomfortable with a pointed discussion of the reality that the social class divide in the United States is larger than ever before (Perrucci & Wysong, 2008). The rich truly are getting richer and the poor, if not getting poorer, are staying the same (Domhoff, 2009). These lawmakers, most of whom themselves have a higher social class than the majority of their constituents, have a vested interest in ignoring evidence that "in every crevice of everyday life we find signs of class difference" (Aronowitz, 2003, pp. 30–31), and that class differences in fact have significant meaning for our lives. Thus, our narrative of a meritocracy denies the multiplicity of factors that influence an individual's socioeconomic reality in our culture.

This reluctance to acknowledge social class as a defining factor in the United States has thus become another element of our society's grand narrative: Talking honestly about class is in many ways a taboo subject (Perrucci & Wysong, 2008). However, demeaning those in social classes other than one's own remains acceptable in many circles. Few reasonable academics would forward jokes or email messages disparaging ethnic minorities or women, for instance, but jokes about "trailer trash" and "Walmart shoppers" still circulate. As bell hooks (2000) said, "Nowhere is there a more intense silence about the reality of class difference than in educational settings." To acknowledge a class distinction in the United States is to confront a fundamental belief held by many in our culture: that everyone in our country has an equal opportunity to succeed. Even the term *poor,* for instance, is often subsumed in the essentially meaningless description "working class," thereby denying the multiple connotations that are implied in the word *poor.*

This uneasiness regarding the topic of social class highlights one of the dynamics that confounds discussions about class and its implications for the helping professions. Do we directly assess a client's social class reality? Or do we indirectly identify class variables and respond to our clients with our own class-bound biases and stereotypes? If we explore opportunities for our poor clients to achieve access to greater resources, are we imposing our own values or ignoring a worldview that has potentially provided our clients with life meaning? How are we challenged to examine our own class background and the values that we hold regarding others' class? If we do not confront our own class identity and all that it means, how will it influence the quality of our work with our clients? Responding thoughtfully to these questions has become foundational for effective counseling practice, for regardless of our strategic or perhaps naïve attempts to avoid discussing it, social class is a relevant consideration in almost every element of our lives (Alves, 2006; hooks, 2000).

In this chapter we define key terms related to socioeconomic class and describe models for understanding class structure and context that affect counselors and clients in the United States. We also present a brief introduction to the complexity that arises when social class is considered vis-à-vis ethnicity and gender. Throughout the chapter we include case studies that illustrate how social class considerations can affect our counseling and supervision work. We also provide opportunities for reflection, for we have found that the subjective experience of the counselor regarding social class may be just as meaningful for the therapeutic relationship as understanding the more objective facts and theories related to social class membership.

SELF-REFLECTION OPPORTUNITY 2.1

Consider your interpretation of the grand narrative of U.S. culture referred to above.

1. What is your understanding of a meritocracy?
2. What stories have influenced your beliefs about whether or not the United States is a meritocracy?
3. Create a three-generation genogram and include messages you received from family members and significant others about the American dream. How does that dream affect you today? How do your training as a mental health professional and your experience in the field fit with those images?

REALITY OF SOCIAL CLASS IN THE UNITED STATES

Although all people may be equal in their inherent worth and dignity, socioeconomic class is a powerful influence on social mobility, physical well-being, and mental health. People who live in poverty, for instance, have greater instances of life-limiting illnesses, such as heart disease and cancer (Kareholt, 2001), receive less effective and less frequent health care, including preventive care (Scott, 2005), have more physically dangerous jobs (Evans & Kantrowitz, 2002; Young, Meryn, & Treadwell, 2008), and generally poorer physical health (Gallo & Matthews, 2003; Liu, 2011). They also are less likely than those with more resources to use mental health services (Garland et al., 2005), and have higher rates of depression. Further, the effects of social class are pervasive in our daily lives, affecting the mundane as well as profound decisions that we make, from the food we eat for breakfast to the clothes we wear to the places we sleep at night. Social class is now considered one of the most salient factors influencing the counseling relationship (Liu, 2011).

SOCIAL CLASS CONCEPTS

Sociologists, the social scientists considered most likely to study social class, have struggled to agree upon a definition of the term *social class* and often choose to focus on class from either a *production* or *functional* model (Perrucci & Wysong, 2008). The production model suggests that people are grouped according to their role in production of goods and services in society. Thus, as in Marx's original views about capitalism (Marx & Engels, 1848/2011), people are either owners or workers. This notion was eventually expanded to include a simplistic tripartite class stratification that many laypeople believe exists today: an upper, middle, and lower class. Many sociologists, however, now believe that the idea of two or three subgroupings of people that are based on production, and by implication the relative income that accompanies one's place in production, is insufficient to capture the complexity of 21st-century life in the United States. For instance, people with "new money or the nouveau riche"—who have wealth that has been accumulated in one or two generations—are sometimes excluded from social organizations and business networks that consist primarily of people with "old money" (Scott, 2005). People who have recently accrued a wealthy income, even though they may actually have greater wealth than those with old money, can have the subjective experience of feeling devalued or even discriminated against as a result of their lack of acceptance into higher echelons of society. Brooks (2000) suggests that the nouveau riche have a difficult time in integrating their newfound wealth and accompanying power with their existing social identities relative to those from old wealth. In response, some theorists have posited the existence of a six- or seven-layered society that ranges from the privileged class to the excluded class that may be more descriptive and therefore provide more utility in examining the constructs offered in this book.

Perrucci and Wysong (2008) described a class structure that included seven segments. The privileged class, comprising 1 to 2% of the population, includes those who own corporations and live on investments. This "superclass" is followed by the credentialed class, which includes the 13 to 15% of society labeled "managers," or chief executive officers of corporations, and the 4 to 5% of society who are "professionals," those whose credentials and connections enable them to have relatively high incomes. Some academics would fall into this category. The next broad class is the new working class, which the authors labeled the "comfort class." This group includes civil servants, teachers, and skilled workers. Those in the helping professions would most likely fit into this stratum. The new working class is about 10% of the population. The largest class, consisting of 50% of the population, is the contingent class, which includes "wage earners" who are usually college graduates working in clerical, sales, and personal service jobs. This group is followed by the "self-employed," the 3 to 4% of the population who have relatively low incomes and no employees. The lowest-paid group, the "excluded class," follows. This group, which represents 10 to 15% of the population, includes those who are transient in the workforce, often working in low- or unskilled jobs.

This class structure presents a helpful, albeit limited, image of the United States as a bottom-heavy structure, with a massive gap between the lowest and highest paid. According to figures from United for a Fair Economy (2011), simple *wealth*, defined as what one owns minus what one owes, is more concentrated in the highest segments of society than it has been since the 1920s, and the wealthiest 1% of the United States has more wealth than the bottom 90% combined (Perrucci & Wysong, 2008). This income-based structure also helps illustrate how the disparity between classes is fairly easily maintained. As those with financial resources have closer, more frequent, and more intimate connections with power sources in the United States, they have the means to influence and benefit from the decisions of those power sources in ways that people from less privileged classes do not. Examining class in this way helps solidify the idea that class mobility is more limited than it may first appear when considering opportunity and equality in the United States.

This wealth gap is startling, but significant disparities also exist within the various classes and subclasses described above. What the class structure above does not address is the diversity that exists among members of the various groups, as well as the cultural capital considerations that affect how individuals actually manifest their social class. The functional model begins to address these considerations.

THE FUNCTIONAL MODEL: MATTERING AND MARGINALIZATION, CULTURAL CAPITAL, AND MOBILITY

The functional model expands on Max Weber's (1978) belief that social class is a more complex construct than mere income and production and must include variables related to education and skills that can lead to access to power. To fully understand an individual using this model, it is necessary to go beyond the individual's level of income and consider the relative prestige conferred upon the individual that gives access to power. The level of prestige or standing in society then becomes a powerful influence upon the individual's self-concept. Relating this idea to the belief in meritocracy offered above, those with privilege are led to believe that they should be proud because they have earned it and have every right to the power and prestige that goes along with it. Similarly, those in need can experience a sense of shame because of their seeming inability to earn more income and access the power and the prestige that should rightfully accompany it. It is this view of social class, which encompasses not only the demographic considerations of income but the subjective experiences of privilege and need, that is perhaps most relevant for counselors.

Aspects of these subjective experiences that are often critically related to clients' class-related issues of shame and pride include *social closure* and *social stratification*. Social closure, a dynamic that serves to perpetuate if not intensify differences among classes, includes *exclusionary* and *inclusionary principles*. Exclusionary principles are the efforts groups make to retain their power by excluding others. Country clubs and housing developments employ exclusionary principles, for instance, when they require referrals for membership or include "upkeep and landscaping fees" that substantially add to the cost of each and serve to restrict access. Exclusionary principles are also at work in schools that charge high tuition rates and require students to have computers or uniforms. Inclusionary principles—actions that purposefully include those with power who have the means to enhance the group identity—are at work when universities offer legacy admissions to the offspring of alumnae and when administrative boards seek socially prestigious individuals for board of director positions in order to strengthen the organization's identity or culture as wealthy or rarefied (Levine, 2006b).

Social stratification involves the study of hierarchies in society in an attempt to explain why unequal distributions of resources exist (Levine, 2006b). Complex societies have historically had systems of relative rank and power, primarily to ensure that goods and services are coordinated in such a way that the society can survive. Those who serve the role of organizing the goods and services obtain power because their organization ultimately influences the behavior of the people who provide the goods and services. Even today we see that management (the organizers) has more power and prestige than the workers (the providers). For our purposes, social stratification helps us remember that social class membership, in and of itself, includes a relative social rank and confers power relative to that rank. Thus, social class membership has implications for how people see themselves as *mattering* or *marginalized*.

Mattering in society, as described by Schlossberg (1989), fundamentally means that one feels important and relevant. People in politics and organizations, who matter, are those whom policy makers and politicians consider when making decisions. People who matter feel valued, are appreciated for their involvement and work, and believe, correctly or incorrectly, that they are worthy as a result of feeling accepted or being accepted. Marginalization, on the other hand, is the subjective experience of being on the fringe of the group and isolated from those who are deemed worthy, recognized, and valued. The feelings that accompany marginalization can include self-consciousness, lack of self-worth, and shame. Mattering and marginalization have potentially profound effects on people because of our tendencies to derive not only our social identity, but also our social self-esteem from our group membership (Gardner, Gabriel, & Hochschild, 2002). If our group membership is such that we feel we do not matter to society, the implications are that we as people are essentially less important or, worse, less than others. The resulting blow to self-esteem is remarkable. The desire to matter can help explain why workers join together to have a collective and powerful voice in unions and why some people from lower socioeconomic classes engage in "reverse snobbery" and poke fun at the wealthy while extolling the virtues of being "poor but happy" and, as Garth Brooks sang, having "friends in low places" (Blackwell, Lee, & Brooks, 1990).

The functional model, including mattering and marginalization, can be further clarified through the concept of *cultural capital*—the degree to which an individual manifests characteristics, traits, and knowledge that thereby provide access to opportunity and information relevant for success. Cultural capital takes into account access to resources as well as income and can illuminate why clients with relatively low income may feel as though they matter (small business owners who have entry with city council), and why clients who have relatively high incomes may feel marginalized (e.g., successful recent immigrants who are excluded from established networks). Cultural capital as described by Bourdieu and Passeron (1977) includes having characteristics and possessions that are deemed as worthy or valuable by others. Children can inherit cultural capital from their parents when they are exposed to art, music, and literature that have the capability of expanding their education and introducing them to higher levels of critical thinking. Middle school students, regardless of their family income, may have cultural capital if they have sought-after clothing or exhibit special skills, such as athleticism, that can make them seem admirably unique to their peers. In the United States, people who speak English as their first language have linguistic capital that automatically gives them an advantage over English language learners. This phenomenon is true in part because cultural capital can become institutionalized, resulting in covert and overt expectations that our clientele and colleagues will speak unaccented English, understand how to behave without disrupting our systems or needing special help, and generally fit in.

Case Study 2.1

Marian, a 27-year-old Cambodian American woman, considers herself financially successful. A first-generation college student, she is proud of her graduate degree in business and feels particularly gratified by her recent employment in a high-power editorial company. Although she has occasionally struggled with the "imposter syndrome" and has had moments in which she feels as though she has lucked into her job and doesn't really deserve it, she can usually acknowledge her own sense of self-efficacy and recognize her professional competence. Since joining this new firm, however, Marian has begun to doubt herself. She sees that her colleagues have access to information and people that she doesn't. Initially she assumed that she was simply witnessing an "old boys' network" in action. Last week, however, she saw that her female colleagues also seem to exhibit a confidence across contexts that she lacks. As she explained to her counselor, "They walk into the room as though they own it. They feel comfortable in social scenes that I'd never even have the nerve to enter. When I thought this was about sexism I could get it, but now that I see the women I work with also having this type of power, I'm beginning to think I really am a fraud. I did just get lucky. I don't belong here."

If you were Marian's counselor, how would you conceptualize her situation? How could access to cultural capital and the phenomena of sexism and racism be at work here? Perhaps more importantly, how would you help Marian explore these concepts?

The fact that our society is stratified and that social class has meaning helps us understand why millions of people each day pursue higher education, cross the border, look for "better" jobs, or buy lottery tickets. These actions reflect many people's fundamental belief in and desire for *class mobility* in the United States, the opportunity to move from one class status to another. Consistent with aspects of the American dream, upward mobility has historically occurred more frequently in the United States than downward mobility. The recent economic crisis may challenge these findings a bit, but according to McNamee and Miller (2009), the greater frequency of upward rather than downward mobility is, in part, a result of industrial expansion and a nationwide increase in the standard of living. It also reflects the ability of those with relative wealth to protect their children, who inherited wealth, from failing and losing their social class status. This protection is heightened by wealthy people's ability to use their cultural capital and take advantage of their status as people who fundamentally matter in society.

Interestingly, social mobility in the United States tends to be much less fluid and dramatic than our mythology leads us to believe (Perrucci & Wysong, 2008). Mobility figures are hard to analyze because mobility can be temporary, and controlling for class distinctions when incomes increase nationwide can be difficult to do with accuracy (Gudrais, 2008). Furthermore, the presence or absence of cultural capital, as alluded to above, can cloud the true effects of changes in income. Simply making significantly more money does not therefore mean that a person will become a member of a higher socioeconomic class, as alluded to above. Exclusionary principles can keep people out of networks and away from opportunities that would solidify a new class standing.

A CULTURE OF SOCIAL CLASS?

Questions of marginalization and mattering, cultural capital, and mobility begin to unveil the comprehensive nature of social class and highlight embedded issues of inequality. One of the reasons that social class remains an uncomfortable issue to discuss is the implication that class suggests more than access to resources;

it suggests beliefs, values, and, even more poignantly, self-worth, prestige, and mattering. Class membership is a type of social identity that can be as influential and profound as ethnicity or gender. However, unlike ethnicity or gender, in the United States many continue to place differential value on people from different classes. Those who are richer must be "better" than those who are poorer. The statement "I've been rich, and I've been poor, and rich is definitely better" lies at the heart of the American dream. The fact that this statement is attributed to personalities as diverse as Mae West, Sophie Tucker, Moms Mabley, and Gertrude Stein suggests the broad nature of its appeal.

Furthermore, class membership is not only value laden, but also loaded with stereotypes and myths. For many people, conjuring images of wealthy "snobs," "poor White trash," and the "vanishing middle class" is easy to the point of feeling automatic, which suggests that whether or not different class statuses have distinct cultures, we often act as though they do. This phenomenon is highlighted in Lorde's (1984) comment that we have a "mythical norm" against which we measure our progress and status. The mythical norm in the United States is, among other things, White, male, and financially secure. To be other is to be marginalized and to matter less.

SELF-REFLECTION OPPORTUNITY 2.2

Think about times in your life when you have been aware of being of a higher social class than those around you. What feelings accompany this memory? Then, think of a time when you were aware of being a lower social class than those around you. What feelings accompany this memory? (Staton, 2009).

Exploring these experiences can help illuminate the poignancy that often accompanies our social class membership. Our class-related experiences of shame and pride, as well as epiphanies regarding privilege, can be particularly profound in shaping our sense of ourselves as worthy.

The mythical norm and its accompanying implications for marginalization help clarify why the United States has struggled since the 1960s to decide, once and for all, whether there truly is such a thing as the "culture of poverty." Although this notion, which was posited by anthropologist Oscar Lewis (1959) and then picked up by politicians such as President Johnson (Cohen, 2010), fell out of favor as being politically incorrect, it has been revisited by politicians and the media in the 21st century. In 2010 social science researchers Harding, Lamont, Small, and Wilson participated in a congressional briefing on culture and poverty (Cohen 2010), and discussed works published in "Reconsidering Culture and Poverty," a special edition of the *Annals of the American Academy of Political and Social Science.* The tone of the briefing suggested that exploring poverty as a culture requires a constructivist view of how people make meaning of the assets and deficits in their lives. To focus only on the structural aspects of poverty, the process by which people become poor and stay poor, without considering how living in poverty shapes decision making, is to ignore the important, systemic considerations that illuminate people's lived experiences.

Case Study 2.2

Jennifer, a counselor in residency, makes home visits as an aspect of her job with the community services board. She is a 25-year-old White woman who has lived most of her life in relative comfort as a member of the upper middle class. Her parents, as well as their parents, were college educated, and many of her relatives have graduate degrees. She considers herself to be open-minded and inquisitive, accepting of difference and aware of concepts such as White privilege. Her clinical work so far has been adequate to impressive. She seems to work particularly well with clients struggling with substance abuse and those who are dually diagnosed. Her home visits, however, which are usually designed to enhance families' resilience and ability to retain or regain custody of children, have caused her to struggle. In a recent supervision session, Jennifer revealed to her supervisor that she felt frustrated with her home visit families. "They don't seem willing to make a change. I visit their houses and see dirty dishes in the sink, the kids eating Cheetos and drinking soda for dinner, the moms sitting on the couch smoking and watching television. There's no drive to improve, no commitment to the future. I get the sense they don't care. They look at me like I'm the enemy, and I think they're making fun of me behind my back. I'm beginning to think their kids are better off somewhere else. Why try to fix these people?"

FOLLOW-UP QUESTIONS

1. If you were Jennifer's supervisor, how would you help her conceptualize the families with whom she works?
2. What assumptions does Jennifer seem to be making about her clients?
3. What is telling about her presentation of what she sees when she visits and how she feels her clients relate to her?

The suggestion that understanding class and culture requires a constructive view is slightly more nuanced than that posited by popular author Ruby Payne (1996). Payne, according to the cover of her book *A Framework for Understanding*

Poverty, is "the leading U.S. expert on the mindsets of poverty, middle class, and wealth" (1996). She has gained notoriety, and some criticism, by offering workshops for educators regarding ways to help poor children, in particular, succeed in school. Although her claims have been challenged for consisting of sweeping generalities and being based on anecdotal rather than scientific evidence (Tough, 2007), Payne can be credited with offering provocative notions of the "hidden rules of social class" and popularizing awareness of the differences between situational and generational poverty. To be fair, throughout her text Payne acknowledges that middle class values are not necessarily better than lower class values. However, she suggests that they should be taught as possible options for people who are trying to succeed. Payne, who has also been accused of not fully acknowledging the fact that the poor are systematically discriminated against, presents a fairly clear-cut depiction of the worldviews and values of lower, middle, and upper class people in the United States, even as she cautions against using this information to stereotype.

In Payne's view, the wealthy are influenced most by financial, political, and social connections. She devotes significantly less of her attention to the wealthy than the lower classes, mirroring Hopps and Liu's (2006) claim that the wealthy are less studied than the other classes. The absence of an extensive body of research regarding this group, especially in the mental health literature, could suggest that the upper classes are perceived as the norm and therefore less worthy of critical attention. Or, perhaps we believe they are having their needs sufficiently met in the current system. This assumption makes sense, given the access that the wealthy typically have to mental health resources, the relative ease with which they can negotiate networks of mental health services, and the fact that wealth can shield people from environmental stressors that can negatively affect mental wellness (Hopps & Liu, 2006).

However, Koplewicz, Gurian, and Williams (2009) wondered if the recent economic crisis in the United States may cause previously affluent families to face emerging stressors that could take a toll on their mental health. Further, there is some evidence that children of the affluent experience relatively high levels of depression, anxiety, and substance abuse, perhaps reflecting the inability of consumerism to sustain happiness over time as well as the negative effects of isolation from parents and the stress of experiencing continued pressure to achieve (Luthar, 2003). Berger (2000) also noted the pressure that upper class working women experience in their efforts to fill multiple roles, sometimes resulting in burnout and self-medication through prescription drugs and alcohol. The relationship between upper social class status and mental health may not be as robust as is generally assumed.

The middle class, which has become a catchall term for those who work for a living and can afford to meet their material and physical needs, is so diverse that to consider it one distinct class is not particularly enlightening. The middle class is the group that, according to Payne's schema, sets the general tone for how business is conducted. Interestingly, this is the group to which most people in the United States will say they belong. In fact, according to Vigeland (2008), in the United States people with incomes of $20,000 and people with incomes of more than $100,000 are likely to define themselves as middle class. Clearly there are significant differences in power and prestige held by those on either ends of this range. Thus, if there is a culture associated with middle class, it must be broadly described as those who define themselves, in part, by what they are not: They are neither rich nor poor. This is the group to which many of our clients belong, bringing with them a range of issues and concerns related to their successes and failures, strivings, and fears of falling.

The fear of falling is a compelling notion for many in the United States because falling from the middle class means becoming poor. To be poor means more than not having enough money or resources. To be poor implies personal failure, loss of privilege, and perhaps inadequacy. It carries with it the shame that one has apparently not lived up to the American dream. Further, being poor may suggest that one is essentially defective and has to be taught basic rules for how to get by in educational and business dealings, a la Ruby Payne (1996). In this way the marginalization of the poor is further institutionalized in society. Rather than examining the education and business leaders' complicity in creating systems that do not meet the needs of all constituents, the disenfranchised are instead taught how to adopt a different way of living.

Granted, being poor carries with it intense environmental and personal stressors. The toll that being poor takes on people's mental and physical health is clear (Liu, 2011). Less clear, however, are the causal links and the directionality of influences that make poverty and health risks inextricably linked. The pressure that we feel to not openly discuss inequality (Gudrais, 2008), and the ways in which we collude to perpetuate the myth that the United States is a meritocracy, serve to silence our ability to thoroughly and systematically examine poverty and our responses to it.

THE COLOR CASTE

A complicating issue in our conceptualization of class as a culture is the existence of what authors in the 1960s (Warner, Meeker, & Eells, 1960) described as a "color caste," the belief that regardless of income, Whites are superior to people of color and naturally will be more likely to be in a higher social rank than those of color. Thus, in some geographic regions it is not necessarily unusual to hear people who are poor claim, "I may be poor, but at least I'm not Black." Furthermore, to ignore the influence of ethnicity and gender in a discussion of social class is to ignore additional aspects of mattering/marginalization and cultural capital that are relevant for our clients. Authors such as Collins (1993), Toporek and Liu (2001), and Constantine (2001) have described the ways in which ethnicity, race, and gender create a complex, interactive system that confounds efforts to study any one of these social identities in isolation. This phenomenon was described by Collins (1993) as a "matrix of domination," illustrating the potential for those with marginalized identities, such as the poor, women, sexual minorities, and people of color, to experience layers of inequality and oppression. If an African American woman experiences discrimination, for instance, is it because she is a woman, or because she is perceived as being poor? Is her ethnicity the target, or her apparent lack of power?

This intersection of identities is evident through the use of expressions such as "working class Whites" or "middle class Blacks." The fact that we seldom feel the need to specify "middle class Whites" or "working class Blacks" suggests that we consider these descriptions to be normative and therefore not necessary to clarify. Our unarticulated assumptions that Blacks are poor and Whites are at least middle class reveal that social class is an elusive characteristic that nonetheless carries profound consequences.

The defining word on whether or not a culture of class exists, or whether it is or is not politically correct to even acknowledge the ongoing debate about culture and class, is not forthcoming in this chapter. A full exploration of this and related questions about social class is elusive, partly because of our grand narrative and the taboo nature of open conversations about class, and partly because we are seldom invited to fully explore our own experiences of social class, even though our lives are saturated with it. To paraphrase Marshall McLuhan (1994), we don't know who discovered water, but we can be sure it wasn't a fish. Fully conceptualizing social class is difficult in part because we enact it every day. We therefore find it most helpful to focus on the basic considerations regarding socioeconomic class that are most relevant for counselors and other helping professionals: What meaning does social class have for counselors and their clients? As counselors we must unpack how our clients experience their social class in relation to the other aspects of their identity and explore the resultant levels of agency, power, oppression, or powerlessness they may feel at any given time.

Case Study 2.3

Jeff is a 35-year-old African American male counselor who works in private practice and has begun teaching as an adjunct faculty member at a local university. In his university work he has recently been given the opportunity to see clients on a low- to no-fee basis at the university's on-campus Center for Counseling and Psychological Services. These sessions are videotaped and will be observed by counseling students in training. Jeff is a licensed professional counselor who has a reasonable amount of counseling self-efficacy. He feels competent in his clinical work and is looking forward to student observation and feedback. Jeff's first on-campus client, however, has challenged him in ways Jeff finds surprising. His client is a 19-year-old White woman who was referred to the center by her physician. She reports being depressed and unable to work in her job at an automotive parts factory and is seeking disability services as a result of what she describes as "uncontrollable anxiety." Jeff, however, feels that her presentation is more one of sullenness than anxiety. She strikes him as fundamentally lazy, and as trying to "work the system." When Jeff tried to assess the client's interest in obtaining her GED in order to get a better, less menial job, his conceptualization was that she had the intelligence to succeed but not the will. This confuses Jeff, since his class background is similar to his client's. Like her, he was reared in a single-family home and had to occasionally live with relatives or in shelters when his mother was temporarily out of work. He, however, identified a goal at a relatively young age of lifting himself out of poverty. He was successful, in part thanks to the school counselors who believed in and encouraged him, and he believes this young woman can be successful too. He feels impatient with her and describes her to his students as a "classic case of learned helplessness coupled with ambivalence."

FOLLOW-UP QUESTIONS

1. How might you confront this conceptualization?
2. How do your own race, class, and gender backgrounds form your own biography?
3. Can you imagine how your life would be different if you were other than who you are?

SELF-REFLECTION OPPORTUNITY 2.3

Lorde (1984) suggested that exploring the ways in which one has been oppressed is often easier than acknowledging the ways in which one has been the oppressor. Some people who have apparent vestiges of privilege, such as whiteness or maleness, take pride in recalling working class roots. What is appealing about claiming a lower social class heritage than one currently has? How might this ease social interaction and soothe guilt?

IMPLICATIONS FOR THE HELPING PROFESSIONS

The helping professions have made significant progress over the last few decades in addressing the needs of underserved or neglected populations. Indeed, training standards, codes of ethics, research efforts, and professional organizations, among other things, have all undergone great change to the benefit of professionals and the clients with which we work. Within this evolution, there has been some attention focused on the role of social class on the lived experience of the individual, but in general, this consideration has taken a back seat or has piggybacked on the seemingly more pressing needs related to ethnicity, race, gender, and sexual orientation within our respective professions.

It is hoped that through the discussion above and the chapters that follow, a compelling case will be made for each of our professions to continue the efforts of the multicultural movement in recognizing social class as an absolutely critical dimension of humanity that requires our ongoing attention. Our ultimate goal, of course, is to prepare and support practitioners in accurately recognizing and effectively responding to a client's socioeconomic realities in the context of the whole person. To do this will require systemic change in each of the helping professions. To bring social class into the foreground and be given equal and rightful consideration with the other multicultural variables, there remains much to be accomplished. To be successful, each of the professions will need to commit to honestly assess its current state of affairs, develop plans to revise its practices as needed, and implement desired changes. This transformative process will take time and effort and will challenge our beliefs and attitudes about social class and how it is addressed by our respective disciplines.

Ultimately, we are suggesting an initiative to systemically accommodate and assimilate a new set of multicultural norms within our professions. We offer the following model consisting of two overarching domains that we hope will facilitate the development of cultural competence in social class issues (see Figure 2.1). The first domain, represented by the blue circles, includes all activities related to gaining cultural competence at various points in the professional development continuum when opportunities for skill development can occur. The second domain includes all of the institutional influences that will support and guide the professional development of social class competence. These are outlined in the attached boxes.

The first opportunity to introduce concepts related to social class is during the professional preparation program in the university or college environment. The concepts can be infused into the training curriculum and reinforced throughout the entirety of the coursework and practicum/internship experiences. Competencies should focus on students demonstrating awareness of social class issues in addition to conceptualization skills and technical skills in implementing therapeutic interventions. The impetus for inclusion of social class issues within the curriculum may be external standards such as accreditation guidelines, certification or licensing requirements, or may emerge organically from the faculty, or may be a combination of the two. Assessment of personal awareness and conceptual and executive skills can occur during coursework, in the fieldwork portion of training, or within the comprehensive examination process requirement for graduation.

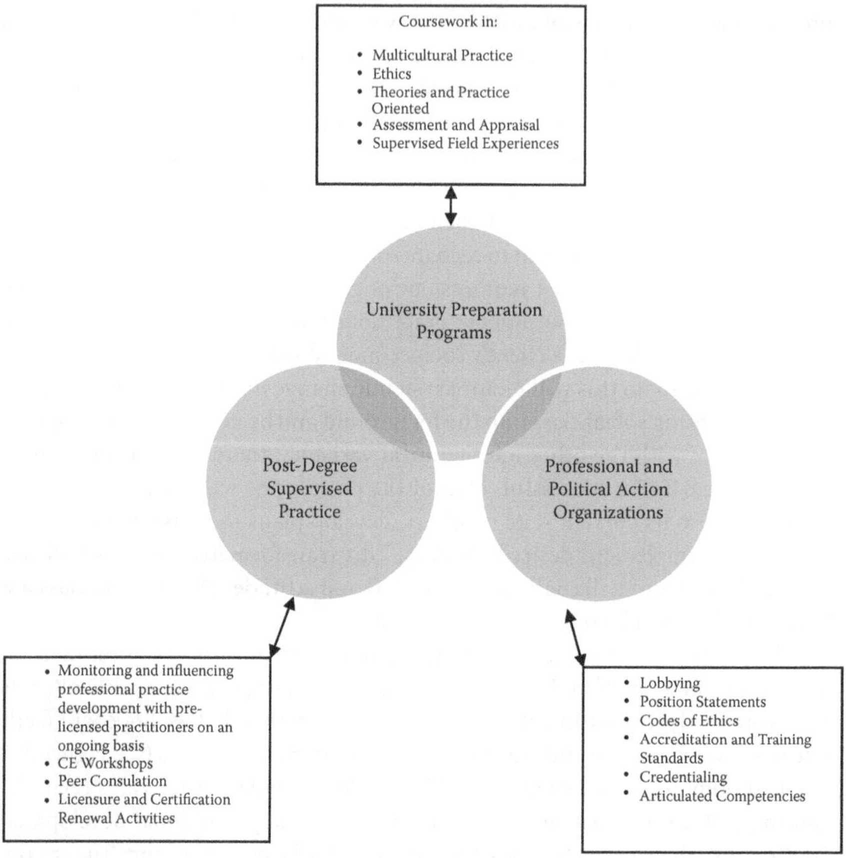

Figure 2.1 Developing cultural competence in social class issues.

The second opportunity to develop social class competence would take place during the supervised practice or postlicensure/certification stage of professional development. Continuing education and workshops focused on issues of social class and classism would expand competence in this area and would be mandated through licensure or certification bodies. In addition to the competencies required by the licensure/certification entities or organization guiding practice of the various helping professions, skills in conceptualizing the role of socioeconomic status in the lives of clients and conducting appropriate therapeutic interventions would occur ongoing through supervision/consultation.

The third and most important area of influence identified on the diagram represents ongoing efforts and practices of the professions themselves that are institutional in nature and affect the course of the professions' direction. Each profession has state and national organizations and a myriad of topical groups or associations within. These organizations exert considerable influence on member norms and practices as well as through lobbying, testimonial presentations in governmental contexts, and position statements on topics disclosed to different constituents. Codes of ethics created for practitioners by professional organizations provide guidance to practitioners in making practice decisions and influence state licensure and certification requirements. Another powerful institutional entity is the accrediting body that determines and monitors training standards for university programs. Standards for training about social class would have considerable effect on the development of practitioners and the cultural competence needed when working with clients. Finally, research in social class and therapy would add to our ongoing understanding about this important dimension of human existence as well as point to the development of best practices in training and practice of counseling and therapy. Acknowledging social class and instituting change at the organizational level may hold the most promise for systemic change in how these pressing issues are incorporated into the consciousness of the various helping professions.

In conclusion, becoming truly competent in multiculturalism necessitates that those in the helping profession first gain an awareness of their own biases and prejudices and examine how these beliefs influence their professional interactions. This chapter highlighted the importance of considering social class as one critical dimension of multiculturalism. Yet, to date, insufficient attention has been given to the influence of social class by institutions and professional organizations charged with training those in the helping professions. It appears that unlike race, ethnicity, and gender, issues of social class and classism have yet to be fully integrated into the recognized tenets of multiculturalism. Reexamining how social class is viewed through the multicultural lens by the various professional disciplines is necessary. This systemic lack of awareness of the cultural considerations associated with social class reduces our organizational response to these issues.

RESOURCES

The United for a Fair Economy website, http://www.faireconomy.org, offers educational resources and reader-friendly views of income and wealth in the United States as well as the reality of social stratification.

Waiting for Superman (2011, Paramount Pictures) is a compelling documentary that, although clearly carrying a political agenda, presents an engaging exploration of social class in relation to public education in the United States.

The Class Action website, http://www.classism.org/, offers resources and information regarding social class and classism in the United States. The organization's website includes articles on a range of topics that address social class, including class and religion, gender, and education.

Nickel and Dimed (2002), by Barbara Ehrenreich, details the author's personal explorations of trying to get by in the United States by working jobs that pay at the minimum wages. Her reflections and experiences in a series of low-paying jobs are thought provoking and illuminating.

Where We Stand: Class Matters (2000), by bell hooks, is a powerful narrative of the author's experiences exploring issues of race, gender, and social class. Her straightforward and tenacious illustration of the connections between these social identities is required reading for those attempting to explore class as culture.

3

Poverty: Urban and Rural

Chanta Pressley and Amy Sifford

Poverty does not discriminate; it permeates, at some level, every race, ethnicity, sexual orientation, religion, region, gender, or any other demographic variable. There are poor people in every county in every state in America. Poverty exists when economic markets are weak and when they are strong. Poverty exists in two-parent households and in single-parent homes. Poverty exists in families with a working parent or parents and in families with unemployed parents. Poverty affects both the elderly and the newborn. Poverty can be temporary as well as chronic. While hard data can provide us with information about who is more likely to be poor, areas of persistent poverty, and utilization rates of programs such as food stamps or Medicaid or Medicare, they do not tell us anything about the poor experience or, just as important, the richness of poor people's lives in terms of courage, values, hopes, dreams, talents, contributions, family ties, or other strengths.

Some of you reading this chapter will have personally, or will have a loved one, who has experienced the sting of the stigma associated with being poor. Other readers may have never been close to anyone that has experienced poverty and are hoping to become more empathic to the experience of impoverished people. Whatever the case may be, the hope is that this section will provide you with an overview of poverty in America and challenge you to consider your views, biases, fears, hopes, and responsibility regarding this topic.

SELF-REFLECTION OPPORTUNITY 3.1

Our views on poverty are often shaped by our personal experiences. Before you begin this chapter, take a few minutes to reflect on the questions below. Be sure to write down your responses. At the end of this section, revisit your responses, ponder the origins of your views, and examine how your views change after your reading.

1. How do you define poverty?
2. In your opinion, what are the differences, if any, between rural and urban poverty?
3. List three adjectives that describe "poor people."
4. Growing up, how would you classify your family's socioeconomic status? What has been your experience with poverty?
5. What are some of the biggest challenges that poor people face?

DEFINING RURAL AND URBAN POVERTY

While the Census Bureau uses a complicated formula to calculate poverty, if you search the dictionary for the word *poverty*, you will find a simple definition: "the state of one who lacks a usual or socially acceptable amount of money or material possessions" (Merriam-Webster, 2005). In the United States, poverty is typically defined by income or whether or to what extent fundamental needs (food, water, shelter, clothing) and access to critical services (health care, education, information) are available.

This much is also true when defining two of poverty's most associated terms, urban and rural. Just as with poverty, rural and *urban*, in terms of definition, are relatively uncomplicated. *Urban* is characteristically defined as "relating to, characteristic of, or constituting a city" (Merriam-Webster, 2005). By definition, *rural* means "of or relating to the country, country people or life, pertaining to less-populated, non-urban areas" (Merriam-Webster, 2005). However, as evidenced by the following responses, to find a consensus on the economical and social definition of these concepts is a much more complex task.

Samantha is a 27-year-old White American female, who was born and raised in South Carolina. Formerly an elementary school teacher, Samantha is currently a counselor education graduate student. When asked about her views on and experience dealing with poverty Samantha notes:

> Poverty exists in people and communities where one or more basic human needs are not or cannot be met due to the lack of funds. Rural poverty seems more common and more of a "way of life," whereas urban poverty seems to cause more violence

> and other acts of abuse. Growing up, I would classify my family's socioeconomic status as middle class. I had a friend in elementary school. I remember going over to her house one day and it was in this one moment that I distinctly remember looking around and I just knew it, she was poor. She did have a house. It was a small house, with cold, concrete floors. Her clothes and jacket seemed like they hadn't been washed in a while. There were not many food choices for lunch—bread and peanut butter. I remember noticing these things, but more than that, I remember how loving and precious my friend was/is despite of what her life was like.

Daniel is a 26-year-old biracial male (Black/Korean) and works as a chemical project engineer in Florida. When asked about his views and experiences with poverty, Daniel explained:

> Poverty is the lack of resources (financial, intellectual, social, etc.) compared to society's standard. I believe that rural and urban poverty are equivalent, except resources seem to be more easily accessible to urban dwellers versus those who live in rural areas. Growing up in a single-parent home, we were definitely what you would consider working poor—my mom was employed but at a low wage. Determined to break the generational cycle of poverty, my mom worked hard to instill in me a strong work ethic and solid values. As a kid I recognized the importance of saving, of hard work and education. For me, living in an urban area made a tremendous difference. While we weren't rich, I had access to a variety of schools, programs (like Tae-Kwon-Do), and good people who cared enough to invest in me. I can't imagine what it would have been like to grow up, in a rural area, without any of that.

Alana is a 42-year-old Black female who serves as a manufacturing supervisor from a small southern town. When asked about her views on and experience with poverty Alana noted:

> There are people who are money poor and there are people who are socially and spiritually poor. From my experiences, it seems that people in urban areas live much harder lives. I grew up "in the country." Being poor was hard, but living in a smaller place helped. In my adult life I have received food stamps, I have received WIC, my children have been on Medicaid. But even with that, even when I did not have money, I had the support of my family. I think that that is a big difference between being poor in a big city and being poor in the country; you have people to help you. Even when you're poor, in the country, you're a part of a community.

Currently, there are no universal definitions for the terms *rural* or *urban poverty.* While there are standard definitions for these singular words, combined, they often ignite a powerful combination of personal experience and intellectual awareness. As with Samantha, Daniel, and Alana, for many, both terms are often defined by what they have read about, witnessed, or endured. According to James

Jennings, the author of *Understanding the Nature of Urban Poverty in America* (1994), "defining poverty has been an exercise involving much debate. It has been defined differently in various historical periods and has reflected a range of ideological orientations" (p. 9). Jennings further notes: "Defining poverty is difficult because the very definition one uses has immediate ideological and public policy implications.... How one defines poverty reflects something about what one feels is the nature of poverty.... How poverty is defined can also predetermine the public policies that will be chosen to eliminate, reduce, or alleviate poverty" (p. 9). Since counseling is a microcosm of our world, the same is true when working with clients who are battling with poverty; how we as counselors define, experience, and understand poverty, and its subclasses, will directly impact our work with impoverished clients.

SELF-REFLECTION OPPORTUNITY 3.2

Before reading ahead, list the demographic characteristics that you believe describe a person most likely to live in poverty (i.e., race, age, gender, geographic region, and so on). After you have listed all of the demographic characteristics that you find relevant, answer the questions below.

1. Examine your list of demographics. Why do you believe that this list best describes person(s) most likely to live in poverty?
2. What are some of your thoughts and beliefs about the impoverished neighborhoods in your city or town? Do you socialize, shop, or attend any events in those areas? Why or why not? What does the local/national media report about the poor? Do you find the media portrayal of the poor in your neighborhood and America to be accurate (or nonexistent)?
3. If you live in an impoverished neighborhood, what are some of the stereotypes you/others hold about your neighborhood?
4. What government programs do you believe are necessary to address the effects of poverty? What kind of antipoverty programs, if any, would you like to see implemented in your community?

POVERTY AND THE MEDIA

If you turn on your television or open a page to your favorite magazine, whether an ad, an article, or a photograph, there will likely be some depiction of poverty. There will likely be some ad asking you to donate money to feed a child or a family, or you may see an article covering the political or social views regarding social welfare programming such as welfare or food stamps. Depending on where you live, your local television station may report on the substandard conditions of your community's schools, unemployment, or crime rate. The question is, what message does that ad or article or photograph convey? Is the message accurate? Does it help or hinder the plight of the impoverished? Although the media's attention has prompted some positive and lasting changes in regards to poverty, over- and underrepresentation and inaccurate portrayals of the poor have had an impact.

In general, the poor are labeled as hopeless, apathetic, uneducated, powerless, lazy people who are either pitied or despised. There is a common belief among American society that "poor people have many undesirable qualities that violate mainstream American ideals" (Clawson & Trice, 2000, p. 54). For instance, many Americans believe that poverty is the result of a "lack of effort" (Kleugel & Smith, 1986, p. 79), that "most people who receive welfare benefits are taking advantage of the system" (Ladd, 1993, p. 86), "that poor single mothers have a child and/or have additional children to gain or extend public assistance—welfare queens" (Clawson & Trice, 2000, p. 54), and that in terms of members, poor families are much larger than middle class families (Sidel, 1996). In behavioral terms, the media regularly describe the impoverished as criminals, alcoholics, and drug addicts, and poor people are frequently associated with pathological behavior in urban areas (Gans, 1995). Additionally, based largely on the media's portrayal of the poor, poverty is often viewed as an urban concern. According to Sayger and Heid (1990), "when one thinks of the nation's poor, images of the urban homeless, families trapped in inner city slums, transients or migrant workers come to mind" (p. 161). Therefore, in terms of visibility, urban poverty issues tend to receive more attention. When rural poverty is highlighted in the media, those who are suffering are often viewed as primitive, backward, and ignorant.

In 2000, Clawson and Trice published a study that addressed the media's portrayals of the poor. Extending from previous research on the topic (Gilens, 1995), Clawson and Trice (2000) "investigated whether common stereotypical traits or behaviors associated with the poor are portrayed in the media" (p. 54). Collecting and examining every story and photograph on the topic of poverty, welfare, and the poor published in *Business Week*, *Newsweek*, *New York Times Magazine*, *Time*, and *U.S. News & World Report* between January 1, 1993 and December 31, 1998, the authors tested "the hypothesis that the media portray poor people inaccurately and stereotypically" (Clawson & Trice, 2000, p. 55). The authors analyzed the demographic characteristics of the poor people being portrayed based on gender (male or female), race (White, Black, Hispanic, Asian American, or undeterminable), age (young, under 18; middle-aged, 18–64; or old, 65 and over), family size, residence (urban or rural), and work status (working/job training or not working). The authors also evaluated whether each individual was represented in other stereotypical ways (i.e., pregnant, engaging in criminal behavior, taking or selling drugs, drinking alcohol, smoking cigarettes, or wearing expensive clothing or jewelry).

While there were no significant findings to indicate an overemphasis on other stereotypical characteristics, Clawson and Trice (2000) determined that Blacks and children were overrepresented, Hispanics, Asian Americans, and the elderly were underrepresented, the amount of women depicted in poverty was exaggerated, magazine depictions implied that poverty was almost exclusively an urban problem, and the media perpetuated the impression that most poor people do not work. "Overall, the photographic images of poor people in these five news magazines do not capture the reality of poverty; instead, they provide a stereotypical and inaccurate picture of poverty which results in negative beliefs about the poor, antipathy toward Blacks and a lack of support for welfare programs" (Clawson & Trice, 2000, p. 62). While there is some truth to the demographic profile presented, it is not representative of poor people or the "poor people experience" in the United States. A greater emphasis on the causes and effects of poverty, particularly those that significantly impact the over- and underrepresented populations, may prove helpful in presenting a more precise depiction of the impoverished.

Although we are surrounded by media, we often forget the power that these stories and images have on our perception of others, on our thinking of who is deserving and undeserving of attention and assistance. Considering the impact of the journalist presentation on the societal worldview of poverty and social programs, imagine the impact that your views on poverty can have on your community and your clients.

THE DEMOGRAPHY OF POVERTY

Impoverished areas exist in every state in the United States; however, there are areas, particularly in the South, that suffer from persistent poverty. Miller, Crandall, and Weber (2002) describe persistent poverty as counties with poverty rates of 20% or higher in each decennial census since 1960. These high-poverty districts are concentrated in southern regions known as the Black Belt, the southern Mississippi Delta, Appalachia, and the low Rio Grande Valley. Additionally, the southwest and Great Plains areas that contain Indian reservations are also areas of persistent poverty. While urban areas are represented within these geographic parameters (i.e., St. Louis), counties in these areas are predominantly rural (Erickson, Reid, Nelson, O'Shaughnessy, & Berube, 2008). Exploring the demographic characteristics of persistent poverty areas is useful in delineating the general similarities and differences between rural and urban poverty.

Poverty and Race

Data from the Economic Research Service (2005) indicates that while there is racial diversity in urban poverty areas, the majority of the rural poor are White. However, given the importance of the intersection of race and poverty, the racial diversity of rural poverty must not be overlooked. Each persistent poverty region encompasses a distinct racial profile. In the Black Belt, the majority of the rural poor are Black. In the lower Rio Grande area, Hispanic poor are the majority. In Appalachia, Whites make up the majority of the poor. Native Americans are the largest impoverished racial group in the southwest and Great Plains areas. It should also be noted that Hispanics are the fastest-growing minority group in rural areas.

To gain a greater understanding of the connection between poverty and race, a look at the statistics regarding children, particularly children being incarcerated, provides great clarity. Researchers have explored the intersection of race and poverty and the collective findings show that while there are more White children living in poverty, minority children are disproportionately poor. The Children's Defense Fund (CDF, 2007) calls the intersection of race and poverty the most dangerous place for a child to try to grow up in America.

In their report *America's Cradle to Prison Pipeline* (2007), the CDF reviewed data that provide compelling reasons to believe that assumptions about race are operating on some level when decisions about how to intervene in the lives of poor minority children are made. Consider these findings highlighted in the report: Black children are more than three times as likely as White children to be born into poverty and to be poor, and are more than four times as likely to live in extreme poverty. Twice as many Black children represent 16% of the general population but 32% of the foster care population. A Black male born in 2001 has a 1 in 3 chance of going to prison in his lifetime; a Black female has a 1 in 17 chance. A Hispanic male born in 2001 has a 1 in 6 chance of going to prison in his lifetime; a Hispanic female has a 1 in 45 chance. Black juveniles are about four times as likely as their White peers to be incarcerated. Black youths are almost five times as likely to be incarcerated as White youths for drug offenses.

Based on these and other findings, to say in general that poverty knows no race is correct, but a closer look into the data reveals that as a group poor racial minorities suffer its impact more frequently and more severely.

Poverty and Work

While rates of un- and underemployment are higher in rural areas, both urban and rural areas have experienced economic exploitation and systematic deprivation of job opportunities (Thorne, Tickamyer, & Thorne, 2004). For example, in Appalachia, when absentee-owned mining, mineral, and forestry operations depleted natural resources and became less dependent on manual labor, the majority of the population was left without any way to earn a living. In reservation areas in the Southwest, having no natural resources from which to profit and because geographic barriers dissuade or make it virtually impossible for industries to locate there, very limited opportunity for work exists (Erickson et al., 2008). In the rural and urban South, manufacturing jobs, once thriving, have all but disappeared and, particularly since the Great Recession, much of the work that was available to citizens and immigrants alike is no longer available

(Erickson et al., 2008; Mattingly & Turcotte-Seabury, 2010). Both urban and rural areas experiencing persistent poverty lack professional or management jobs that offer benefits plus a living wage. Instead, jobs are predominantly service oriented, seasonal agriculture occupations, or climate-dependent construction jobs (Churilla, 2008; Miller et al., 2002).

There is a misconception that people in poverty are either lazy, do not want to work, or are welfare dependent. While these characterizations may describe some poor adults, research challenges these misconceptions. Consider, for example, that in 2006, 80% of low-income children in rural and urban poverty areas combined had at least one working parent (Churilla, 2008). Further, welfare benefits, including food stamps, do not move poor people above the poverty line. Another way of saying this is that poor people remain below the poverty line even when receiving maximum assistance (Greenberg & Robins, 2010). Consider also that in both rural and urban areas, less than half of eligible households are enrolled in the food stamp program (Bean & Mattingly, 2011). One of the primary reasons for not enrolling is due to feeling demoralized or degraded for relying on assistance (McConnell & Ohls, 2002). It is this cycle of limited access, systemic errors, and stigmatization that suspends the opportunity of eventual employment.

Poverty and Education

Low educational achievement perpetuates the cycle of poverty in both rural and urban areas in that even if jobs are available, many would not be qualified to fill them. National education statistics for rural and urban areas indicate that as much as 70% of students in impoverished areas fail to complete high school (Harris, 2005). High school completions rates are lower in rural poverty areas. However, as in unemployment rates, while rural rates are lower, urban poverty areas have graduation rates lower than those of other socioeconomic levels. While researchers and educators agree that education is crucial to a successful exit from poverty (Van de Werfhorst, 2002; Ceballo, 2004), there are multiple barriers facing the impoverished student.

For those students who are the first in their families to attend college, they are very aware of the idea that graduating high school and attending college is an accomplishment to be shared; they are also very aware of the pressure that accompanies that chance. To assist first-generation college students, the Economic Opportunity Act of 1964 (developed in response to the administration's War on Poverty) facilitated the development of several programs (Upward Bound, Educational Talent Search, Student Support Services). While these programs have undoubtedly played a tremendous role in the ability of low-income, first-generation college students to obtain a higher education, impoverished students and their families continue to encounter a host of difficulties that sometimes underscore the significance of the accomplishment of earning an advanced degree.

In his extensive research and work with first-generation college students, Barrat (2007) found that socially constructed barriers contribute to the anxiety and depression often experienced by these students. For instance, these students often are unable to participate in campus social life due to having to work to supplement financial aid. Those that commute or attend a community college often do not have access to a computer at home, making it difficult to study. Faculty and staff often take it for granted that every student has access to technology and financial support. There is often a sense of embarrassment and discomfort when conferences, lunch dates, and material for classroom projects are discussed (Gorski, 2007; Ostrove & Long, 2007). These feelings of isolation, embarrassment, and a sense of not belonging often remain with first-generation students who choose to continue their education (Nelson, Englar-Carson, Tierney, & Hau, 2006). Upon completion of their degrees, be it undergraduate, graduate, or professional, returning to their homes is often not their choice due to lack of professional jobs; thus the best and the brightest members of the impoverished community are most likely the ones to leave (Erickson et al., 2008).

The belief that poor people do not value education is far less accurate than the idea that poor people are often not valued in the educational process. The reality is that education is the most likely exit out of poverty, and because of this, it must be an integral component of the plan to eradicate at most, or reduce at least, poverty and its effects.

Poverty and Health

Research documents that there are physical health disparities in impoverished rural and urban areas. There is an obvious link between these disparities and the lack of insurance or being underinsured. When poor, the high cost of health care or exorbitantly high deductibles are significant barriers to participating in quality preventive care and obtaining necessary intervention procedures. These barriers help explain the higher rates of health issues, such as obesity (Condrasky & Marsh, 2005), cardiovascular disease (Kaplan & Keil, 1993), and higher mortality rates for women with breast cancer (Vona-Davis & Rose, 2009), found in impoverished rural and urban areas. Another factor contributing to these disparities is the lack of general or family doctors and access to those that might be available (Freeman, Ferrer, & Greiner, 2007). Further, as with education, recruitment and retention of qualified health care professionals to impoverished areas is difficult at best. Research also suggests that impoverished minority groups obtain health care at lower rates than their White counterparts (Geiger, 2003; Ross, Bernheim, Bradley, Teng, & Gallo, 2007), only adding to the evidence of persistent racial disparities in impoverished populations.

Poverty and Age

While poverty knows no age, a demographic profile emerges from the data that describes the person most likely to live in poverty in the United States. The population in persistent-poverty counties is young. The percentage of people under the age of 18 is higher and the percentage of people over age 65 is lower than the national average in rural areas. There is no significant difference in age percentages in urban areas from the national average (Miller et al., 2002). Single mothers, whether by choice or through separation, divorce, or death of a spouse or partner, living in rural areas face the highest poverty rates (Mattingly & Bean, 2010). Consequently, children of single mothers, particularly those under the age of 6 and especially those that live in rural areas, are more likely to be poor than such children in suburban or urban areas (Churilla, 2008; Mattingly & Bean, 2010). Further, minority women and children, Black followed by Hispanic women and children, in both rural and urban areas are more likely to be poor than their White counterparts (Jensen, 2006). These findings indicate that in America, the demographic profile of the person most vulnerable to the effects of poverty is minority children under the age of 6 living with a single mother in a remote rural area located in the southern rural United States.

Although each persistent-poverty area in the United States presents its own set of distinctive challenges, one has to acknowledge that this lack of resources and access is the result of many larger sociopolitical processes. Policy, access, infrastructure, and deindustrialization all play a role in the prolonged instances of poverty in the United States, whether rural or urban. For example, the lingering consequences of institutionalized racist policies, government-supported corporate practices that exploit natural resources in urban and rural areas, and the disproportionate amount of Black juveniles who are incarcerated all provide evidence of the larger processes that contribute to the disparities of impoverished groups and the majority.

Whether working with "city poor" or "country poor," there has to be some awareness of the unique financial, political, social, and academic challenges that the impoverished in your community face.

SOCIAL WELFARE PROGRAMS

Social welfare programs provide cash benefits, services, and the administration of public programs that directly benefit individuals and families in poverty. Ideally, they operate to reduce the psychosocial costs of living in poverty and increase the likelihood of leaving poverty. Social welfare programs include Medicaid, food stamps, Supplemental Security Income (SSI), Housing and Urban Development (HUD) programs, Temporary Assistance for Needy Families (TANF), Head Start, Work Study, Medicare, and Social Security. Federal, state, and local taxpayer dollars fund these programs, totaling billions, making poverty a highly politicized issue (Cozzarelli, Wilkinson, & Tagler, 2001).

Theories of poverty intersect with political ideology. Bradshaw (2006) identifies five theories of poverty causation: individual deficiencies, poverty as a culture, political–economic structure, geographic, and cumulative and cyclical. The theory of *individual deficiencies* holds that behavior such as bad choices or laziness and inherent abilities or incompetence leads to poverty. The *culture of poverty* theory holds that impoverished people adopt values that are contrary to productivity, and these values reinforce unproductive and destructive behaviors. *Political–economic structural* theory asserts that systemic barriers in social institutions such as education, housing, health care, political representation, and public safety exclude impoverished groups and leave them out of the discussion about poverty and what to do about it. *Geographic* theories of poverty contend that social disadvantages are created primarily through agglomeration economics and exploitation of natural resources. *Cumulative and cyclical* theories of poverty suggest that poverty spirals in reaction to community changes, such as loss of jobs, inadequate schools, and low tax revenues.

In general, individual and cultural theories appeal to conservative political ideals, while structural theory undergirds liberal political efforts to address poverty. Politically progressive poverty policy involves understanding the interaction between culture, structure, and behavioral factors of poverty, with cultural and behavioral factors secondary to structural conditions (Jordan, 2004). Theoretically, the more causation of poverty is distanced from social and economic inequality, the more emphasis welfare policy and procedures will place on personal responsibility and the less emphasis on systemic change (O'Connor, 2001).

Our current social welfare policies are the result of the Personal Responsibility and Work Opportunity Reconciliation Act (PRWORA), signed into law by President Clinton in 1996. This act challenged the status quo welfare programs that were initiated under New Deal policies and expanded during the Great Society efforts. The PRWORA replaced the Depression-era Aid to Families with Dependent Children (AFDC) program of entitlements with TANF. The PRWORA was reauthorized in 2006 and is essentially a welfare-to-work program that has a 5-year limit of receipt of federal funds and requires recipients to work or seek work within 2 years of receiving benefits.

Research about the effectiveness of welfare reform reveals that while there has been some reduction in welfare expenditures in urban areas, there has been no significant effect detected in the expenditures in rural areas. The lack of effectiveness is attributed to several variables. First, reform efforts and legislation did not address the lack of necessary resources, such as infrastructure, economic resources, child care, transportation, health care, affordable housing, and educational needs in rural areas (Tickamyer, White, Tadlock, Tadlock, & Henderson, 2007). Further, mandatory welfare-to-work programs do better in strong labor markets (Greenberg, Mandell, & Onstott, 2000). In the midst of the current recession, it is unlikely that welfare expenditures in urban areas will continue to decrease. For example, research suggests that the Great Recession has created a 13% increase in participation in the supplemental food program in rural areas and nationally (rural, urban, and suburban areas combined), with more than 1 in 10 households receiving benefits from the program (Bean & Mattingly, 2010). With the possibility of cuts to Social Security, Medicaid, and Medicare, and the lack of a holistic approach to welfare reform, urban and rural poor people are likely to suffer exponentially as our nation, in the grips of a recession, grapples with how to address their needs and fill the gaps in services designed to empower them.

THE HUMAN COST OF POVERTY

Whether living in rural or urban areas, whether temporary or chronic, the consequences of living in poverty on an individual's mental and physical health and well-being are cyclical and dire; therefore it is crucial that those of us in the helping professions understand the relationship between poverty and mental health. Impoverished people are less likely to have educational and employment opportunities, more likely to be exposed to adverse living conditions such as substandard or crowded housing, and have difficulties meeting their basic needs (Melki, Beydoun, Khogali, Tamm, & Yunis, 2004). Because of these conditions, people living in poverty are more likely to suffer from low self-esteem, experience feelings of being powerless, experience chronic anxiety, and suffer from clinical depression.

In response to these conditions, impoverished individuals are more likely to engage in negative coping behaviors such as drug and alcohol abuse. Impoverished people are also highly vulnerable to violence and other forms of victimization and lack both the instrumental and emotional support needed to maintain basic standards of living or break the cycle of poverty (Brody et al., 2001; Eaton, Muntaner, Bovasso, & Smith, 2001; Myers & Gill, 2004). Impoverished people are more likely to be referred for mental health counseling but are less likely to obtain it (Link & Phelan, 2001; Merwin, Hinton, Dembling, & Stern, 2003; Merwin, Snyder, & Katz, 2006).

A myriad of conditions, including access issues such as absence of providers and transportation barriers and internal barriers such as stigma associated with mental health issues and internalized classism, may account for low rates of mental health treatment for impoverished people of all races in rural areas. In urban areas where mental health services are more likely to be available and accessible, Black and Hispanic utilization rates of these services were significantly lower than the utilization rates of their White counterparts, suggesting that systems barriers may be perpetuating this disparity (Petterson, Williams, Hauenstein, Rovnyak, & Merwin, 2009). For children in poverty, their risk of maltreatment is high, as evidenced by a significant correlation between neglect and abuse and county poverty rates (Coulton, Crampton, Irwin, Spilsbury, & Korbin, 2007). In view of these findings, counselors working in areas of economic distress or persistent poverty can expect to encounter a wide range of issues exacerbated by a person's socioeconomic status.

SELF-REFLECTION OPPORTUNITY 3.3

Jacob supplements his family's income through odd jobs such as cutting grass, chopping wood, hauling garbage to the community landfill, washing cars, and collecting scrap metal. Jacob also works as a short-order cook in a local restaurant. Jacob's wife died 2 years ago from breast cancer and Jacob reports, "I ain't had time to grieve." He was referred to counseling by a judge in family court because his son, age 12, and daughter, age 9, have missed over 10 days of school. Jacob faces jail time if his children miss one more day of school. The family court judge postponed Jacob's court hearing pending his participation in counseling.

According to school records, both children are honor students, are not behind in their work, and have no record of behavioral issues. Jacob has explained that his children have missed school due to illness, but he has no doctor's note. Jacob explains that he takes them to stay with his mother, who lives an hour away. His mother has no driver's license, and it is sometimes difficult for others to help with transportation. Jacob explains that he works hard to pay his bills and put food on the table. His wife's medical bills and his and the children's living expenses create the need for him to work whenever he can. Jacob believes that the school authorities should "mind their own business" because his children "are learning and making their grades" and he is "proud of them for it." Jacob also takes pride in the fact he is "doing the best I can and I don't take no handouts from the government or anybody else" and "my young'uns ain't going to either." Jacob agrees to participate in counseling because "if I go to jail I will miss work and if I miss work my bills don't get paid."

You are Jacob's counselor. The court is expecting a formal report from you regarding your assessment and recommendations for Jacob and his family.

FOLLOW-UP QUESTIONS

1. Based on the limited information you have about Jacob, do you believe he lives in a rural or an urban area? Justify your answer. Does it make any difference in your thoughts/feelings about Jacob depending on whether he lives in an urban or rural area?
2. What counseling approach do you believe would best help you build rapport with Jacob? What strengths would you highlight? Would you focus more on the loss of his wife or on his immediate concern about staying out of jail?

3. Given his pride in self-reliance, would you suggest Jacob apply for social welfare programs such as food stamps and Medicaid? Why or why not? How would you broach the subject of social welfare programs with Jacob if you would choose to encourage him to apply? Do you believe that this issue is even pertinent to address given you are a mental health counselor and not a social worker?
4. What are the barriers in the larger culture that may be affecting Jacob and his family?
5. Would you advocate for Jacob's children to be exempt from the law? Why or why not?

CONCLUSION

Regardless of the setting or the geographic location of your current or future work, it is extremely likely, if only for a brief moment, that you will encounter poverty at some level. The important thing to consider is not how we can avoid poverty but how we can become better equipped to be effective in our dealings with the people and issues of poverty. In order to develop competence as a helping professional, it is imperative to explore stereotypes and myths about poverty. Once you have considered your own experience, your personal fears, biases, and hopes regarding the topic, begin with brainstorming what you can do to make a difference on an individual and systemic level.

Members of the helping professions should be prepared to advocate for impoverished clients through political action, such as voting for candidates in local elections that have an agenda that includes addressing the housing, education, and employment needs of impoverished citizens. Poverty researchers suggest the need to develop or strengthen social welfare programs that create jobs and provide room for advancement, plus some benefits or at least family-friendly schedules, and implement pay equity policies in existing ones, coupled with workforce development, public assistance, and takes credit are the ideal solution (Churilla, 2008). Continuing programs such as WIC, Head Start, Medicaid, and in-home services is necessary. In addition, it is important to work simultaneously to eliminate access barriers and strengthen child support enforcement efforts. Targeting female-headed households for intensive education and job training services (Mattingly & Turcotte-Seabury, 2010) and more emphasis on repairing and supporting public education are also crucial to an effective poverty intervention or prevention program. Highlighting the cultural and natural assets, particularly in areas of persistent poverty, could instill a sense of pride and hopefulness (Erickson et al., 2008) and in turn provide incentives for industries to locate in these areas and residents to become more active in the political processes that affect them locally.

Implications for helping professionals include increasing their awareness of the effects of poverty on child development and the impact of internalized stigma about being in poverty on impoverished citizens of all ages. Practitioners in for-profit agencies should consider offering pro bono services to clients without insurance or who are underinsured. Practitioners in both for-profit and nonprofit agencies should develop networks with social services agencies and community organizations that provide services to impoverished citizens. Finally, helping professionals should strive to be able to recognize and mine the strengths of their impoverished clients. Proper grammar, spelling, use of coarse language, and outward appearance are the least important characteristics of the socioeconomically disadvantaged clients you will see. The creativity, resilience, perseverance, wit, dignity, and grace you uncover are the important characteristics.

RESOURCES

Visit http://www.usccb.org/cchd/povertyusa/map.htm and locate your state and determine your state's poverty rate ranking and poverty rates for children and the elderly. Prepare a profile of your state, and your region.

List all of the public and nonprofit organizations in your location that attempt to alleviate the effects of poverty.

Research the following congressional acts and explore how they contributed to the disproportionate economic capital of minority groups in the United States: the Indian Removal Act of 1830 and the Trail of Tears in 1838, the Indian Appropriations Act of 1851, the Jim Crow Laws of 1876 to 1965, the Chinese Exclusion Act of 1882, and the Immigration Exclusion Act of 1924.

Investigate the theories of poverty causation and create a personal poverty proclamation that describes what you believe causes poverty, what can be done to address it more effectively, and what you will do as a counselor to advocate for impoverished clients.

SUGGESTED READINGS

Push by Sapphire

A Raisin in the Sun by Lorraine Hansberry

The Other Wes Moore by Wes Moore

The Corner: A Year in the Life of an Inner-City Neighborhood by David Simon and Edward Burns

Out of Poverty: What Works When Traditional Approaches Fail by Paul Polak

WEB-BASED RESOURCES

A Criticism of Ruby Payne's *The Culture of Poverty Theory* by Paul C. Gorski: http://www.edchange.org/publications/Savage_Unrealities.pdf
The Urban Institute: www.urban.org
Jim Crow in America: http://www.shmoop.com/jim-crow/timeline.html
Living wage calculator: http://www.livingwage.geog.psu.edu/
Class Action: http://www.classism.org/

4

Middle-Class America

Debbie C. Sturm and Elease Slaughter

According to Mason and Sullivan (2011), most Americans tend to define themselves as middle class, but beliefs about what exactly is the middle class vary greatly. Economists and politicians even fail to land on a firm definition. In recent political debates over federal tax cuts, the middle class was defined as those earning above the poverty line but under $250,000; however, J.D. Foster, with the Heritage Foundation, regards the middle 60% of earners as middle class, with incomes between $25,000 and $100,000. But those are economic definitions. Mason and Sullivan also reported that, in addition to financial or income measures, education can serve as a defining line, with those who hold postgraduate degrees seen as upper-middle to upper class, those with traditional college degrees or graduate work as professionals or the middle-middle class, and those with some education as the working class. Nearly every article we read, both scholarly and otherwise, concluded with the statement that the middle class is loosely defined and open to the interpretation of the individual and the context of the situation in which it is being considered. Here are some examples of how people we spoke to defined the middle class:

"Being in the middle class means affording things like college, health benefits and housing of your choice, a certain income, and being able to afford opportunities within your means."

"To me, middle class means I've been raised with many opportunities … but as a young adult I have a responsibility to make the most of what I've been blessed with. Opportunities come with certain responsibilities; a concept often overlooked in our society."

"For African Americans, the goal is to be middle class and those at the top are considered to be rich. But for Whites, it's a minimum expectation to be middle class and a part of the trappings: mortgages, car, eating out … no delayed gratification."

"Being part of the middle class means that I am literally squeezed between two classes … steadily lifting up the lower end and trying not to get crushed by the upper end."

Class-based patterns and identification are most clearly identified at each of the far ends of the continuum—extreme wealth and abject poverty. The area in the middle is, as Hout (2008) describes, "churning" (p. 7). In spite of the broad definitions, the conflicting "official" definitions, and the differences between political, economic, and cultural definitions, most people have some sense of class identity. When asked to identify to which social class they belong, only 3% of Americans failed to identify a particular class (Lareau & Conley, 2008). This means that the vast majority of us have given thought as to which stratus we feel we belong. How we reach that belief, however, varies. For example, college-educated individuals tend to identify with the middle class, while the less educated identify with the working class (Hout, 2008). While education may be a defining factor for some, in other cases the type of work one does drives definition of social class. According to Lareau and Conley (2008), the majority of white-collar and professional workers define themselves as middle to upper middle, whereas blue-collar workers identify as working class. Many women identify social class based on their husband's occupation, particularly if his occupation affords them a higher class standing than hers may. Personal identification and definition of class ultimately align with objective elements such as income, occupation, and education. Ambiguous experiences with these objective elements—such as high income/low education or high education/blue-collar job—can lead to discomfort in identifying class; however, most tend to still choose between working class and middle class.

Class mobility is the degree to which individuals can move between class levels (Newton, 2010). While many people believe the United States offers people the opportunity for a high degree of class mobility within their lifetime, statistics on education, employment, income, and health indicate that family of origin socioeconomic class, or social class, is a much larger predictor of mobility. This means the community in which we live, the schools we attend, opportunities for higher education, and employment are all heavily influenced by the family system within which we were raised.

SELF-REFLECTION OPPORTUNITY 4.1

Given that the highest influence of class and potential for class mobility are experiences within your family of origin and the key indicators for class status in the United States are seen to be education, employment, income, and health, ask yourself this: How would you describe your immediate family of origin in those four domains? And how would you describe your parents' families of origins? What was it like to look at your family through these lenses? How do you think your experience will influence the next generation? You may want to consider constructing a genogram to illustrate the patterns and influences of the four domains in your family.

We have taken a look at the various definitions of middle class, explored some factors influencing class identification, and looked at the patterns in your own family. Ask yourself again the questions posed in Chapter 2: Do we indirectly identify class variables and respond to our clients with our own class-bound biases and stereotypes? Or do we directly assess a client's social class reality?

THE WORKING CLASS

In considering the broad spectrum of interpretation given to what is considered middle class, we wondered about whether the working class ideally belonged as part of the middle class or as part of the chapter devoted to those living in poverty. The working class, often seen interchanged with the term *working poor*, seems to have as much a relationship with poverty, in its desire to stay one step ahead of it, as it does with the middle class, and the pursuit of reaching a stability beyond the immediate paycheck. In David Shipler's (2005) book *The Working Poor: Invisible in America*, he described the working poor or working class in this way:

> The man who washes cars does not own one. The clerk who files cancelled checks at the bank has $2.02 in her own account. The woman who copy edits medical textbooks has not been to a dentist in a decade. This is the forgotten America. At the bottom of its working world, millions live in the shadow of prosperity, in the twilight between poverty and well-being. Whether you're rich, poor, or middle-class, you encounter them every day. They serve you Big Macs and help you find merchandise at Walmart. They harvest your food, clean your offices, and sew your clothes.... They are shaped by their invisible hardships. (p. 3)

One of the interesting experiences that emerged from writing this book was that many of us had to take a close look at our own beginnings, our home towns, the people who surround us every day, and the parts of ourselves that we choose to hide and those that we cherish. L. Smith (2005) indicated that one of the reasons people sometimes distance themselves from or avoid those who are poor or struggling is an internal fear of becoming that person. As we faced our own "stuff," we uncovered a deeper respect for this forgotten America, those who are not poor enough to be considered living in poverty yet not financially stable enough to feel secure in the middle class.

SELF-REFLECTION OPPORTUNITY 4.2

1. What do you think about the differences between the middle class and the working class?
2. Do you view the working class as being at the "top of the poor" or at the "bottom of the middle"? What shapes this belief? Is there a difference?

SELF-REFLECTION OPPORTUNITY 4.2 *(Continued)*

3. When you consider your personal experience with class, what messages did you receive about the difference between those who struggled to get by or who worked blue-collar or hourly jobs and those who had salaries or careers?

The working class is considered to be those who are paid an hourly wage and often work in jobs, such as manufacturing, retail sales, or food service, not necessarily requiring education beyond high school. These individuals and their families have annual incomes at or just above the poverty line, making their financial existence one that requires sacrifice and discipline. They live with the reality that problems such as a minor illness, car troubles, and interruptions in child care can create significant issues for the family. On the other hand, working class families often adhere to a strong work ethic, frequently working multiple jobs when necessary, and impart the importance of working hard and pursuing an education on the next generation. The strong emphasis on hard work and academic success in order to rise above working class status is often a double-edged sword. While children of working class families tend to be supported in their goals and pursuit of the middle class American dream, many find the journey of assimilating into the middle class to be a navigation between two worlds.

> Beginning in high school, I became aware of class markers and began hiding my inherited class and pursuing middle class symbols such as speaking Standard English, wearing classic clothes, and obtaining a formal education. I operated mostly under the model of assimilation, that is, the more one looks and acts like a person from the middle class, the more access one gains to the middle class. (Loomis, 2005, p. 35)

Individuals often experience themselves as hiding evidence of their lower class status in order to achieve a higher or more desired status. Those in the working class or the lower-middle class, when faced with classism, often turn on themselves and their own history, suppressing or internalizing that same classism, in the hopes of assimilating with the desired group. Rather than their history being a source of pride, identity, or honor, it can become something they fear will keep them from being accepted. Perhaps one of the places this is most evident is the educational system. While education is seen as the key to transcending from working class into the middle class, working class students, often the first in their families to attend universities, encounter several unique challenges in their pursuit of higher education. Aside from more obvious logistical challenges, such as financial support, working class students find themselves faced with a conflict between the pursuit of class mobility, class loyalty, and a sense of class betrayal.

Sennett and Cobb (1972) described this as *hidden injuries of class* (in Lehmann, 2009, p. 632). These can be uncomfortable or confusing experiences that range from the process of assimilating middle class peers' dress, ways of speaking, and narratives about career, to more personally harmful experiences, such as feeling a need to downplay working class backgrounds and family narratives or dropping out of the university, in spite of often good grades, as a show of loyalty to their background or conflict over the implications of mobility. The message, perhaps, is that class mobility comes at a price, involving giving up who you are in order to be someone else. Or is it?

In a study of first-generation, working class university students, Lehmann (2009) found that working class students often pursued university educations, first, as a result of encouragement of their families who wanted them to achieve more than they had, and second, as a way of seeking their own social mobility. As educational attainment is seen as a significant factor to class mobility, students of working class backgrounds entering middle class–normed university settings are faced with their own emotional and historical experiences of class while at the same time trying to transcend those within this new context in order to achieve such mobility. Lehmann (2009) described students as having to face structural disadvantages while simultaneously creating their own moral advantages in pursuit of success. For some students, distancing themselves socially and focusing on academic achievement provided a means of doing so. But students who, over time, were able to find comfort within the middle class academic setting and could view themselves as middle class, while still tapping into the strengths of their working class upbringing and utilizing those in their pursuit of academic achievement, found the most balance and satisfaction in the experience. This highlights the often emotional journey many people pursuing social mobility experience whenever they choose to pursue educational levels, employment status, increased potential for income, changes in neighborhoods or communities, or other markers of a desired social class change. It is always a navigation of who you have been, what parts you choose to keep, share, or discard, and those you will pursue and integrate. Some degree of loss is inevitable, and as helpers we can assist clients in understanding the complexities of the process.

In Chapter 2 of this book, the authors talked about the *fear of falling*, as experienced by the middle class in this way:

> Thus, if there is a culture associated with middle class, it must be broadly described as those who define themselves, in part, by what they are not: They are neither rich, nor poor. This is the group to which many of our clients belong, bringing with them a range of issues and concerns related to their successes and failures, strivings, and fears of falling.
>
> The fear of falling is a compelling notion for many in the U.S. because falling from the middle class means becoming poor. To be poor means more than not

> having enough money or resources. To be poor implies personal failure, loss of privilege, and perhaps inadequacy. It carries with it the shame that one has apparently not lived up to the American dream.

If the fear of falling is characteristic of the middle class, then one could argue the working class has a view much closer to the actual edge. Their fear of falling is related more to the feeling of the slippery earth and loose rocks beneath their feet, yet countered by the awareness that they continue to be skilled enough—often just enough—to keep from slipping themselves. They have learned from their own working class parents how to navigate this trail and to climb closer to the summit. They do what needs to be done. And they work hard to instill that same work ethic, that same striving, and the sense of pride in the struggle in their own children, with hopes that the next generation will be the one to reach a more sure-footed spot. Perhaps one of the greatest challenges, then, is to help counter our culture's tendency to reject the places we leave behind, the parts of ourselves we are conditioned to abandon, and instead work to find true appreciation for the working class values, stories, and struggles through the pursuit and achievement of that middle class dream.

PRIVILEGE AND VALUES IN MIDDLE CLASS AMERICA

Peggy McIntosh's (1988) "White Privilege: Unpacking the Invisible Knapsack" is likely one of the key ingredients to most courses in multiculturalism. McIntosh introduces us to the notion that privilege is woven into the fabric of our culture, tied to cultural and social currency, and perpetuated through our social and educational systems. Privilege manifests in an increased sense of self-agency among those who possess it, and a lingering sense of doubt for those who do not. McIntosh focused on White privilege, examining specific privileges that Whites experience simply because they are White; however, Liu, Pickett, and Ivey (2007) discussed the intersection of privilege based on race and that based on class as an added dimension of influence and power in our culture. White middle class privilege, which is different from White privilege, is essentially the privileges that are "taken for granted by the White middle class but are not available to the lower class and working poor" (p. 199). Levine-Rasky (2011) described this in the following way:

> At the intersection of middle-classness and whiteness, it confers legitimacy in its distance from the difficult, immunity from complicity in racism, confirmation of merit and entitlement, a pleasure in itself, and a positive personal identity. It produces forms of knowledge, defines normalcy, delineates inclusion, accords value. Processes of differentiation and normalization, of discrimination and affirmation are coextensive in social relations. (p. 250)

Liu et al. (2007) sought to bring more clarity to what this privilege actually looks like. They derived an extensive list of privileges and categorized them as follows:

1. An expectation of safe neighborhoods and clean housing;
2. The ability to spend money freely and in ways that are self-satisfying and to feel relatively free of the problems of day-to-day needs;
3. An expectation that the government and other systems tend to benefit those in the middle class;
4. The privilege of choice and the expectation of appropriate and respectful treatment by anyone;
5. A familiarity with middle class norms and expectations so that one can successfully navigate the demands and expectations of a middle class culture;
6. The privilege of self-satisfaction and the expectation to pursue and enjoy happiness;
7. The privilege of assuming that one's children or family will be able to somehow benefit from the successes in your life; and
8. The privilege of enjoying leisure time in a way that is voluntary, pleasurable, and does not jeopardize employment. (p. 199)

In addition to this abbreviated list, Liu et al. (2007) compiled a much longer and detailed set of self-statements reflecting White middle class privilege. We have provided the information for you in the "Resources" section at the end of this chapter so that you'll be able to reflect on it as a way to increase your own awareness of these privileges as well and become skilled at understanding the role they play in the lives of the people with whom you work. Accepting that privilege exists is the first step. Examining your own relationship with privilege is a necessary second step. Finally, understanding how privilege shows itself in the therapeutic relationship and becoming comfortable openly discussing both the helpful and harmful ways that middle-classness influences a person's well-being, choice, stability, and support is a powerful, ongoing, and necessary journey for anyone in the helping professions to undertake.

In addition to the underlying existence of White middle class privilege, within-group experiences in the middle class appear in the value of education and interaction with the educational system, the influence of work on families and parenting, ideas about the values of individualism and independence, and even in the training of mental health professionals. While this is far from a comprehensive list, it is a snapshot intended to inspire your curiosity with regard to how privilege and values intersect with the American middle class.

Education

The American middle class has traditionally placed a high value on the pursuit of education—a value also intertwined with varying degrees of privilege. While it is not surprising that educational success is one of the key factors to allowing upward social mobility, it is important to realize that the opportunity for educational achievement is not openly available to all who seek it. One of the privileges to being of the middle class is that many of your internalized class values also align with the middle class values that have shaped and govern our educational systems. Monk, Winslade, and Sinclair (2008) agree that educational attainment is still something that individuals must work hard to achieve, but add that those who have been "groomed in the White middle class culture from birth" have accumulated "cultural capital," providing just enough often unrecognized advantages over students from poor or working class backgrounds to allow a higher likelihood of thriving academically (p. 398). And while this cultural capital is not necessarily something you knowingly learn, it is inherently instilled through the experience of being a middle class person in a middle class–normed culture.

This is much more prevalent for Whites, given it is White middle class norms that have shaped our systems; however, more and more African American families who have achieved upward social mobility are preparing their children for success in a middle class world. For African Americans and other minorities, as we discuss later, this can also mean a loss of other pieces of their identity in order to acculturate or an addition of skills necessary to navigate a White-influenced system. But what we do know is that achievement academically later increases the likelihood of achievement in the workplace, and that understanding how to navigate the norms and expectations of the educational system increases the likelihood of such achievement.

SELF-REFLECTION OPPORTUNITY 4.3

1. Can you identify any particular middle class norms and expectations that were part of your educational experiences?
2. In what ways do you think your experience with social class growing up prepared you for the norms and expectations in the school system?
3. In what ways do you think your experience navigating school has translated to your beliefs about yourself as a professional?

Employment and Parenting

Kohn (1989) established that employment conditions of parents in the middle class and working class influenced the way in which they parented their children. For example, working class individuals are often working in positions where they are not expected to be self-directed, are often told what to do, and supervised directly by their employers. Such workplace experiences may translate to a parenting style emphasizing children doing what is right, what is expected, and what they are told. On the other hand, middle class workers with increasing degrees of self-directedness, responsibility for self, and responsibility for others pass those expectations onto their children. And while this is certainly not a rule, it does indicate that experiences of class in significant and powerful domains of life (such as work) influence the ways in which we approach other areas of life, the ways in which we view power, responsibility, and values of self-directedness and independence. It also reminds us that the middle class values that have shaped our own counseling theories may come in conflict with the lived experiences of many of our working class clients.

Independence

When the topic of American cultural values arises, one of the first things most people will say is that Americans value independence. We are an individualistic society by nature. But independence, as much as it is an American value, is defined in many ways depending on the social and material resources available to an individual in their environment. In a study of working class and middle class individuals, Bowman, Kitayama, and Nisbett (2009) sought to understand differences in how independence is viewed. They found that in working class families where resources are limited, people tend to value being self-reliant and often take action without seeking the advice or assistance of others. There is a strong sense of pride in this self-reliance—an ability to do what it takes to forge ahead and to take care of yourself and your family. In contrast, those in more comfortable middle class positions, where resources are more abundant, view independence more as the ability to exercise a great deal of personal control, rather than as self-reliance.

Middle class individuals put a higher emphasis on social networks and manage those relationships in ways that help them clarify choices and options in their lives. So for working class individuals, independence means being self-reliant, being able to find the resources and solutions one needs, and an ability to get through challenging or difficult times. On the other hand, middle class individuals view that same American value through the lens of navigating networks, fostering social contacts, and putting pieces in place so they can make the best decisions when needed. As we work with individuals and families, it continues to be important to take a constructivist approach to understanding their experience with class and with value systems. It is far too easy to make assumptions that things so commonly discussed as independence or self-reliance mean the same thing for everyone.

Case Study 4.1

Your client is a 40-year-old female with a graduate degree and several years of impressive experience in her field. She is bright, articulate, and friendly. She presents to counseling just a few days after a job interview—one that would represent an appropriate next step in her career—and shares this with you:

> I think the interview went pretty well. But what I realized is that I probably am not quite what they want. I am sure a lot of other people are much stronger on paper and more experienced. I am just grateful to have had the chance to meet with them so maybe they could see that I'm a really hard worker and that what I might lack in comparison to others I would make up for in how hard I work. That's the way it has always been for me, though. Never feeling like I could compete with people who have had more advantages, but just hoping I would have a chance to prove myself. My family always managed to get by. My parents were incredibly hard workers and knew how to stretch a dollar. We had scholarship assistance to attend a better school. But we never had that extra boost that would have allowed me to take advantage of things other kids did. So, I worked a lot and tried extra hard hoping to prove myself as being just as good as everyone else. I continued to do that in college and I guess I still think about it today as an adult in virtually everything I do.

FOLLOW-UP QUESTIONS

1. In what ways does your client's experience with being raised working class or lower-middle class impact her personal narrative today?
2. As her counselor or therapist, how could exploring social class experiences help her with her attempts at upward mobility within the middle class?
3. While we haven't talked about the intersection of race with the middle class, consider for a few seconds how you might conceptualize this client's story differently if she were Black. What if she were Asian? Or Hispanic/Latina?

Middle Class Privilege and the Helping Professions

A final interesting privilege of being part of the middle class is that the majority of graduate programs in the helping professions have been designed by members of the middle class and often prepare students to work well with others of middle class backgrounds. This is not in any way to suggest that graduate programs fail to attend to the needs of the poor and underserved, but instead to underline the fact that our own institutions are also created and normed to those same middle class values and traditions as the remainder of the educational system. According to Monk et al. (2008), "graduate students are drilled in cultural practices requiring self-reliance, standard English, and the middle class work ethic of delayed gratification" (p. 404). Evidence still exists that many counselors prefer to work with "young, verbal, intelligent, and successful clients groups" over those from lower social class standings (Monk et al., p. 404). If we are again considering the privileges of being part of the middle class, then we can add the fact that individuals who belong to the middle class can presumably find mental health assistance that seems aligned to and prepared to address their needs and is likely provided by someone who shares, to a large extent, their class values.

As students, educators, and graduates of programs designed to prepare good helpers, we are additionally called to reflect on our values and experiences in those roles and examine the ways in which the privilege of being a part of the middle class norm influences our definition and approach to helping people who are different than us. As professionals, we need to own and understand this privilege of being professionally identified as part of the middle class culture. And we must also work to understand shame or humiliation we may have with regard to personal experiences of poverty as well as prejudices we may have toward anyone with regard to wealth, privilege, poverty, or economic differences to our own. The reality is that for many in the helping professions, the professional identity with the middle class does not always align with your internal identity or your family identity with class. Examining your personal class identity, your professional class identity, and assumptions made about that identity, as well as the privileges—earned and unearned—inherent to each, makes you stronger not only in the art of knowing your self, but also in the process of empathically assisting others with their own process of understanding. As Monk et al. (2008) state, "the important issue is not *being* privileged as much as how one uses one's privilege" (p. 404).

WITHIN-GROUP DIFFERENCES

Perhaps the piece that struck us most powerfully through the process of creating this chapter was the vast difference in individual definitions and experiences within the middle class. The two of us, of different races and geographical regions, but similar ages, and socioeconomic and educational experiences, interviewed dozens of friends and family members thinking we would find some commonality in the experience of "middle"; however, we uncovered exactly what those who attempt to define middle class contend: that the experience of middle class is incredibly broad and unique to the individual, and inextricably woven with threads of history, family, race, ethnicity, faith, and a myriad of other facts. We also discovered that while general within-group differences are vast, some common themes emerged with regard to racial and cultural backgrounds.

SELF-REFLECTION OPPORTUNITY 4.4

Before we begin our closer look at within-group differences, take a few minutes and reflect on your own circle of friends, family, and colleagues. How many of them would you describe as middle class? How do you think they would describe themselves? How do you think their diverse geographic, racial, and cultural backgrounds may have shaped or influenced their experience? If you have time, ask them! We think it will surprise you as much as it surprised us.

The Black Middle Class

The mass media often depicts the norm of the Black community as "inner-city poor" (Attewell, Lavin, Domina, & Levey, 2004). Rarely do they portray images of Black Americans that reflect the middle class norms that Pattillo-McCoy (1999) describes in her book *Black Picket Fences*: "People who mow their lawns, go to church, marry, vote (they really vote), work, own property and so on and so on" (p. 15). Pattillo-McCoy (1999) described the residents of the Groveland community, a middle class African American community in Chicago where she conducted her research, as engaging in "labor diligent to maintain their families, their investments, and their neighborhood and to further their achievements" (p. 15). This sounds much like the picture of most middle class Americans.

Attewell et al. (2004) report "at least a quarter of today's African-American families are middle class in terms of income, occupation, or education" (p. 6); however, their status does not offer them the same amount of protection from "downward mobility" as their White counterparts (Cole & Omari, 2003, p. 789). Lauret (2011) wrote of Michelle Obama and the controversies that stirred as she spoke about her identity as a middle class Black woman and the middle class Black family. Mrs. Obama's insistence that she and her husband were "representative of a sizeable, if unseen and unsung, African American middle class" was also balanced with an honoring of her working class upbringing, gratitude for those who worked hard to support and encourage her, and free of disengagement from her working class roots (Lauret, 2011, p. 102). She spoke frankly about the reality of barriers to class mobility that exist for African Americans and the belief that even when upward class mobility has been achieved, it is easy to lose.

Financial wealth, which is directly related to one's ability to maintain middle class status, is something that has been somewhat elusive to the African American community. Shapiro (2004) contends that Whites are far more likely than Blacks to receive inherited wealth, thus resulting in greater disparity of wealth distribution than income distribution. The media often ascribes the differentiation of asset attainment to African Americans' excessive consumption or instant gratification; however, Shapiro paints a very different picture.

In his book entitled *The Hidden Cost of Being African American: How Wealth Perpetuates Inequality*, Shapiro (2004) compares two similarly accomplished families: college-educated children attending private schools, and earning similar incomes. When comparing assets, the Black family accumulated $10,000 in their 401(k) that was used to finance the down payment of the purchase of a condominium. They had no other nonretirement savings and still owed $30,000 in student loans. Including the appreciated value of their home, this family has a total net worth of $10,000.

Conversely, the White family has $53,000 in retirement savings and received $10,000 from a family member toward the purchase of their home. This family was fortunate in that their parents absorbed the cost of their education so they have no school-related debt to pay. Additional nonretirement assets include a $95,000 inheritance, and they expect to receive more in the future. With the addition of other nontraditional assets such as professional cameras, flatware, and silver, this family has a total net worth of $140,000. Although each of these couples has put in similar work, their financial outlook is very different. While we don't assume that the financial standing of each of these families is symbolic of all families within each culture, it serves as an illustration of one of the factors contributing to financial discrepancies across racial boundaries.

Gafford (2010) contends the overall experience of the Black middle class is much different from that of Whites. She studied the experience of middle class Black families in a New Orleans neighborhood following Hurricane Katrina and in the wake of a national debate over issues regarding race and class. While much of that debate involved issues that seemed to delineate between the poor Black residents of New Orleans and the middle and upper class White residents, Gafford (2010) believed that it was in fact the experiences of middle class Black families, the families that she described as "a group of residents who are typically perceived to be hardworking Americans who have done just about everything right to accomplish the American Dream" that really illustrated that race and class were inextricably linked. And the middle class experience is different across racial lines (p. 387).

In New Orleans, the Pontchartrain Park neighborhood was different than many of the city's Black neighborhoods highlighted heavily in the media, with a history born of people working their way into the middle class, 92% home ownership rates, low poverty rates, a small baseball stadium, golf course, churches, and a deep sense of community. Gafford's (2010) ethnographic study chronicling the process of recovery within this neighborhood and among its residents illustrated that middle class status did little, if anything, to protect the residents from Hurricane Katrina's long-term impact. Residents struggled with bureaucracy, access to services and aid in recovery, and an influx of non-Blacks interested in purchasing property, thus altering the historic landscape of their community. She adds that this illustrates that Black experiences with middle class are still significantly different than those of the White middle class, and that the myth of meritocracy carries with it some racially influenced fine print. Gafford (2010), however, did note that the strength of the Black middle class lies in its deep commitment to those who have become part of their community and those striving to pull themselves out of poverty. This was true for Pontchartrain Park and is true for the Black middle class in general.

In keeping with this commitment to support their community, African Americans have had to establish different ways to meet their needs not addressed by the larger systems of our society. One such avenue was the creation of historically Black colleges and universities. Given that the public education of African Americans in higher institutions of learning was practically nonexistent, other means of educating were initiated during the mid to late 19th century. Initially created to teach freed slaves how to read and write, today historically Black colleges and universities continue to give "African American students a place to earn a sense of identity, heritage and community" (Cheatle, Fischler, Sucher, & Toub, 2001).

Case Study 4.2

As a young woman about to graduate from high school, Lydia knew that her only option was to attend college. She was extremely excited about the prospect of being the first member of her mother's family to receive a college degree, so choosing the right institution was the biggest decision that she had to make in her life up to that point. Keeping all options open, she visited both predominantly White institutions and historically Black colleges and universities (HBCUs), finally deciding to attend an HBCU. During the deliberation process of which institution she should attend, she would sometimes confer with the educational leaders of her high school. Many of these individuals, most of whom were White, couldn't understand why she would choose to attend a small, all-Black institution when she had so much promise to achieve her aspirations of becoming an engineer. They felt that attending a large university with a well-known name would serve her better in fulfilling her educational and career objectives. But what they didn't understand is that by attending an HBCU, Lydia was following in the footsteps of other African Americans, such as Dr. Martin Luther King, Jr., Zora Neal Hurston, Toni Morrison, Langston Hughes, Thurgood Marshall, and Marion Wright Edelman. It was these individuals, after facing similar challenges, who could serve as her role models for the heights to which she could attain. Lydia's affinity toward these individuals was very similar to what others may have for the founding fathers of this country. Attending an institution steeped in the traditions from which other notable African Americans had risen equipped her with the pride and fortitude to navigate the systems of a majority society. At the HBCU, she was the norm, not the minority, and was able to experience a comfort level that is often taken for granted in traditional institutions.

FOLLOW-UP QUESTIONS

We frequently make certain judgments about African Americans who attend HBCUs. While Lydia placed great value on her educational attainment, her individual choice was to attend a historically Black college or university. When you think about Lydia's story, ask yourself:

1. If Lydia were your client, what are some questions you might ask or techniques you might use to better understand her motivations for choosing a college?
2. In what ways might her previous experiences, such as family, culture, education, or peers, have impacted her decision?
3. What are some ways you could challenge yourself to learn more about social class experiences of the African American population represented in your own community?

Hispanic/Latino Middle Class

Similar to the African American community, the media often generalize the most marginalized parts of the Latino population as the whole. Additionally, they pay little attention to within-group cultural delineations that further distinguish this population. Camayd-Freixas (2006) states:

> Latinos no longer fit into a monolithic description as poor immigrants from agricultural backgrounds settled in central-city enclaves. Many are migrants, fluent in English, more assimilated, and occupationally and economically diverse. Summary profiles show a fuller spectrum of education, occupation, and income—a socioeconomic diversity that underpins a capable population. (p. 10)

Researchers have often lumped members of the Latino community into one homogenous group, ignoring their divergent values and points of views. Roosa, Morgan-Lopez, Cree, and Specter (2002) note:

> Latino families differ on a number of important dimensions, including (a) their place of origin, the ecological niches to which generations of their families have adapted, (b) their reasons for being in the United States, (c) economic circumstances, (d) their degree of socialization in the values and traditions of their ethnic culture and (e) their acculturation level. (p. 27)

G. Gonzalez (2005) describes the emphasis the larger culture places on efforts to engage the Hispanic and Latino populations, particularly Mexican Americans, in educational attainment, as intended not only to improve socioeconomic standings over time, but also to provide a gateway for better acculturation. To many Mexican American families who face stigma and discrimination, education may serve as a "cultural stamp of approval" and an "entry into mainstream culture" (G. Gonzalez, 2005, p. 141). Given that the educational system has its foundation in middle class values, language, idioms, pop culture references, and a mainstream view of arts, culture, and curriculum, Mexican American students learn to exchange their cultural ways of being with middle class ways of being. As mentioned earlier in this chapter, some may learn to discard or hide their history in order to gain desired acceptance and less discrimination by the dominant culture. This is indeed one of the experiences that, although illustrated here with the experiences of Mexican Americans, is not uncommon to Hispanic, Latino, or any other immigrant populations. And while all immigrants find themselves faced with a choice regarding the degree of acculturation, it is important to recognize that the vast majority of our systems, such as educational systems, health care systems, and child care systems, tend to be normed on middle class values and traditions. So, the acculturation process is indeed cultural, but it is also one of class. For many Hispanic and Latino families, the American class system is vastly different than their country of origin class system.

Case Study 4.3

Growing up in America with a Puerto Rican father and Dominican mother, Alta didn't realize that her family may have been considered middle class until she looked back at family photos. She and her sisters attended parochial school, dressed up on Sundays, and had two television sets in their home. During her reflection she realized that private education and material possessions signified her family's middle class status according to American culture; however, the attainment of wealth or being financially comfortable was not stressed in her Latino household.

To better explain, she shared her parents' reasons for coming to the United States. For her father, it was to seek out better employment opportunities. Because Puerto Rico was considered to be a commonwealth of the United States, she compared his migration to someone living in one state and moving to another to find a better job. Her mother was raised from a position of wealth in the Dominican Republic but had to leave for political refuge. Moving to the United States meant she was leaving her wealth behind and had to start over. However, for both of her parents, attaining wealth or achieving a middle class status was never the goal.

For them, the concept of "middle class" was difficult to understand because they had no frame of reference for what it was. She explained that in many Latino countries, you either had money or you didn't. The middle class did not exist. So those who migrated here were not in search of a higher class, they were in search of success. Success was not synonymous with money. It didn't mean striving to become the next Bill Gates because of his financial worth. What it meant was using Bill Gates as an example of success because of how he helps people. Alta went on to explain that success could also mean becoming a priest and running a diocese, or attaining a higher education degree. For them it didn't involve moving from one socioeconomic status to another; however, it was about doing well so that you could help someone else from your country experience his or her own success.

FOLLOW-UP QUESTIONS

So often we lump all Spanish-speaking people into one large group with no consideration of their country of origin. Although Alta may have grown up in the income bracket and with the material possessions that are associated with the American middle class, those values have not carried over into how she identifies her socioeconomic status. In Alta's case, it is still the morals and values that were instilled in her by her parents that signify her definition of the American dream and how that dream should be attained. When you think about Alta's story, ask yourself:

1. If Alta were your client, what are some ways you might explore the influence of her family's history on her sense of how she fits in the American class system?
2. In what ways might the experiences of her parents influence her interaction with American middle class values?
3. What are some ways you could challenge yourself to learn more about social class experiences of the Hispanic and Latino populations represented in your own community?

CONCLUSION

While we consider within-group differences, people working in the helping professions are invited to not only broaden their definition of middle class, but also to challenge notions of meritocracy, the implications of the American dream on different racial and ethnic groups, and the social class markers of education, income, and employment. In addition, we are also asked to consider multiple interaction effects and how those result in individual narratives and identify with social class. People place themselves at various points on the middle class continuum, often with some degree of conflict between their social class upbringing and beliefs about their educational attainment, income level, and employment status or position. Be curious about what each of these things means to the people with whom you are working. Geographical, historical, and community factors influence these narratives as well.

Finally, it is important to keep in mind that the middle class often has a direct intersection with the notion of whiteness. Within-group experiences of middle class mobility and identity are complex. Much of middle class identity has historically been intertwined with White social norms and expectations. Our systems, such as schools and businesses, have been shaped around middle class ideas. It is important that we strive to understand different experiences of middle class, the intersection of values, dreams, and identity, as well as experiences, relationships, successes, and losses that define who we are individually within this group.

RESOURCES

Middle Class

The Center for Working-Class Studies at Youngstown State University hosts a website designed to provide research, political and cultural resources, discussion forums, and more related to the working class. Visit http://cwcs.ysu.edu/

A team of reporters spent more than a year investigating class in the United States. The *New York Times* Class Matters Special Edition resulted in a website rich with information, interactive features, and personal stories (http://www.nytimes.com/pages/national/class/), and the book that followed (titled *Class Matters* and released in 2005) is a must-have for those interested in social class.

"Sample Self-Statements About White Middle-Class Privilege" found in the Appendix of Liu, W.M., Pickett, T., & Ivy, A.E. (2007). White middle-class privilege: Social class bias and implications for training and practice. *Journal of Multicultural Counseling and Development*, *35*, 194–206.

Black Middle Class

Shapiro, T.M. (2004). *The hidden cost of being African American: How wealth perpetuates inequality*. New York: Oxford University Press.

Pattillo-McCoy, M. (1999). *Black Picket Fences: Privilege and peril among the black middle class*. Chicago: University of Chicago Press.

Latino Middle Class

Rodriguez, G. (1996). The emerging Latino middle class. Retrieved from http://publicpolicy.pepperdine.edu/davenport-institute/content/reports/latino.pdf

5

Understanding Wealth and Privilege

Susan Furr, Wanda Briggs, and Virginia Magnus

Money has been hailed as the "last taboo" in society (Krueger, as cited in Weissberg, 1991, p. 245). In American society today, financial information is not disclosed in casual conversation, nor is it the focus of therapeutic interactions (Weissberg, 1991). Yet research demonstrates that money is linked to many health and mental health issues. Most of the research asserts that lower socioeconomic environments contribute to greater emotional distress with the suggestion that there is an inverse, linear relationship between socioeconomic status and emotional disorders (Gallo, Bogart, Vranceanu, & Matthews, 2005). Although research has identified the negative outcomes for those who lack financial resources when compared to those with financial resources, often the assumption is made that those with resources are at low risk for mental health problems (Luthar, 2003). In fact, little is known about the psychopathology that occurs in the context of wealth (McMahon & Luthar, 2006). In this chapter, we will examine definitions of wealth and privilege, explore mental health issues of the wealthy, explore special issues for the children of wealth, and investigate challenges for therapists working with wealthy and privileged clients.

Case Study 5.1

Throughout my years of counseling, I have learned important lessons about hidden biases. I know that the way I conceptualize my clients will make a difference and affect how I respond, how I consider their stories, and the approaches that I choose to engage with them. Several client encounters stand tall in teaching me important lessons that I needed to learn. As you read through the chapter, consider your initial reaction to the three scenarios presented. Upon completing the chapter, see if your view of the client has changed.

Client statement: "It's surreal; how can they believe that I can go to college here and make friends with these people?"

Client situation: Vanessa walked into the counseling center and demanded that she see a counselor immediately. She told me that she had transferred from a highly respected Ivy League college in the Northeast where she had been inducted into the most coveted sorority. For her 20th birthday last year, she had received a luxury sports car and fab shopping spree. She commented that her friends were amazing and always thought she was the funniest, coolest, best person to be around. Now, the summer before her junior year in college, her highly respected family was financially bankrupt. Vanessa had to live at home and attend the public university as a commuter student.

Bias uncovered: I found myself angry by the luxury and entitlement that she took for granted. Racing through my mind, I thought: *Really, give me a break! Why, yesterday I took a student to lunch because she did not have money to eat for the past two days.* Then I stopped. Did I not hear the loss she was experiencing, her shattered sense of self, the aloneness in a new university, and a lifestyle that had disappeared? Regardless of her affluence, my client needed me to hear her pain, her fear, and to acknowledge her circumstances. Suddenly, it became crystal clear to me that social class bias had entered the counseling relationship. I was not prepared to own my socioeconomic values. How could this difference influence the therapeutic relationship?

FOLLOW-UP QUESTIONS

1. How do you position yourself in terms of social class privilege?
2. In what situations does ranking yourself become complicated?
3. How has your response changed over time?

WEALTH AND PRIVILEGE

What level of resources places someone in the wealthy class? Are wealth and privilege synonymous? Does socioeconomic status alone define a person's perception of his or her status in society? In the United States, the political arena is split over any proposal that hints at a redistribution of wealth (Piff, Kraus, Côté, Cheng & Keltner, 2010). These authors cite that households in the top 1% in terms of wealth own 30% of the total wealth in the United States. Other studies have demonstrated a growing social and economic inequality in our country (Liu, Pickett, & Ivy, 2007). Clearly, there is a group of individuals whose wealth distinguishes them from the vast majority of individuals who seek our services.

When trying to research the mental health issues among individuals with higher resources, it is difficult to find a single definition or financial indicator of what constitutes wealth. Gallo and Matthews (2003) propose a two-factor model of socioeconomic status that examines resource-based measures and prestige-based measures. Included in the resource-based measures are one's access to both material and social assets, such as income, education, and wealth. Although prestige-based measures may include access to goods and services, these measures also include the person's status in the social hierarchy that might be related to occupational prestige and education. In their writings, Lapour and Heppner (2009) incorporate the term *social class* and view this term as including the "individual's overall awareness of where he or she falls in the social class hierarchy" (p. 477). The term *privilege* can be defined as having a special status where advantages are conferred to an individual based on a demographic variable, such as race, gender, or social class (Liu et al., 2007; McIntosh, 2003). From this viewpoint, an individual can be privileged without being wealthy (Lapour & Heppner, 2009). For example, an elite college athlete might benefit from special treatment yet financially be far from wealthy at this point in his or her development. Also, college professors might have privilege based on their education and often are viewed as having a respected position in society. Yet their incomes do not allow them to fully pursue interests that they may have in common with the wealthy class, such as travel and the arts.

The term *social class privilege* has evolved to refer to individuals' experiences of privilege that have been internalized through interaction with their environment. Such privilege can include opportunities, material resources, emotional resources, and values that are normalized by family and one's community (Lapour & Heppner, 2009). Individuals may be unaware of this sense of privilege and may view it as a natural right (Liu et al., 2007). Thus privilege becomes more of an attitudinal variable than an economic variable.

SELF-REFLECTION OPPORTUNITY 5.1

1. How do you position yourself in terms of social class privilege?
2. In what situations does ranking yourself become complicated?
3. How has your response changed over time?

What does wealth do for an individual? Johnson and Krueger (2006) found that financial resources were a protective factor that insulated life satisfaction from negative life events. Additionally, perceived financial situation and perceived control over life were mediating variables between financial resources and life satisfaction. Lott (2002) views those in the upper economic strata as having the greatest access to setting the rules that help them maintain their power. She also raises the issue of the special benefits available to the wealthy that have been termed "corporate welfare" (Lott, 2002, p. 107). Such a statement is reinforced by wealthy individuals such as Warren Buffett, who reported that he paid 17.7% of his taxable income in taxes while his receptionist paid 30% (Tse, 2011). Thus having greater resources increases one's ability to exercise greater control over one's life.

In a review of research on the effect of socioeconomic status and cognitive-behavioral factors on cardiovascular health, an inverse relationship was found between socioeconomic status and prevalence of depressive disorders (Gallo & Matthews, 2003). However, several of the studies indicated that higher socioeconomic status is a factor only up to a point of affluence when the effect appears to reverse as income increases (Gallo & Matthews, 2003). Although finding a linear directionality between socioeconomic status, cognitive-emotive factors, and health has proven to be difficult, the construct of *reserve capacity* as proposed by Gallo and Matthews (2003) may help explain the advantage that higher socioeconomic status individuals hold over those with lesser resources (p. 35). Reserve capacity refers to tangible resources, interpersonal resources, and intrapersonal resources that can help buffer stressful environments. Without these reserves, the impact of stressful events is exacerbated and may result in subsequent depressive symptoms. Those with higher socioeconomic status have been shown to have greater intrapersonal characteristics such as self-efficacy and perceived sense of control (Cohen, Kaplan, & Salonen, 1999; Lachman & Weaver, 1998).

In further study, Gallo et al. (2005) found that women in the high socioeconomic group reported the most resources (conditions such as marriage, tangible and financial reserves, social and personal assets), which in turn were strongly predictive of perceived control and positive affect. One interesting contrast was that women in the lower socioeconomic group reported greater positive affect with increasing occupational demands, while women in the higher socioeconomic group reported a decrease in positive affect with greater demands. Such a finding may be related to other studies that indicate that people with low socioeconomic occupations often feel bored; therefore, increased demands may result in greater engagement and interest in the job (Matthews et al., 2000). Conversely, for those with occupations that are already stimulating, additional demands may not strengthen positive feelings.

SELF-REFLECTION OPPORTUNITY 5.2

1. In what way do you believe wealth influences life satisfaction?
2. How does your lived experience shape your viewpoint?
3. How does your work as a counselor inspire your life satisfaction?

Another difference in perception of control is found between lower and upper social class groups. Individuals can explain causes of social events from either an external perspective (contextual explanations) or internal perspectives (dispositional explanations). Kraus, Piff, and Keltner (2009) found that those with lower subjective socioeconomic experiences were more likely to employ a contextualist orientation toward understanding economic inequality as well as personal and social outcomes. In addition, this approach is linked to a perspective that the world is less controllable. Higher subjective socioeconomic experiences had an inverse relationship with contextual explanation of economic inequality, thus indicating that those with higher subjective socioeconomic experiences favored dispositional explanations. Interestingly, when political ideology was considered, it was found that having a liberal political orientation was significantly associated with contextual economic inequality. Finally, Kraus et al. (2009) found that sense of control mediated the relationship between subjective socioeconomic status and contextual economic inequality. Overall, we can conclude that those who perceive that they have greater resources will have a greater sense of control. In turn, those with wealth and privilege may view the world from a dispositional perspective, meaning that individuals can shape the outcomes of their lives, are responsible for their behaviors and emotions, and are more likely to endorse political policies based upon dispositional explanations.

Differences between those in upper social class groups and those in lower social class groups create an interesting reaction. The wealthy may actually trigger a greater negative reaction from others than the reaction triggered by the poor (Luthar, 2003). The term *schadenfreude* evolved to describe the pleasure others may take in the misfortunes of those who are more successful or wealthier than others (Luthar, 2003, p. 1588). Terms that have been applied in describing those with wealth and privilege include *entitled*, *arrogant*, *superficial*, and *narcissistic*. While some affluent individuals may be aware of the resentment others feel toward them, they also have the ability to isolate themselves from these reactions by living in neighborhoods with people similar to themselves, engaging in social activities with those of a similar social class, and sending children to select schools. Thus, the assumptions they make about the world are supported rather than challenged. Yet, those with wealth and privilege may not ultimately be happier than those who have resources that meet a minimum threshold (Csikszentmihaliyi, 1999). Although it seems counterintuitive, there is a low negative correlation between material well-being and subjective well-being. This finding implies that material advantages do not convert directly into more positive social and emotional benefits. Consequently, those who often are viewed as having everything because of greater financial resources may not have corresponding levels of happiness. The incongruence between external resources and internal satisfaction may be a source of discontent that leads an individual to engage counseling services.

SELF-REFLECTION OPPORTUNITY 5.3

1. What stories of misfortune among the wealthy have captured your attention?
2. Describe your reaction after hearing the story.
3. Were you surprised by your response to the experience?

ARE MENTAL HEALTH ISSUES DIFFERENT FOR THE WEALTHY?

From a developmental perspective, everyone passes through the same stages and faces the same developmental challenges. Child development specialists would point out that all children have to master the same developmental milestones. Erikson (1963) extended the Freudian perspective to include the impact of the social world on our emotional development. From his perspective, psychosocial aspects of development occur when the individual encounters specific crises that must be resolved for growth to continue. Each crisis presents a turning point where the individual either resolves the conflict and moves forward or fails to complete this developmental task. For example, the first stage of infancy has been identified as the struggle between *trust and mistrust*. Infants must depend upon others to discover that physical and emotional needs will be met. If the needs are fulfilled, a sense of trust is formed with the world. If needs go unfulfilled, then the world may be viewed as a place that cannot be trusted. Being wanted and loved can occur in any social strata, so many theorists would believe that developmental issues are common across all income levels.

Although developmental tasks may be the same for all individuals, the context in which these developmental tasks occur may vary widely. Contextual factors need to be considered when examining emotional adjustment. Luthar (2003) stated, "Extreme environments of all kinds are likely to have their own set of problems" (p. 1589). Having wealth and privilege may ensure that material needs are met, which then can provide a buffer against life challenges (Piff et al., 2010), yet may not guarantee that emotional needs are fulfilled. Warner (1991) coined the term *affluenza* to describe the problems associated with great wealth (p. 183). He further states that the most frequent contributor to psychological problems is having a deprived childhood and the lack of a close empathetic relationship with parents. This contention is supported by Luthar and Becker's (2002) research identifying both isolation from adults and high achievement pressures as problems experienced by affluent youth.

The most comprehensive study on social class and mental health was conducted in Midtown Manhattan (Srole, Langner, Michael, Opler, & Rennie, 1962). Taking an epidemiological approach, a condition is observed from the viewpoint of the population, and how the environment affects the condition is examined, as well as how the condition impacts the community. In this study, the mental health of a large sample of the population was studied in a cross-sectional design. This research was the first study to test the hypothesis that sociocultural factors impact mental health. Further, comparing the highest social class group with the lowest social class group in terms of mental health functioning, Srole and Langner (1962b) observed that a higher percentage of the lower social class group was rated as severe/incapacitated (30.6% vs. 5.8%), while the highest group was more likely than those in the lower group to be rated as being in the well group (30% vs. 4.6%). When the research focused only on individuals who answered questions that indicated some form of emotional impairment, several significant differences were found between those in the lowest and highest social class groups. From this study, Srole and Langner (1962a) concluded that the affluent group had fewer mentally impaired individuals, that members of the affluent group were more likely to get psychiatric services when needed, and that these services led to more significant and sustained gains.

In her article, McKamy (1976) defined problems of the wealthy as arising from acute or chronic psychodynamic conflicts. Affluent and successful people are "adept at controlling their environment" and find that their own resources are often sufficient to handle problems (McKamy, 1976, p. 1110). Consequently, it is only the complex, psychodynamic breakdowns that bring the wealthy to seek mental health services. The positives that they bring to the therapeutic setting are that the clients are verbal and motivated toward goals they view as worthwhile. Given their history, affluent people are able to envision a positive future and can focus their energies over a long period of time to make changes.

As much as material resources buffer people against environmental traumas, these material advantages do not always result in positive emotional benefits (Csikszentmihaliyi, 1999). He cited time as being one of the scarcest resources for the wealthy. The time demands placed upon those with wealth often create difficult choices in balancing the demands of work and family. If someone places great value in obtaining and maintaining material goods, more time has to be allocated toward that pursuit at the expense of socioemotional pursuits. Diener (2000) has stated that some of the distress experienced by those with wealth comes from the expectations of high productivity that reduces leisure time. Ironically, a low negative relationship has been found between material and subjective well-being, with the conclusion that after a certain minimum threshold, money does not create happiness. Similarly, Luthar (2003) has identified psychological costs of material wealth. On an individual level, the emphasis on material success can limit other rewards, such as close relationships. A lack of intimacy in personal relationships as well as little focus on personal growth may remove sources of satisfaction that others might experience. In fact, those members of the highest wealth and privilege may have difficulty forming trusting relationships due to fear that others like them only because of their wealth. Paradoxically, Kasser, Ryan, Zax, and Sameroff (1995) found that teens who have experienced distant and controlling maternal relationships often become more materialistic, while those who have nurturing relationships come to value more intrinsic rewards. Others have found that unhappy adults tend to seek meaning in obtaining material goods (Diener & Biswas-Diener, 2002). Thus, a cycle might develop where wealth is sought to fulfill one's emotional needs, but the pursuit of wealth may lead to having less ability to be nurturing.

Other pressures faced by the wealthy, particularly women, include substance abuse and eating disorders (Wolfe & Fodor, 1996). Women often are faced with moving from a stimulating educational experience to the role of the spouse of a powerful leader. Their role often is to support the success of the spouse, which relegates them to managing the household, social events, and child-rearing functions. Such a move may lead to social isolation, for which a coping mechanism is substance use. The emphasis on appearance may seem to be a shallow value, but there is a strong emphasis on physical appearance in the upper classes (Wolfe & Fodor, 1996). Women may come to view appearance as necessary to maintaining their marriage and way of life.

On the community level, wealth interferes with forming support networks since any needed service can be purchased (Luthar, 2003). Strong personal relationships often evolve due to helping one another during a time of need because people are emotionally enriched when they are able to share difficult times with others. Altruism, the unselfish giving to another, creates positive feelings in the giver. Conversely, when a community is so self-sufficient that all needs are met, there are few critical incidents to bring communities together to help one another. Members of these affluent communities have little proof that others genuinely care for them. While there may be friendly interactions, there may be an underlying mistrustfulness when friendships are not put to the test. Even the physical nature of these communities may contribute to feelings of isolation; for example, the quest for privacy may be an unintended factor in social loneliness. Although those with wealth and privilege may have numerous social interactions, it is possible that the formation of close, personal connections may be limited.

Luthar (2003) also indicated that on the systemic level, a subculture of affluence may evolve in which wealthy individuals have unlimited options and choices. Because a sense of control has been associated with health and well-being (Lachman & Weaver, 1998), those who are members of this subculture might be expected to be able to control life in a way that leads to happiness. With an emphasis on individualism in the United States, the expectation arises that everything should be the way one wants it to be. Anything less than perfectionism is unacceptable; however, perfectionism is an impossibility. Therefore, when the inevitable failure happens, individuals in this subculture are more likely to attribute the outcome to personal shortcomings rather than external causes (Schwartz, 2000).

Accordingly, Luthar (2003) stated, "Increases in experienced control are accompanied by increases in expectations about control" (p. 1586). Such thinking can actually lead to feelings of depression. When coupled with the unrealistic belief that affluence brings happiness, those with great wealth and privilege may be confused and feel guilty when they do struggle with feelings of distress and unhappiness. With greater resources, the thinking may go, why am I so sad?

ISSUES AFFECTING CHILDREN AND ADOLESCENTS OF WEALTH

Children and adolescents from wealthy families present unique challenges for the clinician. An important detail to keep in mind is that "wealth is not an illness" (Shafran, 1992, p. 269). Children face the same developmental challenges regardless of wealth, and families encounter interpersonal conflicts and disruptions. However, wealth may become a complicating factor in how these developmental issues and interpersonal dynamics are manifested. *Affluenza* is the term coined to describe the condition that affects the very rich (Warner, 1991). This term implies that there are problems that occur because of their affluence. As previously mentioned, sociocultural factors have an impact on mental health, and the culture of wealth is not immune to impacting its members.

One frequently mentioned characteristic found in families of wealth is the lack of consistently available parents (Luthar & Becker, 2002; Luthar, Shoum, & Brown, 2006; Shafran, 1992). Such an absence can easily be disguised among the wealthy since children are not left unattended. Nannies or housekeepers may be relegated to performing many of the parenting duties handled by middle class parents. Children are provided with all of the physical needs but may be deprived of the familial connections that lead to a secure sense of self. On the one hand, these children may be indulged by getting material desires fulfilled, never having to delay gratification. On the other hand, they may question their importance in the family when parents do not contribute to their daily care. Additionally, a corollary to understanding their role in the family may be connected to the fact that wealthy children are not expected to make any sort of meaningful contribution to the family. People are hired to perform the services that children from other social classes have to complete. Although children from any social class may dislike chores, engaging in these behaviors helps children learn that they are able to contribute to the family as well as develop a sense of competence and confidence from seeing their accomplishments.

The lack of clear role models is another complication that occurs when parents are absent (Shafran, 1992). Values, goals, and interpersonal skills are often conveyed to children through interaction with parents. While children may have great admiration for their highly successful and respected parents, in reality they may not know their parents on a personal level. Children may attend boarding schools with excellent academic traditions but miss an opportunity for daily interactions with family. Furthermore, summers may be spent in exciting activities at challenging camps versus family vacations. While the children gain incredible experiences, they fail to benefit from some of the basic experiences of building a sense of self through these important interpersonal interactions with family or parents.

Even career options may appear limited to the children of affluent families (Lapour & Heppner, 2009). For example, a very narrow range of career options may be presented as acceptable to children and adolescents. Any career related to a service that their parents purchase (such as teaching) may not be viewed as acceptable to someone of their status (Lapour & Heppner, 2009). Ironically, children from lower social classes can often find role models outside the home, such as in school, athletics, church, or the community, that help them compensate for models they may not have at home. Children of affluence may not see these same roles as viable alternatives for themselves. Although many of these children will pursue important professions, they may not find as much pleasure in their profession as those who are from middle class backgrounds (Pittman, 1985). Consequently, even though wealth may convey that there are unlimited options in life, choices might actually be restricted regardless of one's talents and interests.

Peer relations may become another source of difficulty. When children come from a legacy of wealth and privilege, it may be difficult for them to know if others like and accept them for who they are rather than for what they have (Shafran, 1992; Warner, 1991). This issue may be compounded by parents who convey that reactions to them by outsiders are not trustworthy (Pittman, 1985). Because children of the wealthy avoid developing friendships outside of their own strata, they often live in a world in which everyone caters to their needs. If they get into trouble, they will be bailed out and not have to face the same consequences as those from lower-income families (Warner, 1991). Such actions can increase their sense of entitlement. Therefore, friendships may be based on mutual activities or shared privilege, leading to a scarcity of peer relationships that are genuine.

Respectively, another challenge to developing an accurate sense of self may be knowing whether or not personal achievements are a result of one's own ability or connected to one's wealth. Often, any preferential treatment that benefits those who may be disadvantaged is criticized; however, preferential treatment of the wealthy is often hidden (Chen & Tyler, 2001). One such hidden advantage is legacy admissions to prestigious colleges. Chen and Tyler (2001) proposed that such admissions are "legitimizing myths," which allow those in positions of power and influence to maintain a high self-esteem by believing their own efforts led to their success, as opposed to examining external factors such as the parents' wealth (Luthar & Latendresse, 2005, p. 243). These myths conceal reality and allow the privileged to attribute success to their own efforts. Larew (1991) found that legacy students at Harvard were significantly less qualified than other admitted students. Support for the ideas for legitimizing myths can be found in the research of Stanley and Danko (1996), in which the process of wealth accumulation was examined. They found that adult children of the super wealthy were able to ignore that they received financial assistance from their families and fully believed that they had earned these privileges on their own merit.

A number of issues have been identified as having prevalence among the children of wealthy families. Luthar and D'Avanzo (1999) found that students living in suburban, affluent communities had higher substance use than students in poor, urban communities. In addition, affluent students in this study had significantly higher levels of anxiety and somewhat higher levels of depression; substance use was related to the anxiety and depression, suggesting an attempt to self-medicate. Another connection for male students was that high substance use was related to popularity, thus suggesting a link to peer pressure. Research indicates that there are some affluent, suburban teens who demonstrate patterns of substance use that have both immediate and long-term risks for their psychological adjustment (McMahon & Luthar, 2006).

Luthar and Latendresse (2005) postulated that two factors may be antecedents to elevated levels of substance use, depression, and anxiety among affluent youth. First, the pressure to achieve has been associated with high perfectionistic behaviors. If a student viewed academic failure as a personal shortcoming, then that student was more likely to display high levels of depression, anxiety, and substance use (Luthar & Becker, 2002). A second aspect of achievement pressure was related to parental emphasis on achievement. Students may feel that their parents value them more for what they achieve than who they are, thus basing self-worth on accomplishments.

The second potential antecedent identified was isolation from parents (Luthar & Latendresse, 2005). Parents often believe that allowing their students to be unsupervised after school allows them to become more self-sufficient, thus justifying their long hours from home. Additionally, parents in highly demanding careers or social responsibilities often have little time left for unstructured family time, thus losing the opportunity for building emotional closeness. Luthar and Latendresse (2005) found that the simple family routine of eating dinner with at least one parent on most nights was positively linked to a student's self-reported adjustment and performance at school.

Another interesting finding concerning affluent youth was in terms of their rebellious behaviors (Luthar & Latendresse, 2005). Almost 10% of these students demonstrated high levels of behavior disturbances and were at risk for poor grades, and 20% of these students exhibited persistently high levels of substance use across time. The authors of this study stated, "Youth at the socioeconomic extremes were more similar than different" (Luthar & Latendresse, 2005, p. 51). However, one of the differences between those on the high end of the social class spectrum and those at the low end of the spectrum was that the wealthy youth were able to counterbalance the negative consequences of their delinquent behaviors due to the resources available to them. They were more likely to receive high-quality treatment and less likely to face legal consequences.

One common belief is that children from affluent families are highly overscheduled. In their book *The Overscheduled Child*, Rosenfeld and Wise (2001) discuss how children from upper SES families are expected to spend extensive time in outside activities as a way to build resumes for future opportunities. According to Luthar et al. (2006), emotional closeness within the family may suffer as children are transported to a variety of lessons and activities; however, research has shown that the issue is more complex than just the number of activities. While modest links were found between the number of outside activities and adjustment outcomes, the more important variable was the child's perception of the parents' attitude toward achievement. Furthermore, the perceived level of parental criticism was particularly detrimental to the child. In fact, the general effects of extracurricular activities were positive. Luthar et al. (2006) also found that expectations and criticism had opposite effects. Whereas high expectations did not create problems for children, children felt diminished or unworthy when criticized by parents for not reaching their expectations. This criticism in turn was associated with distress.

Physical appearance is an issue that is particularly salient for adolescent females. Physical attractiveness and popularity have been found to be strongly linked among affluent girls (Luthar & Latendresse, 2005). The drive for physical attractiveness can contribute to the development of eating disorders as evidenced by the phrase "you can't be too rich or too thin" (attributed to the Duchess of Windsor, previously Wallis Simpson).

Nonsuicidal self-injury (NSSI) has also emerged as an issue among affluent youth. Yates, Tracy, and Luthar (2008) found that almost one-third of the affluent students in their study engaged in NSSI during the past year. Although levels were higher in girls, boys also engaged in the behavior at sufficient levels for concern. Perceived parental criticism was a significant predictor of NSSI. Respectively, an emerging associated factor, reported by students in the study, was alienation toward parents.

Whereas many of the issues faced by children and adolescents are common for those in all social classes, the tendency is to ignore these problems in children of wealth due to the vast resources available to them. Resources can be utilized to cover up problems and to minimize the outward impact of the problems. Unfortunately, any unresolved issues will continue to be present in adulthood, thus perpetuating the mental health concerns found in the upper class. The affluent, neglected child becomes the affluent, detached parent. The child with an eating disorder may evolve into the glamorous, perfect host who secretly starves herself. The youth who finds risk-taking behaviors thrilling may develop into a brilliant CEO with a hidden side that engages in illicit behaviors just because he can. Regrettably, problems that are not addressed do not necessarily disappear.

CHALLENGES FOR THERAPISTS

In the recent movie *The King's Speech*, speech therapist Lionel Logue states to the Duke of York "my castle, my rules" when establishing the treatment protocol for the future king of England. This example highlights one essential issue when working with clients of wealth and privilege. Establishing the therapeutic alliance when the client has a sense of entitlement with an expectation of special privileges may become complicated (Warner, 1991). The very rich are accustomed to having the best and therefore may search for the therapist they consider "in vogue" (Warner, 1991, p. 185), regardless of whether this professional is best suited for treating the presenting problem. In addition, the client can just as easily "fire" the therapist and "hire" another if the therapist does not say what the client wants to hear. Establishing one's self as the expert is crucial from the beginning of treatment and needs to be accompanied by having clear ground rules (Shafran, 1992).

Because those with wealth are accustomed to having control of situations, these clients may place greater demands on the therapist for accommodations such as schedule changes or providing the type of treatment desired (McKamy, 1976). Clients may not want to give up the control they are used to having and may want to dictate treatment, such as receiving the latest medications. They may even threaten litigation if they do not like the treatment they receive (Warner, 1991). For example, a college student at a prestigious private university was sent to the campus counseling center after being arrested for illegal behavior. When the therapist confronted the student on his actions, the student replied that the therapist could not talk to him that way and that his father was a major CEO who would have her job. Students like this one may be accustomed to someone else taking care of their problems rather than having to face consequences. Therapists in these types of situations need to be confident in their own skills and secure in the knowledge that their organizations will support their actions rather than give in to wealthy clients or their parents.

The prevalent tendency of wealthy individuals is to see self as functioning just fine as opposed to having mental health issues. Parents might see a child's problem as unrelated to their own behavior and believe the therapist should "fix" the child. In fact, the parent may resent being told that a child has a mental health problem, may deny that it exists, and insist it is just a "phase" (Warner, 1991, p. 186). Although this type of denial is not limited to the wealthy, these individuals do have the ability to gather support for their view of the situation. Learning to pace the delivery of confrontation along with building the therapeutic alliance is necessary, or clients who are used to hearing what they want will quickly seek other treatment.

Case Study 5.2

Client statement: "... and you know my dad can have your job in a minute!"

Client situation: Rome, on academic probation, was required to attend weekly counseling sessions. He set the tone for counseling in his initial session where he diffidently responded only when necessary. He was smart, handsome, savvy, popular, and rich. He displayed an air of entitlement and privilege; however, it was not planned—it was just there, a natural response to his social status. By all standards, in every way Rome exuded his position, he finished the session stating ...

Bias uncovered: Any client can fire you. I have experienced this in the past; some clients I challenged or confronted never returned. Why was this different for me? Immediately, I felt an urgent need to show my position as expert in this counseling relationship. I even remember changing my physical distance to Rome. Now as I consider that first session, I wonder if the expression on my face showed my disgust. Did Rome experience the distance that I placed between us? What did I model for him in that moment? My theoretical stance is not that of counselor as expert; so from where were these responses coming? Did my actions move him toward introspection? Did they move his thoughts toward others in his life who established high expectations and the pressure to succeed no matter what?

FOLLOW-UP QUESTIONS

1. What are the circumstances for unconditional positive regard?
2. Does a wealth and privilege stereotype shape my values?
3. What effect do these values have on my identity as a counselor?
4. Do these values have an effect on the therapeutic relationship?
5. Would you be willing to share your thoughts in supervision?

Fees

Setting fees can be a complicated issue in therapy. Even Freud had to deal with the issue of fee setting and collecting in a day when clients paid for services from their own pocket (Chodoff, 1991). Freud viewed money matters as important in that the analyst had to recognize personal material needs and take responsibility for them with the patient. He favored addressing fees as part of setting up the initial psychoanalytic situation (Lerner, 1991). It is important to consider that financial arrangements for therapy are essentially a business agreement that needs to be discussed openly (Weissberg, 1991).

Fees need to be stated clearly at the beginning of therapy along with expectations about the timeframe for payment (Shainess, 1991). The actual amount of the fee is also a complicated issue. If the wealthy client believes the fee has been increased due to the client's financial status, the client may view this as further evidence that others cannot be trusted not to exploit those who have money. However, the opposite view can be just as powerful. Unless the fee is high, those with wealth may not believe they are getting the best therapy (Horner, 1991). The therapist may benefit from knowing the prevailing rates in the community for therapy and set a fee that is consistent with the local area. Raising rates for wealthier clients may result in the therapist becoming more economically dependent on the client, thus clouding therapeutic judgment.

An interesting correlate to money issues is the client's view of having to pay for therapy. Even though money is not a financial issue, it may be an emotional issue. If the client has an illusion of specialness, the need to pay for a therapeutic relationship may trigger narcissistic wounds (Horner, 1991). The client may question whether the therapist really cares about the client if the client is paying for the service. Concerns about only being liked because of wealth may arise that will need to be examined throughout the therapeutic process. Finally, the wealthy may have casual attitudes about money that can lead to sporadic payment, which will need to be addressed if these patterns evolve (Shafran, 1992). Because money is always available when needed, wealthy clients may not be concerned about those who depend upon a regular payment for income.

Ethical Issues

Therapy with wealthy clients raises a number of ethical issues for therapists. First, the therapist needs to examine personal beliefs about those with wealth. One problem of countertransference may be envy of the client's financial resources accompanied by contempt if the client's values are contrary to the therapist's values (Shafran, 1992). Because of these differing values, the client and therapist may have different worldviews that could impede progress (Liu et al., 2007). Likewise, the therapist's own work ethic may interfere with understanding the client's life perspective. It is essential that therapists recognize and acknowledge personal feelings that the client's wealth may trigger. Although it may be difficult, the therapist needs to be willing to see the world through the client's eyes.

How to avoid minimizing the client's problems is another challenge. Weitzman (as cited in Luthar, 2003) found that service providers underestimated domestic violence among affluent women, believing that these women had the resources to leave if they chose to do so. Second, signs of trouble in school children may not be pursued when recognized because of the fear of how parents will react (Luthar & Latendresse, 2005). Third, when a problem is chronic mental illness, the family may reject the client, leading the treatment team to exclude the family from any therapeutic tasks (McKamy, 1976). Finally, fearing the impact of confronting clients of affluence, treatment may not produce improvement in a timely manner (Warner, 1991). Ironically, families of wealth and privilege may be underserved due to the belief that their wealth prevents them from experiencing normative life crises.

Therapists working with affluent clients need to be aware of their own strengths and vulnerabilities. In many circumstances, therapists are respected due to their education and expertise. In contrast, when working with wealthy clients, the therapist may actually be assisting the client to excel beyond the level the therapist has achieved (McKamy, 1976). There may be pressure for the therapist to "prove his worth" (Warner, 1991, p. 193) to these clients, whereas clients from lower and middle social class groups are more likely to view the therapist as the expert. Being unaware of the difference of status is the true problem. Maintaining a strong professional identify along with preserving a strong self-image is important to therapeutic success (McKamy, 1976).

Additionally, there are temptations that may arise from working with the wealthy that necessitate counselor awareness. Therapists are often privileged to information that is not available to the public. Wealthy clients have access to financial dealings that could provide "insider" information. It is both illegal and unethical to act upon this information. In addition, wealthy clients may want to show appreciation through gifts that may seem innocuous to them, such as event tickets or products produced by their company. Accepting such gifts has the potential to create an imbalance in the therapeutic relationship (Drellich, 1991). Having a clear policy on gifts as part of the informed consent may be a method of eliminating this issue.

When working with clients who are known public figures, there may be an allure to being associated with their fame. Warner (1991) addressed the issue of "name-dropping" (p. 180) as a way to increase one's own status. Not only is the therapist connected to wealth by this association, the therapist also has access to extremely personal information. For example, an adolescent from a well-known family shared information about sexual infidelities among adults in her community with her therapist. Whenever the therapist saw these individuals in the news, the temptation to share their stories was present, though the therapist maintained confidentiality long after the therapy terminated. In this electronic age of easy access to personal secrets, the therapist could be tempted to disclose information inappropriately to colleagues under the guise of seeking consultation. Even if clients share their own therapeutic experience with the public, the therapist is still bound by confidentiality not to disclose information discussed in sessions.

Case Study 5.3

Client statement: "The people in this town would be incensed if they only knew the man my stepfather really is."

Client situation: Tiffany sat angrily in my counseling office. She complained that her stepfather had tremendous power over her mother.

He had paid for several plastic surgeries, he expected her mother to dress in certain ways, he only allowed her to associate with selected friends, he scheduled all their social events, and so on. Tiffany went on to talk about all the politics, scandals, society events, and the secrets her mother had shared with her. Tiffany conveyed her resentment of the financial control her stepfather held over her, yet she would not have her college education and the privileges she enjoyed without his financial support.

Bias uncovered: As I listened to Tiffany, I was surprised and enraged. I could not believe my ears—the violation of political office, the breach of ethics, the scandal. What was I to do with this information? I had suddenly gained personal knowledge about extortion, conspiracy, illegal hiring and firing, and the ongoing sexual affairs. I know—it is called confidentiality.

FOLLOW-UP QUESTIONS

1. Have you ever experienced knowing personal information that is so "hot" that your urge to tell has caused you to pause?
2. Are there increased professional challenges to the explicit promise of safeguarding of confidentiality and holding the privilege when counseling individuals with wealth and privilege?
3. How does knowledge of secrets influence your need to know more?
4. How do you safeguard confidential and privileged communication when "to tell" could afford you the financial resources to educate your child?

CONCLUSION

Wealth does not preordain that individuals will encounter mental health problems. Nevertheless, wealth may become a complicating factor when emotional problems are encountered. Children raised with affluence may face challenges related to the financial status of the family and may carry these issues into adulthood. On the positive side, wealthy clients can afford treatment designed to meet their needs. They often are resourceful and have the ability to focus on goals for an extended time period and can envision a positive future for themselves. For a therapist to be effective with this population, it is important to maintain sensitivity to personal feelings about wealth as well as be aware of the client's fears and anxieties. Wealth does not prevent the impact of life's complexities; therefore it is essential that the therapist understand and accept the uniqueness of this cultural group.

II

II

6

The Intersection of Class and Race

Shawn L. Spurgeon

In this chapter, the relationship between race and social class will be examined as it relates to individual development in the United States. Professional counselors will see how an increased awareness of the intersection of these two variables can enrich clinical experiences with their clients and can provide a framework for a more comprehensive understanding of their clients' core issues. An understanding of the relevance of this intersection provides the necessary tools for engaging in rich and deep discussions with your clients.

Case Study 6.1

I remember my excitement as I took my first clinical position as a counselor in a family services agency. I was armed with a lot of knowledge from my master's program about human behavior, development, and the interaction of those variables as they relate to family. My first couple was Jim and Terry. They were a young, African American, dual-career couple who wanted to explore issues within their marriage related to communication and finances. I thought, "This should last about three sessions."

Well, 6 months and 15 sessions later, they still had the same issues and problems. Progress seemed to be going very slow. Both of them were hard-working individuals, they clearly loved and cared for each other, and they seemed to respect their marriage. I had hit the wall because I had tried different things in session with them to help them communicate better. For example, I used the traditional "I statements" exercise and it worked really well in session. When they got home and tried to do it, they failed miserably. I could not understand how two people who cared about each other so much could be so adamant about not listening. Initially, I did not bring this case up in supervision because I felt (as an African American male) that I could relate to them and help them through their concerns with no problems. Obviously, I was wrong.

I met with my supervisor at the usual time, and this case was the first one I discussed. I explained the situation, their presenting problem, and my struggles with helping them learn to communicate effectively. My supervisor listened intently as I expressed my concern for their well-being and questioned my competence to help them. Then, she made a simple statement that helped me understand my dilemma: "Tell me what you know about Jim and what you know about Terry." As I began to explain what I knew about this couple, she stopped me and restated, "Tell me what you know about Jim and what you know about Terry." Again, I started to talk about the couple, and again she stopped and repeated the same statement.

FOLLOW-UP QUESTIONS

1. What message was my supervisor trying to convey to me?
2. What information did I miss that I needed to know more about?
3. How do you think my culture (African American) and social class (middle) influenced my initial thoughts about my effectiveness?

Though the United States has worked hard to rid itself of the race-based hatred and cruel injustices that have plagued minorities over the years, the fact remains that this country is based on race and social class (Harley, Jolivette, McCormick, & Tice, 2002). This concept is prominent in the literature as researchers make connections with other aspects of life, such as domestic violence (Sokoloff & Dupont, 2005), crime (Burgess-Proctor, 2006), labor inequality (Poster & Wilson, 2008), and network building (Damaske, 2009). These variables permeate every aspect of our selves and influence decision making, self-concept, and overall wellness. Harley et al. (2002) note that people often find ways to justify their decisions to behave a certain way with a certain population of individuals when in fact the roots of their decisions can be traced back to racism and classism.

Constantine (2002) argues that any experiences and phenomena that occur in society should be viewed through the race and social class lens because it is through these lenses that we begin to fully understand and appreciate the complexities of life. The intersection of these identities shapes our lives and forms the realities we experience (Fukuyama & Ferguson, 2000). For example, Damaske (2009) argued that though African American males have a more difficult time establishing networks for business opportunities, the within-group differences for this population of individuals are more profound than the differences between African American males and Caucasian males. Sokoloff and Dupont (2005) argue for a social structural model of domestic violence against women that has at its roots the intersection of race and social class. It is important for counselors to understand the intersection of these variables and the effect that intersection will have on their clients.

RACE

When we think of race, we think of biologically defined aspects of ourselves that are unchangeable in nature. These aspects include physical, mental, and behavioral attributes that influence the way other people evaluate us visually (Herrnstein & Murray, 1994). There are some who would argue that race in the United States is a social and political construct that is constantly changing (McGoldrick & Giordano, 1996). The definition of race has undergone multiple evaluations and analyses, but most of those definitions highlight the notion of race as both a biological and cultural entity (Harley et al., 2002).

It is important to note that the terms *race*, *ethnicity*, and *culture* each have a specific meaning and should not be considered synonymous. Helms and Cook (1999) define ethnicity as "the national, regional, or tribal origins of one's remembered ancestors and the customs, traditions, and rituals (i.e., subjective culture) handed down by these ancestors, which among ethnic group members, are assumed to be their culture" (p. 19). The definition implies that adherence to customs and traditions serves as a strong indicator of one's commitment to and how well one identifies himself or herself. This identity is distinctive from racial identity, which is conceptualized as an avenue through which an individual becomes aware of and develops salience for his or her race (Vandiver, Fhagen-Smith, Cokley, Cross, & Worrell, 2002).

Racial identity has been thoroughly researched and conceptualized over the last 35 years (Whittaker & Neville, 2010). For example, Cross's (1971) model of Nigrescence served as the focal point for future research on racial identity development among individuals in society. His initial research focused on African Americans and their racial identity development; since that time, the concept of racial identity has been applied to Caucasian Americans (Helms, 1990), Hispanic Americans, and Korean Americans. Though most counselors have a clear understanding of the relevance of race, many of them struggle with the role social class plays in their clients' individual development (Liu, Pickett, & Ivy, 2007).

SELF-REFLECTION OPPORTUNITY 6.1

What do you think of when you hear the term *race*? What images come to mind? Ask your friends about what it means to have a racial identity and note their responses. What conclusions can you draw from your friends' responses about race as well as your own understanding of race?

SOCIAL CLASS

Dittmar (1995) argues that the United States has created a conundrum in which it avoids acknowledging the class and economic issues in society by funneling all of their discussions under the umbrella of poverty. This country has worked to ignore the obvious differences that exist among individuals in society. Given the disparity and unequal distribution of resources, wealth, fringe benefits, and privilege, it is clear that the United States operates in a vacuum of assumed equality for all. However, there are multiple examples of inequality, and these examples seem to increase as this country continues to experience economic growth (McGoldrick & Giordano, 1996).

Class has been conceptualized in different ways and by different individuals. Inherent in those conceptualizations is the notion that there are both personal aspects and natural aspects that seem to contribute to differences among the social classes. Though the United States has implemented programs designed to level the playing field for everyone, the pervasiveness of social class continues to manifest itself in society (Dittmar, 1995). We live in a society in which a positive correlation relationship exists between worth and social status.

SELF-REFLECTION OPPORTUNITY 6.2

Think about this statement: 10% of the people in this world own 90% of the wealth. What does that statement mean to you? Think about a time when you were judged based on the type of clothes you wore. What was that experience like for you? Think about a time when you judged someone based on the type of clothes they wore. What was that experience like for you? Now compare the similarities and differences between these two experiences.

RACE AND SOCIAL CLASS

The intersection between race and social class is clear and powerful. Harley et al. (2002) argue that race and social class are interconnected and cannot be discussed within separate vacuums. Similarly, Holvino (2008) concluded that this intersection influences organizational structure and practices, particularly for women. Strolovitch (2006) believed that the political advocacy of interest groups is influenced greatly by the racial makeup and level of marginalization of its members. The truth of the matter is that many of the racial minority clients we see come from impoverished backgrounds.

Constantine (2002) argues that race and social class represent important cultural group memberships in this country and cannot be ignored. When we choose to individualize these variables, it prevents us from fully understanding the dynamic nature of their interaction, and thus prevents us from fully understanding our clients' core issues. Arredondo (1999) concluded that effective multicultural counseling cannot occur if we do not respect and examine the intersection of these variables with our clients.

SELF-REFLECTION OPPORTUNITY 6.3

Think about the media coverage of the victims of Hurricane Katrina in New Orleans, Louisiana, in 2005. What kinds of things did the news media focus on? What terms were used to describe the victims of this tragedy? Now think about the flooding victims in Nashville, Tennessee, in 2008. What kinds of things did the news media focus on? What terms were used to describe the victims of this tragedy? Now compare and contrast these two events.

CLINICAL IMPLICATIONS

The human services profession has played an important role in helping to maintain the stereotypes related to racial and cultural differences (Helms & Cook, 1999). Though there has been a strong emphasis on multiculturalism and respect for diversity in recent research, many of the theories on which we base our understanding of human behavior were written by Caucasian males (Corey, 2009). Clinical training for professionals focuses on increased self-awareness and ownership of values, beliefs, and attitudes; yet there are still instances where our individual biases as clinicians affect our therapeutic connection with our clients (S. Sue, 1999). The nature of counseling itself could lead one to engage in discriminatory treatment, given the emphasis on equal treatment for all clients (Harley et al., 2002). This state of affairs rings true when we talk about social class and the influence it has on the development of a therapeutic relationship with our clients.

The notion of social class bias can manifest itself in many forms in the therapeutic relationship. Liu, Hernandez, Mahmood, and Stinson (2006) support the idea that some counselors struggle with an upward mobility bias. The completion of a master's degree affords a certain level of status and professional recognition, which could work to create situations in which counselors see themselves as different than or even better than their clients. There is a power differential inherent in the counselor-client relationship that trainees are taught to understand and respect (Constantine, 2002); however, there have been numerous instances in which the abuse of this power resulted in the client being harmed by the counselor (Remley & Herlihy, 2010).

Case Study 6.2

In my work as a mental health clinician in a small rural community, I had the fortunate opportunity to work with Melissa. She was a 16-year-old Caucasian female who was having some serious conflicts with her mother. She was a straight-A student and wanted to attend college, first attending the local community college and then going on to a four-year university. She really wanted to leave her small town as soon as she could and embark on a journey of education, growth, and self-discovery. She talked about traveling to New York and maybe doing graduate work at a school in Philadelphia.

The problem was that she hated her mother and everything she stood for. Her mother had the same ambitions and dreams but decided to stay and marry the local football hero after graduating from high school. When Melissa was 6 years old, her father left the family and never returned. Since then, her mother had struggled over the 10 years trying to provide for Melissa and herself. Melissa felt that her mother tried to "live through her" by telling her who she could be friends with, giving her silly curfews, and constantly nagging her about making good grades. Melissa was clear: "I love my mother, but she gets on my nerves."

FOLLOW-UP QUESTIONS

1. Do you think this family is experiencing a conflict between social class and race? If so, in what way?
2. I consider myself to be a middle class African American male. What types of things do I need to pay attention to as I am working with this client?
3. Consider yourself and how you might work with this client. What types of things would you focus on, and what do you need to be aware of?

CONSIDERATIONS

There is a paucity of literature that details the intersection between race and social class in counselor education (Lui, Ali, et al., 2004). Constantine (2001) states that counselors would be less likely to ignore the relevance of the intersection of these variables if they were introduced to the idea in their graduate training programs. Given the changing and diversifying mental health needs of clients, it is important that clinicians and researchers alike explore these issues and provide more direction for their trainees. There are aspects of race and social class that need to be identified and taken into consideration when working with clients.

Multiple Identities

It is important for counselors to understand that their clients come to sessions with aspects of their identity that need to be considered within the context of their primary concerns. These aspects include gender issues and family of origin issues. Oftentimes, clients are hesitant to process these issues with their counselors because they get the message that the issue is not relevant or will not be received warmly (L. Weber, 1998). It is the intersection of these identities that provides rich and valuable information for the client and can serve as the impetus for effective treatment planning.

Structure

It is important for counselors to understand that the traditional ways of gathering information and structuring sessions will not be effective for all clients. Given the intersection of race and social class, it is important for counselors to be willing to integrate creative and meaningful ways for working with clients. This includes a blending of theoretical perspectives that will incorporate all aspects of identity, including social class and race. When counselors begin to understand this notion and are willing to approach their work with clients in a nontraditional fashion, a wealth of clinical information can be discovered to help with effective diagnosis and treatment (Arredondo, 1999).

Bias and Privilege

Oftentimes, when counselors complete their master's degrees and begin their clinical work, they move from a lower class to a middle class style of living (Liu et al., 2006). This movement is subtle but cannot be ignored by the counselor. It is important that counselors begin to understand the impact of this change and how this change can affect the counselor's worldview. Additionally, this change has the potential to influence the view that counselors have about their clients. Counselors need to be willing to explore their own potential biases because these biases have the potential to affect the therapeutic relationship.

Relationship Building

The therapeutic relationship established between the client and the counselor continues to be the heart of effective clinical work (Cochran & Cochran, 2006). Oftentimes, counselors complete comprehensive assessments on their clients without developing a strong therapeutic relationship. This relationship is steeped in trust and mutual respect and allows the counselor to further understand the client's worldview. An important part of that understanding is an astute analysis and awareness of the way the client sees himself or herself according to society's standards of living. Sometimes, due in part to a need to press forward and rapidly develop a treatment plan, clinicians want to simply make observations about the client's social class without processing these issues with the client. Mental health professionals need to understand that differences exist across social class and race, and that those differences have an effect on how quickly a therapeutic relationship can be established.

Case Study 6.3

Mike, a Caucasian American male, is a new counselor and is just beginning working with his first client, a 32-year-old African American female single mother with four children. He reads from her intake sheet that she gets public assistance, is not currently employed, and receives child support payments from two of the fathers of her children. I know from conversations with Mike that he has a middle class background and has struggled with class issues in his program of study. During a lunch break and before he sees the client, he stopped me in the break room and asked if I would be willing to take over the case and see this client. I was curious as to why he wanted me to work with this client, and he stated, "She is African American and so are you, so I thought that maybe there would be a stronger therapeutic relationship between the two of you. You could probably do more for her than I ever could." I asked him if he had a bias against her and he adamantly denied any such bias.

Since I refused to take the case, Mike went ahead with his scheduled appointment. Later on that day, I saw him in the break room. I asked him how his first session with a real client went. He stated, "Not well. She did not want to talk to me and I couldn't get anything out of her. I think she may have been intimated by me, so I asked her if she wanted to see someone else. She agreed that maybe we were not a good fit, and so I turned her file back in and asked the intake specialist to assign her to someone else. I got the feeling that she didn't like men, so I think she may do well with a female counselor."

FOLLOW-UP QUESTIONS

1. What do you think I should say to Mike about this situation? What would you say?
2. Do you think Mike has an issue with her class or her race or with neither of those?
3. What does Mike need to be more aware of in his future work with clients?

ADDENDUM

The client was assigned to another Caucasian male counselor in the agency and this is what he found out after his first session:

1. She was in the second year of a master's degree in education, with an emphasis on English education.
2. Her children were the result of three failed marriages, two of which were domestic violence situations (which was her presenting problem; she wanted to find out why she involved herself with violent men).

3. She is on scholarship and her program is designed such that the second year of the program is dedicated to student teaching and supervision and students are discouraged from working.
4. She used the money from her husbands' child support to pay for apartment rental and food and used the public assistance she received to help pay for her children's medical expenses.

CONCLUSION

Social class and race continue to be salient variables in this country, and their role in the identity development of clients cannot be overstated. It is important for counselors to recognize the relevance of this intersection in their clients' lives and to be willing to attend to it. Counselors need to explore opportunities in training, including practicum and internship experiences, to develop a stronger understanding of the role these variables will have and how they will ultimately affect the lives of their clients. An important part of that understanding is an increased awareness of the role social class and race have played in their own development. Through this lens, counselors can broaden their conceptual frameworks and provide an opportunity to be more effective with their clients.

RESOURCES

The following books are highly recommended reading on this topic:

Dilg, M. (2010). *Our worlds in our words: Exploring race, class, gender, and sexual orientation in multicultural classrooms.* New York: Teachers College Press.

Grant, C. A., & Sleeter, C. E. (2007). *Turning on learning: Five approaches for multicultural teaching plans for race, class, gender, and disability* (4th ed.). Indianapolis, IN: Jossey-Bass.

Hughes, D. (2008). Cultural versus social class contexts for extra-curricular activity participation. In A. Booth & A. C. Crouter (Eds), *Disparities in school readiness* (pp. 189–198). New York: Lawrence Erlbaum Associates.

Kincheloe, J. L., & Steinberg, S. R. (Eds.). (2007). *Cutting class: Socioeconomic status and education.* Lanham, MD: Rowman & Littlefield.

7

Chasing the American Dream: Social Class and Career Counseling

Colette T. Dollarhide

In Chapter 7, the roles of class and opportunity are examined through the lens of the metaphor "the American dream" as they relate to clients' views of career, success, and opportunity. With an awareness of the positive and negative connotations of this popular metaphor, counselors can adopt more inclusive and empowering perspectives of the clients' future, and can use the provided career counseling tools to empower clients to value their pursuit of their own dream.

Case Study 7.1

From 1988 to the mid-1990s I worked as a career counselor in Reno, Nevada. One of the most interesting local characters was a man known at the time as "the Waver," who walked back and forth from Reno to Carson City (40 miles) though summer heat and winter snow. I assumed he was homeless due to his daily walk and his "eclectic" clothing. What do people say about the homeless? "Poor thing! Does he have a mental health problem? He must be starving! Where does he sleep? How does he survive the weather? Shouldn't someone help him?"

On his daily walk for over 20 years, he waved and smiled at oncoming drivers, prompting many to wave, smile, and honk in reply. My husband worked in a business on his walking route and got to know him, where the Waver affirmed that, "I do just fine! No need to worry about me!" He said that he saw it as his life's *work* to spread love and happiness, and he did this by waving to make people smile. People gave him clothes to stay warm and a bed to sleep in at night. To pay for his food, he gave people stones that he found on his daily walk. That was his job, given to him by God—to walk and smile and wave.

I have some of those stones still today. I owe them to *him* for teaching me about the meaning of "work."

FOLLOW-UP QUESTIONS

1. What are your reactions to the homeless? Does homelessness equate to purposelessness?
2. Does this person need counseling? If so, what would be your counseling agenda?
3. How would you like to see this story end? What does that say about your values?

Many counselors and helping professionals offer career counseling within the context of holistic mental health services. In its most inclusive sense, career counseling is far more than offering advice on resumes and interviewing; it is inter- and intrapersonal counseling to help a client examine his or her life direction to find a good fit between vocational and avocational life roles (Fouad et al., 2007; Super, Savickas, & Super, 1996). In this process, the counselor may inadvertently influence the client's progress when unexamined and unchallenged assumptions about that goodness of fit are predicated on the counselor's implicit biases (Boysen, 2010).

Implicit bias is a manifestation of unintentional and unconscious values that are a product of early values programming—the internalization of spoken and unspoken social messages embedded in school, music, family stories and lessons, movies, books, and everyday social interactions (Boysen, 2010). The implicit nature of these internalized messages means that we can be *consciously* open-minded, accepting, and receptive to others, yet still engage in stereotyping or disrespectful actions because implicit biases are below our awareness (Sue et al., 2007). Research has revealed the insidious nature of implicit biases in terms of multiculturalism (Boysen, 2010), but any common image or metaphor can result in buried attitudes that emerge unbidden during routine life. One such metaphor related to classism is the concept of the American dream.

The American dream exists for both counselors and clients in this country, and for many, serves as a template for measuring "success" in this culture. It can create expectations of material possessions, status, and prestige that may perpetuate classist career counseling (by the counselor) and unproductive career decision making (by the client) that could skew the client's perception of his or her best interests. To understand the power of this image, we must examine its source, historical meaning, and current manifestations.

SELF-REFLECTION OPPORTUNITY 7.1

What do you think of when you hear *American dream*? What images come to mind for you? Can you recall the first time you heard that expression? Ask friends and family about their understanding of the term. Note their responses—both the content and the emotional connotations in their replies. What conclusions can you draw from this experience?

THE SOCIOPOLITICAL HISTORY OF A NATIONAL MOTTO

The term *American dream* is deeply embedded in our national consciousness, to the point that this ubiquitous phrase has lost much of its original meaning (Cullen, 2003). Currently, it is used to celebrate athletic successes, justify financial conquests, and excuse political intrigue and imbroglio, evoking images of poverty to riches, acquisitiveness, cut-throat competition, and winning at any cost—what Zakaria (2010) termed the "opening credits of Dallas ... open land, shiny skyscrapers, fancy cars, cowboy businessmen" (p. 30). Variously, it is also used to evoke idealized images of suburbia—the house in the suburbs, two cars, two children, and a docile family pet—the product of television programming of the 1950s (Wright, 2009). In order to understand how this concept has influenced our perceptions of other terms, like *social class*, *prestige*, *success*, and *career*—and how those terms influence the work we do with our clients when we offer career counseling—we need to understand this national icon. Coined in 1931 by James Truslow Adams (Cullen, 2003; Wright, 2009), the phrase originally meant

> that dream of a land in which life should be better and richer and fuller for every man [*sic*], with opportunity for each according to his [*sic*] ability or achievement ... a dream of social order in which each man and each woman shall be able to attain to the fullest stature of which they are innately capable, and be recognized by others for what they are, regardless of the fortuitous circumstances of birth or position.... We cannot become a great democracy by giving ourselves up as individuals to selfishness, physical comfort, and cheap amusements. (Wright, p. 197)

As you can see from this quote, the original context of the term is a calling to citizens' higher purpose: status as a result of achievement and hard work, plus some measure of equality of opportunity. Explicit also is a warning about the excesses of rampant self-service as a danger to democracy. This speaks to the dual nature of this metaphor, as historically, this symbol of American life has both positive and negative sources and contexts.

Cullen (2003) traces the origins of the various images embedded within this myth. Because of its ambiguous and omnipresent nature, Cullen examines the history of the American experience to describe the various facets of the dream.

From the lessons and lives of the Puritans came faith in social reform and the belief that things can be different with hard work; the negative side of this aspect of the dream was that hard work and enjoyment were mutually exclusive. From the words of the Constitution came the belief that men were "created equal" and endowed with unalienable rights, including the pursuit of happiness (even if the words "equal" and "men" were heavily qualified in the minds of the framers of the document) (Cullen, 2003). Germane to the dream, the *right* to pursue self-oriented goals was born, along with the negative belief that one's individual rights could supersede the rights of the whole. From the upward mobility of notable public persons (Benjamin Franklin and Abraham Lincoln) came the belief that those with humble beginnings—through hard work, dedication, and living a good (virtuous) life—could be successful. The negative side of this facet of the dream came from the rise of the robber barons who piloted the industrial revolution (Andrew Carnegie, John D. Rockefeller, Cornelius Vanderbilt, John Jacob Astor). These "captains of industry" showed the country that upward mobility was earned by merciless greed and ruthlessness. This became the path to financial happiness: being a "self-made man." The "good life" is financial, not spiritual; when we are "good," God allows us to make money. In the capitalist American dream, virtue is defined by money—lots of it.

During this same time in history, African Americans and persons of cultural diversity dreamed their own American dream—that of literal freedom, economic and social equality, as articulated by freedom writers and Dr. Martin Luther King, Jr. (Cullen, 2003). These dreams are far from reality, even today (Keene, 2008; Roxas, 2008). From land lotteries, westward expansion (also known as Manifest Destiny) and the birth of the automobile came the dream of home ownership and mobility, increasing White flight to the newly developing suburbs to escape urban social and economic problems (Cullen, 2003). Finally, from being a nation of risk takers and gamblers (from the frontier to the corporate boardroom), lessons learned in the California Gold Rush, the rise of the gambling industry in the desert, and the movie industry in Hollywood (Cullen, 2003) came the dream of easy money without working, ways to "get your money for nothing and your chicks for free" (Dire Straits, 1998).

The positive legacy of the American dream is the emphasis on hard work, the belief that change is possible, and the faith that modest beginnings will not dictate life trajectory. There are the seeds of social consciousness and social justice in the rising awareness that the American dream has long been denied to others on the basis of skin tone, gender, religion, national origin, sexual orientation, physical or mental ability, and other diversity constructs. The negative legacy of the dream is that many believe that we have the right to trample the rights of others to get what makes us happy; that we can take what we want, and if done legally, we have the right to keep what we take; and that it is possible to get all the goodies without working at all if we are smart enough, fast enough, and ruthless enough. Winner takes all.

SELF-REFLECTION OPPORTUNITY 7.2

What are some current examples of the positive side of the dream that you have recently heard in the news? What are some examples of the negative side that you have heard in the news?

THE CURRENT STATE OF THE AMERICAN DREAM

What is the nation's current understanding of the American dream? Social critics would argue that the consumer-focused derivation of the American dream has created a greater sense of social malaise and classism (Fox, 1994; Wright, 2009), while others argue that socially informed, moderated forms of the dream are still socially, economically, and practically viable (Zakaria, 2010). What do Americans themselves think?

While there are various implications, to many Americans, the dream is getting less attainable. Hanson and Zogby (2010) examined 2 decades of American's answers to the questions: "What is the American dream?" "Is the American dream achievable?" and "What is the role of government and politics in the American dream?" They found that over the past 2 decades, trends can be discerned. The first trend is that when asked if the American dream is about material success or spiritual attainment, more than half indicated spiritual attainment in the 1990s, but that percentage is less than half as of 2004. The second trend is while two-thirds of those polled believe that working hard is the most important part of getting ahead, that number is declining. The alternative explanation of the source of success, "forces outside our control," is rising. The third trend is that over the past 20 years, over half of respondents agreed that the American dream has become impossible for most people to achieve, and as respondents' pessimism about the future has increased, support for programs that assist minorities has declined (Hanson & Zogby, 2010). Fully twice as many respondents blame Blacks, not discrimination, for their condition (Hanson & Zogby, 2010). Over the 2 decades of opinion polls, support for the Democratic Party increased, as this political party became associated with doing a better job to help more people attain the American dream (p. 581). Finally, 75% of respondents agree that is it necessary to get a college education to attain the dream (Hanson & Zogby, 2010). These trends highlight the political, economic, educational, and multicultural implications that influence our understanding of this metaphor.

In terms of economics, current calls for the restoration of the American dream feature a return to the economic stability of the "middle class," which is the source of many of the underlying assumptions and inherent influence of the term (Zakaria, 2010). The foundation of the economic structure of a capitalist society is the striving for affluence, which rests on the concept of upward mobility—the working class aspiring to the middle class, and the middle class working hard to mimic the lifestyle of the upper class (Wright, 2009). Zakaria argues that restoring the true American dream (that every person can be successful) requires the very antithesis of the consumer-driven foundation of the dream and a return to the socially responsible original meaning as presented by Adams.

In terms of the educational implications of the American dream, higher education and training for jobs of the future is a common theme. Keene (2008) highlights the role that the community college system plays as the gateway to the American dream for students from diverse or low-income families. In terms of access to higher education—and, by extension, to the American dream—Gibbons and Borders (2010) found important perceptions that directly influenced the college aspirations for prospective first-generation college students in the seventh grade. These students, who were more likely to be diverse and from low-income families, reported their intent to attend some type of school after high school, yet they perceived significant barriers to this goal, including lower parental support, finances, family issues, racial/ethnic discrimination, lack of college-educated role models, lack of college planning guidance, negative educational role models, and lack of preparation (p. 204). These barriers reflect the reality of many American students of diversity who see the American dream as out of their reach.

If challenges exist for citizens in terms of access to higher education and the American dream, the implications for international and immigrant people, for whom the American dream provided the courage and fortitude to move across the globe, are even more significant. For example, Roxas (2008) found that social discrimination hampers Somali students' attempts to adapt to schools in the United States. The various challenges they face include very few diverse teachers to serve as role models, problems learning English, numerous competing family responsibilities, and the lack of educational opportunities in their home country and refugee camps. As a result, these Somali students may also find the American dream, as a product of American education, out of their reach.

SELF-REFLECTION OPPORTUNITY 7.3

1. What are your opinions about immigration reform?
2. Do we live the words found in the museum at the base of the Statue of Liberty, lines from Lazarus's poem "The New Colossus"? "Give me your tired, your poor, Your huddled masses yearning to breathe free, The wretched refuse of your teeming shore. Send these, the homeless, tempest-tost to me, I lift my lamp beside the golden door!" (Lazarus, n.d.).

3. Consider that when the economy is doing well, immigration restrictions are expanded to allow more foreign (and less expensive) labor to enter the country; conversely, when the economy is not doing well, immigration is restricted to slow the influx of "cheap" labor and protect American wages. So is immigration policy dictated by the economy, the workforce, or humanitarianism?
4. How does your answer to that question inform your thoughts about immigration reform?
5. How does that influence your understanding of the American dream?

THE AMERICAN DREAM, UPWARD MOBILITY, AND OCCUPATIONAL PRESTIGE

The concept of upward mobility has deep roots in the American psyche and in our capitalist economic system. Occupational mobility "has long been a part of the U.S. heritage. In the dynamic, expanding and classless society that has existed in the United States for the past two centuries, such opportunities have existed" (Isaacson & Brown, 2000, p. 78). These authors examine upward mobility as the interaction between the individual and the environment of the work, highlighting the active nature of the individual in the career process involving information, planning, educational opportunities, and support from significant others for "effective and satisfying career development" (p. 79). (Notice that in 2000, career counseling textbooks promoted the notion that U.S. society was "classless." It is important to recognize the inaccuracy of that idea.)

In addition, one of the enduring artifacts of the consumer-driven American dream is the belief that in order to attain upward mobility and reach the American dream, young people need to strive for prestigious occupations. One convenient measure of prestige is found in research that documents occupational prestige (Isaacson & Brown, 2000).

Occupational prestige is defined as the esteem or social status accorded to an occupation by the general public (Isaacson & Brown, 2000). Qualities that contribute to the prestige of an occupation include the following (Garbin & Bates, as cited by Isaacson & Brown, 2000):

1. Desirable to associate with
2. Intelligence required
3. Scarcity of personnel who can do the job
4. Interesting and challenging work
5. Training required

6. Education required
7. Originality and initiative; autonomy
8. Tasks that improve the lives of others
9. Having influence over others
10. Security
11. Opportunities for advancement

These prestige rankings have been documented as stable over time and across cultures (Isaacson & Brown, 2000). The five occupations that have consistently been in the top five prestigious jobs since 1925, in various orders, include banker, physician, lawyer, superintendent of schools, civil engineer, and army captain. The occupations that have consistently been in the bottom five jobs across the same time span include truck driver, coal miner, janitor, hod carrier (physical laborer), and ditch digger (p. 77). It is interesting to note that although pay or income is not specifically noted in the qualities that influence the prestige of an occupation, the qualities themselves, such as education and autonomy, suggest higher income. A review of the highest and lowest prestige occupations listed above would confirm a strong correlation between prestige and income.

All of these qualities influence how we perceive success in this culture. Some would argue that someone who has a job with all the qualities of a high-prestige occupation, including high income, is successful. Others would challenge that definition of success. How do we know that someone has attained the American dream? What is success?

SELF-REFLECTION OPPORTUNITY 7.4

1. Note your reactions to this list of prestigious occupations. In your opinion, what are the highest prestige occupations currently? The occupations with the lowest prestige?
2. Given the fluid nature of labor statistics, how do you think the research-based rankings have changed since 2000?
3. In addition, what are the standards by which *you* measure success: Work? Family? Possessions? Toys?
4. Most importantly, how will your answer influence the counseling you provide to your clients?

THE AMERICAN DREAM AND CLASSISM

Although there are positive aspects of the American dream, there are also negative ramifications. The most significant negative ramification for the purpose of this chapter includes social and economic stratification that occurs on the basis of income and lifestyle, also known as classism (Liu & Pope-Davis, 2004). According to Watts (1994), people develop a worldview about their economic context from the patterns of beliefs and perceptions that are shared by a population "based on similar socialization and life experiences" (p. 53). It would be safe to consider the American dream, as a capitalist manifesto, is a powerful socializing force across time for Americans and for persons around the world. This socializing force defines worldwide economic and social expectations for defining success (financial wealth) and achieving success (hard work, upward mobility, prestige, risk taking, and fierce competition).

Recall that the American dream predicts the haves and the have-nots in this society on the basis of income, status, and prestige. When an individual senses competition, feels threatened, or is frustrated in attempts to meet the demands of the economic culture, classist behavior (prejudicial behavior toward others on the basis of economic and social class) results as a means of reducing dissonance (Liu & Pope-Davis, 2004, p. 300). Such prejudicial behavior can manifest as downward classism (treating those who are perceived as inferior as unworthy or invisible), upward classism (treating those from "higher" social groups as snobs, spoiled, elitist), lateral classism (treating those within our own subjective social group as inferior if they don't conform to the norms of the social group), and internalized classism (experiencing feelings of shame, despair, and fear of exposure when in more "privileged" environments) (Liu & Pope-Davis, 2004).

Because we have grown up in this capitalist society, we might not realize that these hierarchies are *artificially* and *socially constructed* groupings (Delgado & Stephancic, 2001), unquestioningly acting instead as if they had intuitive validity based on some objective criteria (Liu & Pope-Davis, 2004). When we do this, we are engaging in classism, as destructive as racism, sexism, heterosexism, linguicism, and other forms of social stratification, disrespect, and hatred.

SELF-REFLECTION OPPORTUNITY 7.5

1. What is your understanding of social justice?
2. How committed are you to the words of James Truslow Adams quoted in the original definition of the American dream?
3. What happens to a society when it experiences rampant "selfishness, physical comfort, and cheap amusements"?

Case Study 7.2

In my work as a career counselor for the state's flagship university, I met numerous students who were unsure of their ultimate goal(s) for attending the university. One of the most memorable students was a young, beautiful, intelligent Black woman from Las Vegas, who was majoring in business. When we talked about her goals, she indicated that she had always wanted to be a bank teller. Why? Because in her home community, bank tellers had the best of all possible worlds: they wore professional clothing, they worked in an air-conditioned building, they had a prestigious job, and everyone knew they were smart. In this client's world, this job represented success for young women.

What struck me most about her story was how severely she seemed to be underestimating her potential; after all, a university bachelor's degree was not required to become a bank teller. Her story speaks to the career reality of youth in the inner city of any American community, where jobs and opportunity structures are limited (Reece & Gambhir, 2008). Young people develop a picture of their future based on *what they see today in their world,* not based on *the future others see for them from the adult world.*

FOLLOW-UP QUESTIONS

1. What would you say to this client? What is your counseling goal?
2. What would you estimate is her level of self-esteem, based on the case study? Why?
3. Have you lived in a community of poverty? If you have not, how can your inform yourself about what life is like for those from poverty?

POSSIBLE SELVES AND CAREERS

The connection between the haves and the have-nots relative to diversity and poverty is strong in the literature. If the pathway to the American dream is hard work and higher education (Hanson & Zogby, 2010; Zakaria, 2010), then it is important to understand the subjective images that can influence clients to strive for their best possible future (Perry & Vance, 2010), one in which college and hard work will result in a secure and comfortable life.

Markus and Nurius (1986) posited that the organizing construct of autonomous behavior is "possible selves": individuals' ideas of what they would like to become (*hoped-for selves*), what they expect to become (*expected selves*), and what they are afraid of becoming (*feared selves*) (Perry & Vance, 2010). According to Markus and Nurius (1986), "an individual is free to create any variety of possible selves, yet the pool of possible selves derives from the categories made salient by the individual's particular sociocultural and historical context and from the models, images, and symbols provided by the media and by the individual's immediate social experiences" (p. 954). Enter the American dream as a primary source of images and symbols defining what it means to be successful in this country.

These possible selves are the product of both cognitive and affective (emotional) processes. They reflect thoughts about the self in the past, present, and future, and are shaped by the valence or value of various possibilities (Markus & Nurius, 1986, p. 957). Individuals have "ideas, beliefs, and images about their potential and about their goals, hopes, and fears" (p. 955), and the possible selves provide an interpretive framework for making sense of past behavior and a "means-ends pattern for new behavior" (p. 955). It provides important insights to consider the use of possible selves as a framework for discussing careers (Perry & Vance, 2010).

In this exploration of possible selves, the importance of sociopolitical realities, historical realities, and the models, images, and symbols from society at large become germane. It is in this reflection on career counseling that the relevance of implicit biases and the cultural icon of the American dream become visible. As career counselors work with clients, their implicit biases about the American dream mythos ("Pull yourself up by the bootstraps"; "Hard work will see you through") and "success" (fast-track, high-income, prestigious careers, competition, material acquisition) can unintentionally perpetuate classism in American society by imposing a narrow, Eurocentric definition of success on clients. How?

Using possible selves as a template for a transtheoretical structure for career counseling, the "unaware" career counselor initiates a discussion of hoped-for selves, expected selves, and feared selves. When the client shares his or her dreams for the future, the counselor scoffs at careers that don't make a lot of money, focuses on careers that are driven by the market, or minimizes the potential for success in unusual or nontraditional careers. When the client shares his or her expectations of the future, the unaware counselor highlights the potential for disaster or affirms subtly, with a sad shake of the head, "People like you often struggle in college. You're going to need lots of help [with studying, finances, child care, time management, etc.]." When discussing fears, the unaware career counselor projects classist fears that the client won't be able to pay his or her way or the client will fail miserably, utterly humiliating his or her family, after accruing huge student loan debt.

Conversely, the "aware" career counselor has an understanding of those sociopolitical messages that shape the client's worldview, including diversity, economic realities, and myths like the American dream. With an awareness of diversity, for example, the counselor is able to help the client construct a meaningful success identity that does not conform to the dominant societal narrative of White superiority in school (Carter Andrews, 2009). With an understanding of economic realities, for example, the career counselor is able to understand the opportunity structures (i.e., access to stable jobs, safe housing, high-performing schools, and health and social services) (Reece & Gambhir, 2008) within communities that influence how the client might construct possible selves, informing the client's construction of the hoped-for self, the expected self, and the feared self. With an understanding of the metaphor of the American dream as it is promoted in advertising (want more, buy more, be more), the aware career counselor can free the counseling dialogue from the focus on prestigious jobs, material accumulation, and consumerism as indicators of success, and focus instead on empowerment of the client for the betterment of the community, the country, and society (Fox, 1994; Zakaria, 2010).

The challenge is to address implicit biases about the American dream to provide mindful career counseling, becoming an "aware" career counselor in the process.

ADDRESSING IMPLICIT BIASES AND MINDFUL CAREER COUNSELING

Implicit biases fade in the bright light of self-reflection and analysis; although they lose their power through self-awareness (Boysen, 2010), the ethical counselor must be ever mindful of these deeply embedded images and perceptions, ready to counter them whenever they emerge. Mindful career counseling would be an important way to provide career counseling that is vigilant against the influence of unhelpful biases, including the negative classist assumptions of the American dream.

In a review of the practice and research in 15 national and international career counseling and development journals, Patton and McIlveen (2009) did not identify mindful career counseling as appearing in any article. However, there is support for the use of mindfulness strategies as a general strategy for self-awareness and stress reduction. For example, in a meta-analysis, Grossman, Niemann, Schmidt, and Walach (2004) found that mindfulness-based stress reduction may help a broad range of clients to cope with both clinical and nonclinical issues. Similarly, Collard, Avny, and Boniwell (2008) found that teaching mindfulness to students resulted in higher levels of mindfulness overall and a significant decrease in negative affect, and Jacobs and Blustein (2008) suggest mindfulness as a means of reducing job-related stress and anxiety. Most importantly, however, are results of a study by Schure, Christopher, and Christopher (2008), in which counseling students of a 3-credit course in mindfulness techniques reported being less defensive, less reactive, more open to experience, more compassionate, more accepting of self and others, more empathic, more spiritual, and more confident.

According to mindfulness practitioners, mindfulness is a state of present-moment awareness, a relaxed state of mind, in which we are conscious of all of our experiences as they arise, including thoughts, feelings, sensations, breathing, and surroundings, all with nonresistance, nonjudgment, peace, and acceptance (Hanh, 1991; Schure et al., 2008). Importantly, mindfulness practice allows counselors to become aware of images, self-talk, assumptions, and perceptions in the moment with the client, and then dismiss those images, self-messages, assumptions, and perceptions that are not helpful to the counseling process. It allows the counselor to become aware of thoughts and images that are borne out of implicit biases, and then to nonjudgmentally dismiss those to refocus on a more compassionate reality with the client in the moment.

With this ability to notice and dismiss implicit biases from the American dream and classist perceptions, career counselors can then replace those nonproductive images with informed perceptions about multiculturalism, opportunity structures, and empowering possible selves.

SELF-REFLECTION OPPORTUNITY 7.6

Have you ever practiced mindfulness? There are a number of good resources, both in print and online, that can introduce you to the practice. Is now the time for you to consider becoming more mindful of your counseling work?

Case Study 7.3

As a career counselor, I got to work with the adult son of a very wealthy family. He described a life of searching for meaning, not wanting to enter the family business, but not needing to work. His existence shrank into semi-agoraphobia, at first not needing to leave the family compound, then later, finding it hard to leave due to his anxiety. In our counseling work, he struggled to define his life separately from his family's business, but eventually he shared a highly creative product that he wanted to patent and produce. After some empowerment and cheerleading, he ended counseling with the determination to move forward with his invention.

During this counseling, I became aware of my own implicit biases against those I termed "the idle rich." What I found to counter this bias was a kind and creative person whose environment had stunted his existential growth, in many ways similar to the client from poverty.

FOLLOW-UP QUESTIONS

1. What is your reaction to the term *the idle rich*? What are your internal images or impressions?
2. How would you have worked with this client? What approaches would you use?
3. What challenges do you face with your implicit biases?

CONCLUSION

In a study examining the life and work values of a national sample of counselor trainees, the four highest values were found to be benevolence (preservation and enhancement of the welfare of people), self-direction (independent thought), achievement (personal success through demonstrating competence according to social standards), and universalism (understanding, appreciation, tolerance, and protection of the welfare of people and nature) (Busacca, Beebe, & Toman, 2010, p. 7). In this list appear two values addressed in this chapter: achievement (personal success through demonstrating competence according to social standards) and universalism (understanding, appreciation, tolerance, and protection of the welfare of people and nature). For some, achievement may speak directly to the American dream and classism, especially as it relates to social standards. Although no one would advocate that counselors should be values-free (this is neither desirable nor possible), it is important that counselors are able to identify values and work to counteract those that emerge from implicit biases.

Perhaps the strength, or valence, of these two values might be weighed on the fulcrum of client benefit: Concurrently, we can work to lighten the valence of the achievement value as we work to increase the valence of the universalism value. In the end, through mindful career counseling, we can support the positive elements of the American dream without perpetuating the classism.

RESOURCES

On Implicit Biases

Boysen, G. A. (2010). Integrating implicit bias into counselor education. *Counselor Education and Supervision*, *49*, 210–227.

On the History of the American Dream

Cullen, J. (2003). *The American dream: A short history of an idea that shaped a nation*. New York: Oxford University Press.

On an Alternative Vision of Work to Replace Consumerism

Fox, M. (1994). *The reinvention of work: A new vision of livelihood for our time*. San Francisco: Harper.

On Possible Selves

Markus, H., & Nurius, P. (1986). Possible selves. *American Psychologist*, *41*, 954–969. doi: 10.1037/0003-066X.41.9.954

On Work and Class

Terkel, S. (1974). *Working: People talk about what they do all day and how they feel about what they do.* New York: The New Press.

On Mindfulness

Schure, M. B., Christopher, J., & Christopher, S. (2008). Mind-body medicine and the art of self-care: Teaching mindfulness to counseling students through yoga, meditation, and qigong. *Journal of Counseling and Development, 86*, 47–56.

On Diversity

Delgado, R., & Stephancic, J. (2001). *Critical race theory: An introduction.* New York: New York University Press.

Sue, D. W., Capodilupo, C. M., Torino, G. C., Bucceri, J. M., Holder, A. M. B., Nadal, K. L., et al. (2007). Racial microaggressions in everyday life: Implications for clinical practice. *American Psychologist, 62*(4), 271–286. doi: 10.1073/00003-066X.62.4.271

On Poverty and Opportunity Structures

Reece, J., & Gambhir, S. (2008). *The geography of opportunity: Review of opportunity mapping research initiatives.* Retrieved from the Kirwan Institute for the Study of Race and Ethnicity website: http://4909e99d35cada63e7f757471b7243be73e53e14.gripelements.com/pdfs/Opportunity_Mapping_Research_Initiatives.pdf

8

Social Class and Mental Health

Carl Sheperis and Donna Sheperis

If you or one of your family members needed medical treatment for cancer or a heart condition, you would want the best-trained medical doctor to oversee your treatment. Of course, there are hospitals throughout the world that specialize in these issues, but the cost of such specialized treatment may be out of reach for you. How would it feel to know that one of these specialized hospitals is in your city but that, because of your financial situation, you would have to settle for a different hospital and a medical doctor who is simply assigned to your treatment rather than one that you get to select? Of course this would be difficult for anyone. Hopefully this analogy depicts how social class impacts medical treatment. If this analogy is clear, then it would not be difficult for you to understand that the same holds true for social class and mental health. The relationship between social class and mental health has long been discussed in the professional literature. As professionals, it is imperative that counselors understand the role of social class in mental health and mental illness as well as the treatment implications impacted by social class issues.

OVERVIEW OF SOCIAL CLASS

Social class divides are inevitable components of contemporary social systems. There are likely no societies, historical or present day, that have not or do not experience discrepancies based on social class. Professional helpers are acutely aware of social class differences. Counselors may find themselves working within a particular social demographic and would need to attend to the needs of that demographic. For example, counselors working in women's treatment centers must be aware of treatment implications and treatment practices that relate to gender. Counselors working in urban, inner-city environments must be aware of treatment interventions and practices related to that population. Whether working with clients of upper socioeconomic status, with specific gender role issues, or with clients of minority racial/ethnic status, contemporary counselors can best serve clients when they understand the role of social class.

Previous chapter authors in this text have discussed social class in depth, and we invite you to refer back to those chapters as we discuss social class. For the purpose of this chapter, we focus on the social class issues that are most closely related to mental health and well-being: social economic status, gender, and race (Muntaner, Borrell, & Chung, 2007).

Socioeconomic status (SES) traditionally describes an individual or family's level of income as well as education, which correlates to income earning potential. In a most general sense, socioeconomic status is broken down into three categories: high SES, middle SES, and low SES. It is likely that you've encountered these categories when reading research about populations, looking at the U.S. Census, or taking a survey of some sort. You probably also possess your own relationship to these categories based on your lived experiences. For example, as a child, what SES category did your family likely fall under? Has that status changed in your adult life? What are the differences between going from low or middle SES to high SES between childhood and adulthood? What are the implications when we go from high childhood SES to a lower or middle adulthood SES? As professional helpers, what values or biases do we have toward any of these categories?

As we discuss social class and mental health, we must consider the role of gender. Historically, research is focused on the minority gender, or women's issues. However, there are also considerations for providing mental health treatment to males. As such, a focus on client gender and the role of social oppression is necessary in conceptualizing and providing appropriate treatment. In the United States, the male gender has typically enjoyed the benefits associated with the dominant gender role. Women are often viewed as the minority gender, often the weaker gender, and often have greater social oppression. For decades in the United States, there has been a push for gender equality, yet there are still many facets of American life where women face obstacles based on gender. Thus, it makes sense, then, that the majority of research has been related to social class and women.

As we discuss treatment implications and the relationship between gender and mental health, we address both male and female role concerns. Let's look at an example of how gender may be important in this discussion. In relation to social economic status, it is a fact that women are more likely to be found in poverty. We know that poverty is strongly correlated with increased health risks and reduced quality of life (Muennig, Fiscella, Tancredi, & Franks, 2010). This reality has significant impact on the types of mental health concerns presented by women in treatment and the types of interventions that might be most appropriate. While our discussion for this chapter focuses on male and female role concerns, we would be remiss if we did not also address the potential for mental health concerns in the transgender population. To be a transgender individual does not mean there are mental health concerns: however, the social pressures on our transgender community are great. This is an emerging area of research that deserves further study.

The final area of social class that we discuss in this chapter is that of race. The history of systemic, institutional, and other forms of oppression based on race in the United States has left its mark on families, individuals, and systems, including institutions, education, and the provision of mental health treatment. Racial minorities in the United States have had and continue to have more significant pressures, stressors, and oppression than the majority, or Caucasian race. The relationship between minority race and diagnosis of more severe pathology is well reported in counseling literature (Good, 1996; Feinstein & Holloway, 2002). Treatment is rarely specialized by culture and may not meet the needs of minority race clients. As such, our focus for this chapter is on the differences in mental health diagnosis and treatment for members of minority races.

Before we look more closely at the components of social class that impact, or are impacted by, mental health, it is important to investigate further the relationship between the two.

RELATIONSHIP BETWEEN SOCIAL CLASS AND MENTAL HEALTH

There is much discussion of mental health and causes of mental illness in counseling and related literature. A factor that has been shown to correlate with mental illness is social class. Because correlation does not indicate a cause-and-effect relationship, it is important to look at how class and mental health are linked. One of the most common arguments is akin to the age-old question: "Which came first, the chicken or the egg?" The question as it relates to relationship between social class and mental health is whether or not social class impacts mental health or whether mental health impacts social class. To examine this relationship, we will first look at the two opposing arguments of the drift hypothesis and social causation theory.

Drift Hypothesis

The drift hypothesis, in its simplest form, states that mental illness causes one to have a lessening of social class status. The idea is that the mental illness is not caused by social class, but because of the mental illness, the individual has a lower social class status than would be expected without the mental illness. The original research on the drift hypothesis, conducted in the 1960s, examined men who were placed as inpatients for schizophrenia. The researchers explored the occupation of these patients as well as their fathers' occupations. They were interested in looking at whether or not there was a "drift" downward in social class due to the patient's schizophrenia. The researchers did this by looking at childhood social class with the assumption that most persons do not stray far from their social class origins. They discovered that the childhood social class of these persons with mental illness mirrored that of the general population. However, the adult social class of these persons was uniformly low. Their findings were that the current adult class of the mentally ill person was because of the mental illness (Goldberg & Morrison, 1963).

From a practical perspective, you might see how this could be the case. As an individual develops schizophrenia in his early 20s, he is less likely to be able to attend to the complexities of an advanced occupation. We know that the typical first psychotic break for persons later diagnosed with schizophrenia occurs between the ages of 18 and 24 (American Psychiatric Association (APA), 2000). A high school graduate enters college with ambitions of completing a degree program that will result in a profitable and fulfilling career. This college student may come from a middle to upper class background. During the course of the college years, the student develops psychotic symptoms and is later hospitalized for schizophrenia. The likelihood that this student could continue his college career is in jeopardy. While this student may have, without the onset of mental illness, gone on to finish the degree program and earn a middle to upper class living, the illness of schizophrenia creates an impact. Instead, this same person is now faced with making career choices that are less complex and generally less profitable. This student who came from a middle to upper class background may now find himself working for minimum wage at a grocery store. His standard of living will by necessity be lowered, and thus his social economic status, or class level, will be lowered. This is an example of the drift hypothesis in action.

Social Causation Thesis

In 1990, John Cox of the University of Northern Colorado took exception to the drift hypothesis and developed the social causation thesis. Cox (1990) based his challenge on an analysis of the methods used during the original research on drift hypothesis. Using more advanced analytical techniques, he found that there was no direct proof that mental illness caused a downward drift in social class status. Conversely, this research provided support for a social causation thesis. The social causation thesis posits that it is actually social class that contributes to the mental illness. For example, the experience of poverty has been shown to increase levels of mental and physical stress (Murali & Oyebode, 2004). As a result, mental illness may be present and, at the very least, mental health is compromised because of poverty.

As we did with the drift hypothesis, let's take a practical look at how the social causation thesis may play out in the client's mental health status. Within the United States, there is an extreme amount of poverty. Murali and Oyebode (2004) discuss the relationship between being poor in our country and inequality. They report the fact that there are less occupational, educational, and social opportunities available to the poor. In addition, according to Murali and Oyebode (2004), it is the poor in our country that are often exposed to the most dangerous living environments, as impoverished neighborhoods have higher rates of crime. Living conditions may be challenging in poorer communities. Consequently, there is an extreme amount of stress that accompanies the phenomenon of poverty. Simply affording the necessary food and shelter, the basics of Maslow's hierarchy of needs, may be difficult for individuals in poverty.

We also know that mental illness occurs at higher rates in communities primarily inhabited by families who fall below the poverty level, and that these psychiatric illnesses may "cluster together, usually in disintegrating inner-city communities" (Murali & Oyebode, 2004, p. 217). Imagine the myriad of stressors placed on those who live below the poverty level. Housing opportunities, medical and mental health, and access to resources may all be compromised. Although having money does not guarantee mental health, there's a distinct relationship between poverty, stress, and mental health.

When exploring these two theories related to social class and mental illness, we can see the potential that having a mental illness causes social class status to decline (drift hypothesis) and that lower social class status can contribute to declining mental health (social causation theory). Both social causation theory and the drift hypothesis have promising arguments related to social class and mental health. However, neither fully explains the phenomenon completely. It is possible that the relationship between social class and mental health is not a simple linear structure and that multiple explanations are needed. Social class status can both impact mental well-being and be impacted by an individual's mental well-being. As such, we will look at this phenomenon through the lens of systems theory and circular causation.

SYSTEMS THEORY AND CIRCULAR CAUSATION

As helping professionals, you've likely studied systems theory in relation to family dynamics. Systems theory was first proposed by a biologist and focused on the arrangement of and relationships between parts or elements that create a system, and the system itself is an entity independent of its parts (von Bertalanffy, 1950). In family therapy classes you have probably studied how the dynamics among and between family members create a system that is more than just the personalities of each person. This phenomenon is known as circular causation. Circular causation means that within the system, impact is bidirectional; that is, one element does not simply impact the next but is also influenced by that impact. Circular causation implies a cause-and-effect relationship between all components of the system.

Here is an example: the following graphic illustrates a relationship between a husband and a wife that are having difficulties. There is tension between the two elements of the system, the husband and the wife. The wife wants to talk to the husband about the relationship. Her desire to talk frustrates the husband, who instead chooses to isolate. His isolation frustrates the wife, who is then even more desirous of talking. Her repeated attempts to talk about the relationship push him further into isolation. The husband's increasing isolation further frustrates the wife. Here we have a system where each part is affecting the other part and the system is spiraling downward. The end result is likely an argument: the wife trying to get the husband to talk and the husband trying to get the wife to leave him alone. Each wants his or her own needs met within the system, but the needs of one create problems for the other. Thus the husband and wife have a reciprocal effect on each other, and there is a balance in the system that is maintained by their interaction (Figure 8.1).

For the purposes of this discussion we will be viewing another system composed of two elements: social class and mental health. As we previously discussed, there are higher rates of mental illness in communities of lower socioeconomic class. Within each community, there are neighborhoods that fit this description. Take a few minutes to consider your own community. Within those neighborhoods, where do individuals find treatment? You will likely say that these individuals receive their mental health treatment at some form of a community-based agency.

Community-based mental health care has its roots in the 1950s. Prior to the early 1950s, most mental health services were provided at state hospitals and

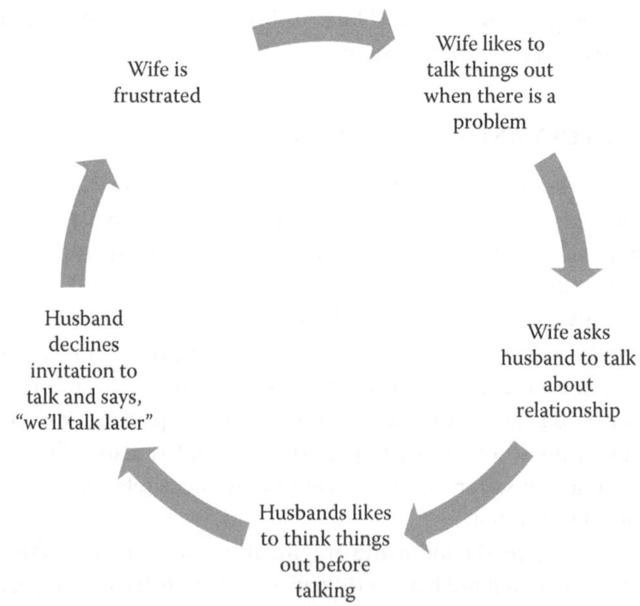

Figure 8.1 Reciprocal causality.

institutions. If a family member suffered a mental illness, it is likely that the family member would be shipped off to a hospital in the largest communities in the state (Litchfield & Watson, 2009). Virtually all mental health care was relegated to these institutional settings. Aside from being institutionalized, the individuals with mental illness were isolated from their families. Because transportation was not as evolved as today, the distance impacted family involvement in treatment. Today, family involvement in treatment is both integral to positive therapeutic outcome and ethically mandated (American Counseling Association [ACA], 2005).

President John F. Kennedy instituted the Community Mental Health Centers Act of 1963, which decentralized mental health care away from these institutional settings. Rather than being treated in a hospital, individuals with mental illness could now receive their care in community-based outpatient clinics (Litchfield & Watson, 2009). Previously, individuals were sent away to a hospital, returned to some state of mental well-being, and sent back to their home community where symptoms often returned. The intention behind the Community Mental Health Centers Act was to provide treatment within the person's home community so that mental health could be maintained in that home community.

Consider what these community-based mental health agencies are like in your hometown. Most practicing counselors had a start in some form of the community-based agency setting. Many of our internships were in such settings. In fact, this training model is common to agency practice. In order to serve a large community need, inexperienced counselors in training are offered an opportunity to learn and accrue hours for licensure. Thus, these agencies may be staffed by students in training, or young practitioners who are novice counselors. We will use the state of Mississippi as an example. In the state of Mississippi, the mental health systems operate under a state department of mental health that is able to provide services to residents who receive disability benefits and are placed on Medicaid. Professional counselors who work within this state department are required to have a master's degree in counseling or a related mental health field. However, counselors in Mississippi state agencies are not required to be independently licensed. To be independently licensed as a licensed professional counselor, the state of Mississippi requires that one have a master's degree in counseling (not a related discipline) that meets the standards of Council for Accreditation of Counseling and Related Educational Programs (CACREP), have successfully passed the National Counselor Examination (NCE), and have 3,500 hours of supervised clinical experience, which is mostly accrued post–master's degree. Those who successfully complete these advanced requirements and are granted LPC status in Mississippi can operate a private practice (Mississippi State Board of Examiners for Licensed Professional Counselors, 2011).

Someone with a new master's degree in counseling in Mississippi might go to work for a community-based agency to accrue those clinical hours needed toward licensure. During that period of early training, these prelicensed counselors could see Medicaid recipients. By definition, these prelicensed counselors are less well trained than their licensed counterparts. It is likely no surprise either that these prelicensed counselors are paid less as well due to their young status of the profession. Upon reaching licensure, that LPC may decide to open a private practice. In Mississippi, LPCs are not granted the right to treat individuals who receive Medicaid benefits. They are not able to bill Medicaid for their services. In other words, once they gain the experience necessary to open a private practice, they can no longer treat the poorest of their community. The discriminatory practice is that the poor are left to receive their services within a community agency that is staffed by often less trained personnel.

When looking at clients who are college students and thus of middle to upper educational class, there does not seem to be a difference in outcome when treatment is provided by students in training, new, or licensed professionals (Nyman, Nafziger, & Smith, 2010). However, in this research study, the novice practitioners received at least doctoral student supervision and in some cases were supervised by doctoral level professionals. The same cannot be assumed in a community mental health agency. In fact, many states do not have requirements for supervisor credentialing within agency settings. As a result, novice counselors receive supervision from other master's-level practitioners who often have no background in supervision theory or best practice in counselor training.

How does this relate to systems theory and circular causation? We have described a situation where the poorest in the community receive their services at the community mental health agency. The community mental health agency is staffed by less trained and often unlicensed practitioners. The quality of care may be presumed to be compromised given that mental health clients do not have their choice of providers. The assumption is that if they could, they might choose someone with more training, experience, and credentials. They might choose to receive the type of services provided to clients in college counseling settings, as described in the Nyman et al. (2010) study. The quality of care impacts the client. The client's mental health and well-being are affected by the quality of care, and yet the client can only seek services through the very system that may provide a lesser quality of care. As a result, we can see a circular pattern between the elements within the system.

In summary, clients with mental illness who are of lower social economic status are typically chronic, perennial clients that remain tied to the system for life. In many cases they have no way to break the cycle of treatment and quality of care because of elements of the system that are beyond their control (e.g., state laws related to Medicaid provider status). The poor in our country are not offered the privilege of decision making about their treatment and care. As we have discussed, the same is not true for those of us of middle or upper social economic status who have insurance, in and out of network provider lists, and the power of choice within our healthcare system. As we continue in this discussion of social class, it is important to explore specific elements of social class such as gender, race, and the role of poverty.

ELEMENTS OF SOCIAL CLASS RELATED TO MENTAL HEALTH

Gender

Historically, men and women have experienced compromised mental health in distinctly different ways. Women are more likely than men to be diagnosed with mood disorders, for example (Wittchen, 2010). Women experience stressors unlike those of their male counterparts. Single parenting is a common source of stress for American women. Women also have more employment disadvantages than men and are paid less than men with similar education (Thompson, 2009). Women may show coping strategies in ways that differ from men and may present as diagnostic criteria (e.g., crying, sleep and appetite disturbance) (Wittchen, 2010). Finally, women are more willing to seek treatment and may present for diagnosis more frequently (World Health Organization [WHO], 2011).

You may wonder why it matters what we are diagnosed with, by gender, as long as the diagnosis is made. According to the WHO (2011), "gender determines the differential power and control men and women have over the socioeconomic determinants of their mental health and lives, their social position, status and treatment in society and their susceptibility and exposure to specific mental health risks." In other words, our gender plays a role in whether or not we receive a diagnosis, the type of diagnosis we receive, and the availability of appropriate treatment measures for the diagnosis.

Researchers (Klose & Jacobi, 2004; Wittchen, 2010) and the American Psychiatric Association as editors of the *Diagnostic and Statistical Manual of Mental Disorders IV*—Text Revision (2000) offer clear distinctions between prevalence rates of disorders among men and women. Women are more often diagnosed with mood disorders, such as anxiety and depression, while men are more frequently diagnosed with antisocial personality disorder and substance abuse disorders than women (Klose & Jacobi, 2004).

Further, according to the WHO, gender creates role pressures for women and results in discrimination. Gender is also related to the associated factors of poverty, abuse, and malnutrition that impact mental health. We know that there is a direct correlation between the presence of such factors and compromised mental health in women (WHO, 2011).

Race

Race and social class are clearly intertwined and have been throughout time. In today's society, race is a complex factor that requires extended discussion as it is related to social class and mental health. The prevalence rates of mental illness in specific racial and ethnic subgroups are widely discussed in the professional literature. Prevalence rate refers to the total number of cases in a population at a given time. The prevalence rate for schizophrenia in Caucasians, for example, is 1.4%, but that number rises to 2.1% when looking at the African American population (Singleton-Bowie, 1995). Similarly, the prevalence rate for phonic disorders in Caucasians is between 9 and 10%, yet is reported to be between 16 and 24% in African Americans (D. R. Williams, 1995), a substantially higher percentage.

The DSM IV-TR (2000) does consider these numbers when guiding clinicians. For example, it is reported in the DSM-IV-TR that schizophrenia may be overdiagnosed in some ethnic groups, particularly African American and Asian American populations. The American Psychiatric Association (2000) does not take the position that these are true differences in prevalence, stating "it is not clear, however, whether these findings represent true differences among racial groups or whether they are the result of clinician bias or cultural insensitivity" (p. 307). Regardless of whether these are true differences in the disorder's presence or overdiagnosis based on clinician error, minority clients are more likely to receive the diagnosis than Caucasian clients. This means that the inherent stigma, barriers to treatment, and expense are shouldered more frequently by persons of color and of minority race. There are greater rates of treatment attrition, meaning that persons of minority race do not always receive the full benefit of the treatment available to them. Regardless of form (e.g., insurance inequities or stigma), race impacts both mental health diagnosis and quality of care received for all people.

Poverty

According to the U.S. Census Bureau (2010), poverty in this country is calculated by taking a family's annual income and comparing it to predetermined thresholds. These thresholds are set annually based on the family's size, number of children, and the age of the head of the household. In 2009, 14.3% of the population, or 42.9 million people, fell under this poverty threshold. These rates ranged from a state low of 8.5% in New Hampshire to a 21.9% high in Mississippi.

In a study of risk factors related to overall health, poverty is the factor that links most strongly with increased health risks and reduced quality of life (Muennig et al., 2010). In fact, poverty was the strongest link to these issues with higher correlations than other factors, such as race/ethnicity and education. As previously mentioned, resources are rarely allocated at higher rates in more impoverished areas, and the quality of care may be compromised in communities of poverty.

Poverty level, or socioeconomic status level, is also impacted by mental illness. Families with a member who has received a mental health diagnosis have significantly higher poverty rates than families without a diagnosed member (Vick, Jones, & Mitra, 2010). In addition, the odds of being poor for families with a psychiatric diagnosis are 1.76 times the odds of other families being poor, after controlling for other relevant variables ($p < .01$). Finally, Vick et al. (2010) found that while there is a strong correlation between poverty and mood (e.g., major depression, anxiety disorder) or psychotic (e.g., schizophrenia) disorders, there is no significant correlation between poverty and adjustment or anxiety disorder diagnoses.

SELF-REFLECTION OPPORTUNITY 8.1

At this point in the reading, you are well informed about elements of social class that impact, and are impacted by, mental illness. Take some time to think about your own family of origin. How was mental illness viewed in your family system? Did you have a family member with a mental illness? Prior to entering this program, what social class barriers were you aware of for persons with mental illness? What were you aware of with regard to race, gender, poverty, and mental illness? Did you ever think that mental illness was somehow their fault?

Case Study 8.1

Belinda grew up in a rural, impoverished area with little occupational opportunities. The daughter of two public school teachers, she lived a typical middle class life. Both she and her family valued education. Belinda did well at the local high school, although she was not a popular young lady. Other students found her odd and, unless they needed help on a test, generally left her alone. At the end of her senior year, Belinda received an invitation to a summer study program at Harvard. Her family jumped at the chance to give Belinda this opportunity. Belinda found Cambridge to be a more stressful environment than her rural hometown. She quit bathing and other participants in the program began to notice that she often talked to herself or seemingly talked to no one at all.

Finally the administrators of the summer program decided there was a problem and sent Belinda home for an evaluation. She was 19 years old with a high school diploma when she walked into the local mental health center. Belinda was subsequently diagnosed with schizophrenia, paranoid type. She lived with her parents until she acquired disability benefits. At that point, she was able to afford subsidized housing in town. Belinda was in and out of hospitals for the next 30 years while maintaining outpatient care between hospitalizations. She moved to an even smaller town where the rents were cheaper and there was a public health facility that could treat her medical concerns.

Belinda began in a middle class household but by her early 20s was living in poverty with no hope for gainful employment.

FOLLOW-UP QUESTIONS

1. What are typical post–high school plans for children of middle class families? What family expectations and values impact those plans?
2. What prevention or community efforts may have helped Belinda identify her disorder earlier and mitigate the stigma attached?
3. What opportunities are available for young people with schizophrenia?

ADVOCACY

From a social justice perspective, helping professionals have the obligation to be informed about the relationship between social class and mental health issues. However, being simply informed is not sufficient. Those in the helping professions must be agents of social change and advocate for clients' rights in relation to disparate services, treatment, and resources. Often clients are unaware of their rights or are not able to advocate for themselves in an effective manner. As an advocate, you may be required to make phone calls, write letters, or attend a nonbillable meeting to help your client receive appropriate services or resources. If these types of activities seem like a strange role for a therapist to play, consider that the Ethical Code of the American Counseling Association dictates that counselors have an ethical obligation to promote the welfare of clients both individually (client advocacy) and collectively (institutional advocacy).

In our professional work, we have been involved with client advocacy for many years. As a case in point, we were invited to testify in front of a state senate committee about the training, roles, and scope of responsibilities of professional counselors. In this particular state, professional counselors weren't reimbursable by Medicaid. Because counselors couldn't be reimbursed, individuals who received Medicaid benefits were restricted in their choice of treatment. In this state, counselors who worked for a community mental health clinic could provide services through a state license and psychiatrist's oversight. Because the community mental health clinics were primarily staffed by fledgling professionals, the clients served by Medicaid were relegated to services that may have been qualitatively different from those provided by more experienced licensed professional counselors.

RECOMMENDATIONS AND STRATEGIES FOR MENTAL HEALTH PROFESSIONALS

Now that you know that you should act as an advocate, it is important to understand how to advocate. Following are some suggestions we have for the advocacy role of a professional helper:

1. Contact your state professional association and ask about legislative issues of concern to professional counselors and other helping professions.
2. Call or write your state representatives and senators and let them know that you are a voter and that you are interested in their votes on issues related to your profession.
3. Consider participating in either a state counseling association or the American Counseling Association (ACA) leadership training seminar. Legislative training is an aspect of the ACA seminar and it is an aspect of many state-level seminars.
4. Learn about national legislative issues for counselors through the ACA website (www.counseling.org).
5. Consider becoming a part of a community health services advisory board. These take different forms or have different names across the country, but many communities have one.
6. Teach your clients about their rights and offer to assist them in any issues that may require advocacy.
7. Develop or adopt a client bill of rights for your office or agency. Make sure to share it with your clients.
8. Become familiar with the resources available in your community and keep a list available in your office.
9. Consider becoming involved in a community action group that is active in your area.
10. Join the American Counseling Association. A united group of counselors can be a powerful force for advocacy.

SELF-REFLECTION OPPORTUNITY 8.2

You have been reading about advocacy and have considered some strategies for such. Of the 10 strategies presented in this chapter, which can you do immediately? Place a star by those. Which can you do later? Place a question mark by those along with a note as to when that might be something you could accomplish or what current barriers prevent you from accomplishing it now. If there are any that you do not ever see yourself doing, ask others if they are likely to choose this path of advocacy and why. Doing so may open your eyes to advocacy opportunities you have not thought possible.

COUNSELORS FOR SOCIAL JUSTICE

Counselors for Social Justice (CSJ) is one of the 19 divisions of the American Counseling Association. The primary aim of the organization is to promote social justice. The division and its members are committed to social change through confrontation of systems that manifest oppression of counselors and clients through power and privilege. The main focus of CSJ is to promote social justice. According to the CSJ website (http://counselorsforsocialjustice.com/):

> Social justice counseling represents a multifaceted approach to counseling in which practitioners strive to simultaneously promote human development and the common good through addressing challenges related to both individual and distributive justice. Social justice counseling includes empowerment of the individual as well as active confrontation of injustice and inequality in society as they impact clientele as well as those in their systemic contexts. In doing so, social justice counselors direct attention to the promotion of four critical principles that guide their work; equity, access, participation, and harmony. This work is done with a focus on the cultural, contextual, and individual needs of those served.

If you are interested in learning more about the Counselors for Social Justice, visit their website at http://counselorsforsocialjustice.com/.

ADVOCACY IN ACTION

Head Start, a federally funded educational program for preschool children, is the longest running program offering early intervention to families living in poverty. As part of this initiative, Head Start operates early intervention mental health programs directed at children from birth to age 5. Since 2000, we have provided comprehensive mental health services to Head Start organizations throughout Mississippi. We have had the privilege of interacting with thousands of teachers, children, and families through our services.

We established our mental health services as a form of social entrepreneurship. Our private practice was established to address a social problem that was prevalent in Mississippi. There were a large number of children in need of mental health services but few counselors were trained to provide these services. Social entrepreneurship is the development of a business venture using entrepreneurial principles to create social change. The primary focus of a social entrepreneurial venture is to create social capital. In our case, we needed to develop a sustainable community-based service that would address the mental health needs of underprivileged children. According to federal guidelines, all Head Start children must at least receive mental health screening. In addition, the guidelines require Head Start organizations to provide access to mental health services for children and families in need of those services. Because there was a paucity of highly trained counselors able to conduct the screenings and to provide the required intervention services, the plan had to expand beyond a traditional practice approach. In other words, we could not effectively or efficiently provide the necessary services by ourselves.

As is the case in most entrepreneurial ventures, necessity drives new developments and new ideas. In this case, we decided to develop a for-profit social entrepreneurship venture that would lead to sustainable mental health services for children enrolled in Head Start throughout Mississippi. In order to operate our business venture, it was necessary to procure mental health service contracts from Head Start agencies. As part of our proposal to the agencies, we committed to providing a degree of in-kind services that would count as donations to each agency. While professional staff members were provided a modest salary for their work, the primary funds were used to provide tuition funds and stipends to graduate students training to develop specializations in pediatric mental health counseling. As part of their employment, students were able to garner supervised practicum and internship hours toward their degree requirements. Students received ongoing training and supervision throughout their tenure with our company.

By developing a social entrepreneurial venture, we were able to devise a sustainable plan that benefited the stakeholders (children and families), the Head Start agencies, the students training to specialize in pediatric mental health counseling, and the communities where we operated. Between 2000 and 2010, our company was able to donate over $1,000,000 of in-kind services back to the Head Start agencies in Mississippi. The fact that the company was developed as a for-profit venture allowed the services and in-kind contributions to continue for over 10 years. In addition to the benefits of the contributions and sustainable company, there are now a number of professional counselors who have developed the requisite skill sets to provide independent mental health services to children.

While it might be easy to determine the benefits of our social entrepreneurial venture from the overview provided, we believe it is important to also give a specific example of the systemic manner in which the services operated. One of our functions in working with the Head Start organizations was to provide early assessment and intervention services for children with autism. The Centers for Disease Control and Prevention (CDC, 2009) now estimates that 1 in every 80 children is diagnosed with autism. Because the prevalence of autism is growing at an exponential rate, it is important to have highly qualified counselors who can provide effective services to children. As stated earlier, very few counselors existed in Mississippi who even specialized in pediatric mental health, and only a handful of counselors with knowledge of autism treatment were available throughout the state. To complicate matters, researchers have shown that effective behavioral intervention for autism requires up to 30 hours of services per week. Because the time commitment is so extreme, costs for services are also extreme. Thus, families in poverty have little opportunity to receive the services they need to help their children make adequate clinical progress.

Case Study 8.2

Demarcus was a four-year-old African American child who was enrolled in a federally funded pre-K classroom. Demarcus was very quiet and kept to himself. In the first month of the school year, the teachers were trying to develop some structure to the school day and to acclimate all of the children to the pre-K environment, so he didn't receive much attention from his teachers. In fact, they appreciated having a quiet child who didn't cause any trouble for them. I (Carl Sheperis) was working with the pre-K system as a mental health consultant at the time. Part of my duties was to observe and evaluate each classroom at the school and to make recommendations to the teachers about appropriate strategies for managing behavior. As I was observing Demarcus's classroom, I immediately noticed him. He was sitting by himself at the desk and spinning a small toy on top of the desk. He had an intense focus on the toy and didn't seem to have any awareness of the other things happening in the room. I conducted a 15-minute observation of the classroom and noted that Demarcus never stopped spinning the toy. At the conclusion of my observation, I had a chance to interact with the teacher. I said to her, "When did you get the child with autism in your classroom?" She looked at me quizzically and said, "We don't have any autistic children." I saw several key signs of autism during my observation and was quite surprised that there wasn't a diagnosis for this child. I carefully pointed to Demarcus spinning the toy and asked, "What about that child? What have you seen from him?" The teacher said, "Oh Demarcus! He is just quiet and likes to play by himself." I then asked the teacher if she would mind me talking with Demarcus's parents and asking for a chance to evaluate him.

About a week later, I had the opportunity to schedule a meeting with my intervention team and Demarcus's father. I tried to be cautious in how I approached the conversation and didn't want to worry the parent before any formal assessment was conducted. I said to him, "I would like to evaluate your child and potentially provide some in-school services for him if necessary. I have noticed some behaviors in class that have me curious and I believe a formal assessment would help to clarify my observations." The father looked at me and asked, "What do you believe is wrong with Demarcus?" I wasn't ready to provide any diagnostic information, so I said, "I don't have any diagnostic information yet and really just want a chance to do a formal evaluation before offering any insights. However, I think that there may be some developmental problems and just want to rule out anything that might impact his education." The parent wouldn't allow me to sidestep his question and said, "I know you can't offer a diagnosis but I want to know from your professional experience, what you think is wrong with Demarcus." After pausing for a few second, I said, "I think Demarcus might have autism and I want to rule it out." The father just smiled at me and said, "Demarcus is just quiet, he doesn't have autism. His older brother has autism and he is nothing like Demarcus."

I proceeded to explain to the father that autism is a spectrum disorder and that symptoms can vary from person to person. I provided some examples of what autism could look like in terms of child behavior. At the end of our discussion, the father understood the range of potential symptoms and permitted the evaluation. After conducting three thorough observations of Demarcus, a clinical interview with the parents and teachers, and having the parents complete some rating scales, I came to the conclusion that Demarcus did indeed have autism. Furthermore, I realized that Demarcus only used echolalic responses and had no spontaneous speech of his own. Echolalia involved the repetition of sounds. In this case, if you said, "Good morning, Demarcus." He would respond with, "Good morning, Demarcus."

After providing the assessment results to Demarcus's parents and to the teacher, I worked with my intervention team to develop a plan of action for Demarcus. In this case, I believed that the best choice would be to provide 30 hours of intervention per week using techniques from applied behavior analysis. Researchers have found that 30 hours per week of initial intervention is necessary to produce positive results for children diagnosed with autism. However, as you might guess, 30 hours of services per week is an exorbitant cost. For the average counselor in private practice, a one-hour session could cost over $100. This would mean that services for Demarcus could cost upward of $3,000 per week.

In order to make sure that Demarcus received the services he needed, I had to advocate on an individual level with his teachers and parents to get their support for my recommendations. Next, I had to advocate for Demarcus with the school administration and find a way to get them on board for such a costly treatment approach. As you might guess, it was no easy task. Because the federal education guidelines require a free and appropriate public education for all children and require that schools provide for appropriate intervention services for children with disabilities, I was able to negotiate an appropriate treatment strategy. In the end, I managed to have a master's-level intern assigned to him for the 30 hours. The school agreed to pay a stipend for her internship, and I agreed to work with the intern and closely supervise the interventions. While this would not be the optimal approach, it was a win-win for the school and Demarcus.

We used a multipronged treatment approach with varying aspects of applied behavior analysis. One of the strategies was to teach Demarcus a picture system as a means of communicating. We also used sign language as an intervention strategy. Each week, Demarcus was able to make progress and learn new signs and new words. By the end of the school year, he had over 30 words and signs that he could communicate with spontaneously. While progress was slow, our advocacy efforts helped a child who was being seen as "quiet" to receive appropriate services and appropriate educational support.

QUESTIONS

The case study did not reflect some of the other resources that were accessed through advocacy efforts.

1. What types of community resources might Demarcus need?
2. How would you help him to receive them?
3. What types of resources might Demarcus's parents need?
4. How could you advocate on their behalf?
5. What would you have done differently with regard to advocacy in this case?
6. Were there any aspects of the advocacy efforts that you found surprising?

Case Study 8.3

Maria is a 19-year-old junior college student from a rural southern town. She has recently discovered that she is pregnant with her second child. Maria has a two-year-old son, Jesse, from a previous relationship. Maria and her son live with her mother, her 13-year-old sister, her 9-year-old brother, and Maria's uncle, who is 100% military disabled.

Maria had a school counselor in high school that helped inspire her to go to junior college following the birth of her son. However, she has never met with a mental health counselor. When Maria discovered she was pregnant, she was distraught. Her mother has helped her raise Jesse since he was born. Maria's mom works for the local paper plant on the assembly line. Her salary plus the uncle's disability benefits support the family of five. They live modestly and Maria has received Pell grants to support her education.

Jesse is enrolled at the local Head Start. Maria knows that she cannot afford daycare and will need to enroll the new baby in Head Start, but there is a waiting list for newborns. Maria is distressed that she is pregnant as she was not looking for a long-term relationship with the baby's father. She is worried that the new baby will interfere with her college plans and that she will have to go to work in the factory with her mom. She approaches her son's Head Start asking for help.

The family service worker (a bachelor's degree–level social worker position) recognizes that Maria has needs that are different from other pregnant women in the area. Maria has few resources, lives below the poverty threshold, and has limited access to medical care. Already 6 months pregnant, the family service worker discovers that Maria has not received any prenatal care. In addition, she has missed several classes this term and her grades suffered.

FOLLOW-UP QUESTIONS

1. As the mental health consultant for this program, you are asked for some recommendations from the family service worker. What should be the first steps that the service worker should take?
2. What might be some potential areas that would require advocacy for Maria?
3. What advocacy efforts might you engage in from an institutional level? What community level advocacy efforts might be needed?
4. Could there be some legislative advocacy in this case?
5. What parts of advocacy in this case would be difficult for you? How could you learn more about how to be effective in this role?

TRAINING OF HELPING PROFESSIONALS

As we discuss the relationship between social class and mental health, it is paramount that we also discuss the training the helping professionals receive to work with various populations. For the most part, counselor training programs and other graduate programs are skewed toward the middle to upper class direction. Consider the makeup of counselor education training programs in our country. Most counselor educators have a PhD or EdD degree, which places them in an upper educational class. Counselor educators are training students to become master's-level counselors, which is also an upper educational class. Racially, counselor educators are primarily of the majority, or Caucasian, culture. In fact, recent data have been reported that only 3% of the 160,000 higher education faculty employed at Research I and Research II institutions are of ethnic minority status. In the counselor education field, Latinos/as and African American faculty are the most underrepresented (Bradley & Holcomb-McCoy, 2002).

Thus, we have a system where counselor educators of majority status are training students using majority models (e.g., Rogers, Freud) that were developed using a Western, European, middle to upper class, male worldview. These theories of counseling are directed toward the treatment of the same type of client as the theorist.

Lower social economic status clients are typically of the minority culture living in impoverished areas. These majority theories do not address the challenges and struggles indigenous to the populations described in this chapter. Newer theories, such as those in the solution-focused family, were developed and designed specifically to work across social class. However, counseling students and other students in the helping professions receive limited training in these newer theories, as the older, even antiquated, theories are those that are stressed in the majority of counseling texts.

One method of improving on the training counselors and other helping professions receive is through the supervision of their clinical work. Traditionally, supervision has been conducted from a theoretical-based standpoint, which contains some of the inherent flaws mentioned in our discussion of counselor education and counseling theories. However, there has been a movement toward culturally sensitive supervision as well as supervision that addresses social change and advocacy perspectives (Glosoff & Durham, 2010). In fact, the terms *social justice counselor* and *social justice counseling advocate* have recently been introduced into the supervision literature as those who work "with or on behalf of clients, or within the broader social system, to minimize oppression, discrimination, and disenfranchisement with the goal of obtaining fair, just, and equitable treatment and access to services" (Glossof & Durham, 2010, p. 116). As we consider the interplay between social class and mental health, the idea of becoming social justice counselors and social justice counseling advocates should remain at the forefront of the discussion.

SELF-REFLECTION OPPORTUNITY 8.3

Consider the faculty makeup of your university. What are the ethnicities, genders, ages, races, and religions of those who teach in your program? Now consider the student body within the program. Again, consider their ethnicities, genders, ages, races, and religions. How do the faculty and student groups complement or contradict one another in terms of statuses? Finally, consider the client populations you will likely work with. How similar are faculty and students to the potential clients? How are they different? What challenges might these similarities and differences bring up? How would you begin to evaluate the impact of any identified differences?

CONCLUSION

Mental health issues can affect anyone regardless of race, culture, or gender. However, the severity to which those mental health issues impact someone can be influenced by social class. Access to resources is clearly different for people of different economic means. The privilege of choice of treatment and treatment provider is often only given to those of substantial economic means. People victimized by poverty often are relegated to seeking treatment from community mental health systems where less experienced providers are the only option.

Our intention in this chapter was to demonstrate the clear relationship between mental health and social class. We had no intention of denigrating community mental health systems. Without them, many individuals with serious mental health conditions would have no treatment options and would likely be detained in criminal justice systems. We applaud the creation of these mental health systems and at the same time believe that these systems need to be strengthened through greater community and governmental support. Providing the right kind of support for these systems would serve to bridge the gap in resources between those with a choice of mental health care and those who are limited in choice due to social class.

Through this chapter, we discussed the theories that explain how social class and mental health issues are related and how differences due to social class have occurred. We also provided some context for understanding how the current system of mental health care remains in a homeostatic state. Our belief is that all counselors must adopt a lens of social change as they engage in their vocational efforts. As beginning professionals, we have stressed that you must include advocacy as a key role in your work if the social class differences in the mental health system are ever to be overcome. We strongly encourage all readers to become active advocates for social change and active members of your professional associations. While singular efforts are required, the power of a united voice will be the only way to develop overall system change.

RESOURCES

Counselors for Social Justice Website: http://counselorsforsocialjustice.com/

Hollingshead, A.B., & Redlich, F.C. (1958). *Social class and mental illness: A community study.* Washington, DC: APA.

Mental Health Advocacy Coalition, 4500 Euclid Avenue, Cleveland, OH 44103; phone: 216.432.7262, fax: 216.432.7252; email: info@mentalhealthadvocacy.org; website: www.mentalhealthadvocacy.org

National Alliance on Mental Illness. (2011). State advocacy 2010. Retrieved April 20, 2010, from http://www.nami.org/template.cfm?section=about_the_issues

World Health Organization. (2003). WHO Mental Health Policy and Service Guidance Package: Advocacy for mental health. Retrieved from http://www.who.int/mental_health/policy/services/essentialpackage1v7/en/index.html

9

Social Class and the Family

Julie M. L. Martin, Sara McKeown,
and Debbie C. Sturm

Social class experiences tend to have a significant influence on family dynamics, as family structure, roles, rules, and expectations often vary across social class status. Generations shape family narratives about class, affecting how family members define themselves, their shared values, and the manner in which they approach the challenges of daily life (Kliman, 1998). These narratives create an intergenerational process of defining what is acceptable and expected within the family, whether it be education, vocation, or future decisions about family. The traditional view of social class in the helping professions stratifies people into social class groups and then infers that people within a particular group will see and react to the world similarly. This tendency is referred to as the stratification paradigm (Liu, 2002) and can lead helping professionals to make assumptions based on class, such as the familiar assumption that lower class families have higher degrees of disorganization and dysfunction. However, many family issues that arise in family counseling are quite similar across clientele of various social standings. It is the coping mechanisms and resources that are available to these families that differ. Helping professionals who work closely with family systems are tasked to look beyond the traditional stratification paradigms to the specific experiences of families, and then work closely with families to bring about change that is meaningful and appropriate for them.

This chapter will discuss family structure through the lens of upper, middle, and lower social classes. The impact of family-of-origin social class on future family dynamics will be explored. And we will review the practice of family counseling with an invitation to consider the power of the therapist's social class status on the therapeutic relationship.

Case Study 9.1

Many people view social standing and social class as the same thing and will do whatever it takes to keep up appearances and protect their perceived status. During this reflection, imagine your practice involves working with families from a variety of social class backgrounds. Recognizing that becoming a culturally competent helping professional involves a degree of introspection, also consider yourself and your experience with social class as your read the following scenario:

> An upper-middle class couple comes in for counseling. They admit to struggling financially and are faced with the choice between paying their $1,200 mortgage or buying tickets for the country club gala. This is not the first time they have had to make such decisions, and in the past have relied on relatives to help them with the basic bills to prevent embarrassment. They reveal that they have decided to buy the tickets even though this could mean missing their mortgage payment. They feel that maintaining the public perception of financial security is more important than privately struggling with finances. As you listen to their decision-making process, you think about another family you are seeing that same day that lives in subsidized housing and places a high value on paying their bills on time and never owing anyone money.

FOLLOW-UP QUESTIONS

1. What thoughts or feelings emerge as you consider the dilemma and subsequent choices of the first family described?
2. Which of the two families can you most relate to as you consider your family of origin? Does this impact your automatic reaction to each presented family?
3. Do you agree with the notion that social class and social standing are the same thing? What role have these played in your own life?

Social class is determined by many factors, such as the area and house one lives in, the type of work one does and the salary earned, the school one attended and level of education achieved, and one's family of origin (McAuliffe, 2008). Social class often defines a family's way of thinking about their opportunities or limitations in life. It can also define who the family feels they are and the resources they expect to be available to them.

The social status of an individual's family of origin influences his or her opportunities for friendship, travel, education, and employment. It is also a powerful predictor of the social class of future generations, as families write scripts for their members to follow, which is known as *family legacy.* Generally, an individual will follow the legacy set forth by his or her family; however, there is permission and opportunity for promotion in some families. The perceived social class may "label" individuals or make it difficult for them to transition into a different social class. Sometimes this transition is aided by different opportunities that are presented or provided to an individual. If he or she attains a higher level of education or income than his or her family of origin and takes advantage of opportunities provided, then this transition to a higher social status or educational level can be considered an upward change (Liu, Soleck, Hopps, Dunston, & Pickett, 2004). Likewise, families who fall below the perceived social class experience of their family of origin, regardless of the reason, would be considered downwardly mobile. Beliefs about class and mobility more often than not place a higher value on upward mobility over remaining the same or becoming downwardly mobile.

The following sections describe how family appears and functions within each social class. These sections will also explore the power of the family of origin's social status on future generations as well as the types of family legacy and transition opportunities available to each social class.

UPPER CLASS AND THE FAMILY

A typical assumption about upper class families is that they have enough money or other resources to access their wants and needs; therefore, they should not have any particularly significant problems. Members of upper class families tend to have more opportunities afforded to them due to more ready access to resources, such as financial, social, educational, and political resources. At times members of these families may experience a sense of entitlement to more than they have actually earned, a characteristic that tends to trigger negative reactions from those in lower social classes who take pride in working hard for what they achieve. While the very nature of high social class standings implies the likelihood of more power and means to ensure their needs are sufficiently met, this same dynamic may cause pressures within families to act a certain way in order to maintain their status. A characteristic of the upper class is increased resources, which leads to more perceived control over one's life. Unfortunately, there has been very little research about upper class families in counseling.

As highlighted in previous chapters, membership in the upper class has positive aspects and negative trade-offs. For example, children have material fulfillment, but the consequence is often lack of parental involvement. There are high expectations for children of upper class families, but also heavy criticism upon failure. The higher levels of employment within the upper class create and perpetuate higher income, but the consequence is less family interaction and nurturance for children. The ultimate consequence for children of upper class families is the neglect received at the hands of uninvolved parents. This leads to detached adults, which cycles to a new family, therein repeating the unhealthy family pattern.

The family structure of the upper class is typically considered to be traditional, including both parents, one or two children, and an older generation of grandparents. However, the family structure in upper class families can actually be as diverse as others and include large families, single-parent families, stepfamilies, blended families with children from previous relationships, same-sex partnerships, and grandparents raising grandchildren. Family therapists define family structure as not only those members included in the family, but also how each member interacts to maintain the family system. It is important for family therapists and other helping professionals to look past expectations of family structure and instead inquire with the family about who they consider to be significant within the system.

Popular media has suggested that upper class families tend to demonstrate a structure that is overbearing and oppressive, in which the older generation dictates proper behavior to the younger generations. It is accurate to suggest that upper class families tend to recluse themselves and interact mostly with other upper class families, but family closeness is not a necessary part of this structure. More often, the parental generation works hard, through their professional and social connections, to maintain their position among the upper class. This may cause a lack of family interaction due to long work hours, travel, or social expectations. As with other family structures, a lack of parental time or attention can elicit acting out behavior by the younger generation, with the purpose of gaining attention and support from the older generations (Yates, Tracy, & Luthar, 2008).

The power of family legacy is probably the strongest among the upper class. The highest social echelon is determined as such due to the sustainability of social prestige and a family legacy of power and income over many generations. There is increased pressure for the youngest generation of an upper class family to maintain the social class standing of the generations before them. Children of upper class families are generally educated at higher performing or private schools and accepted into Ivy League or other prestigious universities due to the family name and understanding how to gain access to higher levels of opportunity. There is an expectation that the youngest generation will make similar career and marital choices as their parents and grandparents; therefore, a choice to be different may invoke harsh disapproval (Lapour & Heppner, 2009). It may be considered failure if a member of the upper class "falls" to middle or lower class, which creates pressure to do as well or better than the previous generations, either educationally or financially. The expectations from within one's family of origin, as well as from society, are a heavy burden and can push a younger generation to succeed or fail, particularly among children whose parents have a public identity.

The increased resources available to members of the upper class can also create confusion when the parental generation is faced with acting out behavior of the younger generation (Yates et al., 2008). Family therapists know that developmentally an adolescent will push the boundaries in order to assert oneself as a young adult and to fully understand limitations. The added pressure of the family of origin is knowing when and how to allow a member of the younger generation to receive consequences of a misdeed, which may expose the family to ridicule among social peers or the society at large. The choice to rescue an adolescent or young adult from societal consequences may preserve the family name, but it does not teach the young person limitations to his or her behavior, which is a necessary tool for transition into adulthood.

MIDDLE CLASS AND THE FAMILY

There are a wide range of experiences within the middle class, as those in the upper-middle class can have similar incomes and prestige as upper class families, and members of the lower-middle class can have lifestyles similar to those of lower class families with regard to financial stability and resources. Though middle class families often have more resources available to them than those who are considered working class or poor, these families tend to work hard to keep things going by putting many hours into making their small businesses successful or continuing their employment status to maintain a certain income level. Education, income, and type of employment are means to advance one's social class (Liu, Soleck, et al., 2004), but generally most people experience mobility within the middle class rather than beyond the middle class.

As highlighted in previous chapters, middle class is defined as being between the upper and lower classes, and trying not to lose ground. Members of the middle class range from professionals to salaried employees, and all those in between. As a middle class family, one privilege is that most of society is geared toward supporting the family unit, as it is considered the "norm." The American dream is the unspoken goal of most of our society, as we secretly hope that if we work hard enough our youngest generation will enjoy more comfort and stability than the previous generation (McAuliffe, 2008).

Family legacy is strong within the middle class, but not as strong as within the upper class. The younger generations of middle class families tend to take direction from their parental generation and parents serve as influential role models and advocates for their children. Adolescents and young adults are given the option to "be who you want to be" as part of the American dream, provided they are willing to work for it (McAuliffe, 2008). The younger generation is given a wide range of choices, as education can be private or public, and can range from Ivy League schools, to community colleges, to trade schools. One constant across the middle class experience is a multigenerational family focus on education as the seed of upward mobility.

A member of the younger generation receives a similar message about work and vocational choices, as he or she is encouraged to work as hard as he or she wants in order to achieve a status comparable to his or her family's older generations. The ultimate decision is that of the individual, and choices can be modified throughout one's life cycle, which provides hope and freedom for members within the middle class.

Family structure of the middle class is very diverse, as the public image of the family is not as pressing as in the upper class family. The family arrangement is wider due to greater choices and acceptance in society. The maintenance of a family system is just as diverse, as family therapists work with families who are enmeshed to disengaged within the same workweek. The choices a family makes to maintain its structure are as unique as middle class families themselves.

Case Study 9.2

You have been seeing a couple several times and they begin expressing a high degree of concern over their teenage daughter's lack of interest in school. She is a delightful girl, popular, athletic, and without any significant behavior issues; however, she has simply lost interest in her academic performance. The parents are distraught as they have carefully instilled the message that education is the key to success and worked hard to be sure their daughter would have more options than they did. While they can clearly see her other strengths, they cannot help but be fearful about her options if she fails to maintain a good academic standing.

FOLLOW-UP QUESTIONS

1. What does their daughter's lack of interest in academics mean to these parents? In what ways are your own beliefs about education as a key to mobility intersected in their story?
2. How can you help the parents maintain a strength-based perspective with regard to their daughter while simultaneously addressing their concern over her academics?
3. If you were to bring the daughter into the session, what would that conversation look like?

POVERTY AND THE FAMILY

Lower social class and those living in poverty are often characterized by a lack of financial resources, power, prestige, and privilege (Kraus, Piff, & Keltner, 2009). In fact, even the use of the term *lower* class implies something "less than." And while they may experience a lack of resources, the types of resources and the impact on the family system vary significantly throughout this stratum. Many helping professionals still ascribe to the belief of poverty as a culture, meaning that those who are poor share predictable beliefs, values, and behaviors. Gorski (2008) suggests that this myth is perpetuated by a collection of other stereotypes regarding lower social class, such as believing that individuals who belong to the lower social class are lazy and do not work hard enough to make money to help their situation. The reality is that many work very hard at low-paying jobs and often have to work more than two jobs just to pay for basic necessities, such as rent and food. According to Piff et al. (2010), while upper class individuals are characterized by economic independence, elevated personal control, and freedoms of personal choice, individuals and families living in poverty experience less personal control and may often need to depend on others to achieve desired outcomes. This encourages these individuals to behave in ways that increase social engagement and connection with others.

Family of origin among those living in poverty provides a strong message to younger generations (Scaramella, Neppi, Ontai, & Conger, 2008). If a member of the younger generation chooses to pursue education or achieve a status higher than his or her family of origin, there is a chance of losing the bond formed within the family or experiencing oppression by the upper and middle classes as they seek upward mobility. Members of the lower social class give the younger generation a similar message that young in the middle class receive, which is the message of the American dream. However, there is an invisible glass ceiling that is present for members of the social class that does not exist for the other classes. The lack of privilege and opportunity for upward mobility coupled with the oppression of upper classes causes the majority of younger lower class generations to repeat the same family cycle in which they were raised.

The working poor and those living in poverty are faced with many challenges in our society. From one day to the next, they must deal with the challenge of survival. This includes low-paying wages that poorly meet the financial needs of housing, adequate nutrition, clothing, transportation, child care, medical expenses, and safety, just to name a few. Unfortunately, there is the additional challenge of discrimination by other social classes. Classism is defined as a set of characteristics of worth and ability based on social class as well as the oppression by the other, more dominant social classes (Smith, Foley, & Chaney, 2008). The automatic assumptions that are made about those living in poverty add to the stress that these families already feel and contribute to the oppression of this class. Additional stressors are the labels that are often given the poor, including "white trash," "rednecks," "trailer trash," and "the wrong kind of people."

Classism is a form of oppression, like racism and sexism, but added to it is power. Prejudice can exist between dominant and subordinate social classes, but oppression exists when the dominant groups have cultural power over the subordinate group (L. Smith, 2005). Though some working poor and those living in poverty face issues with substance abuse, early pregnancy, or high school dropout, these crises do not equate to a limited future for children of lower social families. Instead, these are opportunities for helping professionals to identify resources, advocate, and empower clients in order to help break these patterns.

OPPRESSION AND CLASSISM

As mentioned throughout this book, classism is defined as prejudice and discrimination based on social class and refers not only to cognitions but also to associated affects such as shame, guilt, depression, and anxiety (Liu, 2002). While classism may not be the most readily identified form of marginalization, it is that same lack of awareness that perpetuates its pervasiveness. Members of both dominant and subordinated groups are capable of prejudice, but only dominant groups have the institutional and cultural power to enforce their prejudices via oppression (L. Smith, 2005). The upper and middle classes have the power to oppress the lowest class, which ensures separation and distance. Liu (2002) suggests a modern classism theory, which states that there are four types of classism: upward classism, which is directed toward people of a higher social class; downward classism, which is directed toward those of lower social class; lateral classism, which occurs among people in a similar social class for the purpose of realigning a target's social class worldview to be congruent with others; and internalized classism, which is feelings of anger, frustration, depression, despair, disappointment, and anxiety experienced when one is unable to meet and fulfill the social class expectations of one's economic culture.

Classist behaviors are mostly learned through parents and family, while others are socialized through peer groups (Liu, 2002) and larger systems. Treating poor people as somehow deficient or lesser than oneself is central to the concept and practice of classism (Lott, 2002). According to Liu (2002), social class and classism have an impact on not only the psychological self but on other aspects of health as well. It has been found by many researchers that those who are poor tend to have poor health behaviors, high rates of coronary heart disease, more frequent use of alcohol, and high rates of premature death and mortality. They experience higher rates of work stress and conflict, participate in dangerous sexual behavior more frequently, may have higher rates of poor social support, a higher frequency of depression, anxiety, and aggression, and are exposed to chronic stressors and hostility (Liu, 2002). Again, it is important to consider not only the existence of classism within our culture, but the impact it has on family systems. If adults have been oppressed by the larger culture, their view of the world, of possibilities, and of acceptance is sure to influence the way in which they create and foster those same things within their own family. An awareness of this is critical to therapists honestly confronting the weight of classism on families struggling to successfully overcome obstacles.

SELF-REFLECTION OPPORTUNITY 9.1

Take a moment to reflect on the words of family therapist Harry Aponte (personal communication, May 15, 2011):

> Class influences people's mindset about their issues (such as their expectations about the possibility of positive change—hopefulness versus despair). Class has a great deal to do with the kinds of resources (internal and external) that people have available to address their issues. Class directly affects the mindset and approach of the therapist to the client and the client's issue, depending on the therapist's class (affecting the ability of the therapist to understand and empathize with the client) and the social roots of the therapeutic approach the therapist is using (example: psychoanalysis born to treat the middle class, versus structural family therapy born to address the struggles of disadvantaged families).

FOLLOW-UP QUESTIONS

1. How do Aponte's words strike you? How do you think his work with lower social families impacts his viewpoint?
2. What is your opinion on the power of the social class of the therapist in comparison to the client family?
3. How do you plan to address your own bias regarding social privilege?

THE PRACTICE OF FAMILY COUNSELING

Family therapists have been known to say that there is no benefit to labeling a family with an artificial term, as it has nothing to do with the character, or heart, of the family. Labeling and expectations associated with class can affect treatment of others in the education, work, and community settings, creating a "self-fulfilling prophecy" that may derail opportunities for these individuals and their families. Some suggest that even the process of dividing individuals into social classes is a method of discrimination. Other counselors recognize the separate social classes and state that working with many different social classes helps them become more empathetic to others. These counselors think that a family makes sacrifices in order to provide better opportunities for their children, which may have been modeled by the families of these particular counselors. They believe that social class is as present as any other form of cultural identity in a counseling session; therefore, it is important to address and discuss class status as part of establishing a working relationship. Understanding and removing the bias of the counselor created by a middle class social standing is critical in truly being able to connect with and effectively counsel families of various social levels.

Therapist Family of Origin

Family therapists and other helping professionals often miss the mark when they place their own goals for counseling on the family, which tend to be based on the counselor's social class instead of their clients' class system. The working poor cope with a variety of oppressive factors from day to day. The stereotypes and social expectations they face create an environment of continued disappointments and shame. Yet many lower social status families exemplify resilience by virtue of their survival under harsh daily conditions. The economic, political, social, and racial crises of the dominant class continue to be borne by people of color, the working poor—those who have jobs but do not earn enough money to support their families—and women (Harley, Jolivette, McCormick, & Tice, 2002). Thus, upward mobility may not be the goal of every social class, and the challenge for therapists is to deal with the clients' goals of therapy. In fact, it is possible to argue that imposing the belief that upward mobility is a preferred goal fails to value families of all social class statuses who value their status and are simply struggling with other issues.

Family therapists and other helping professionals need to be aware of the impact that social class has on the lives of all men and women, as well as the power of classism on the emotional and cognitive state of clients (Liu, 2002). It is an automatic response when meeting an individual who is struggling to want to help them. Therapists have this dilemma as well, as often the clients' goals for therapy are overshadowed by the goals of the therapist for the family. The challenge in this situation is to recognize when we are shifting focus to meet our own value system. The counselor and client may have opposing worldviews and goals that may impede counseling, leading to impasses and incongruence (Liu et al., 2007).

SELF-REFLECTION OPPORTUNITY 9.2

In my family, we have decided that I have somehow "outgrown" the social class from which I was raised. This is not something that I place into the dynamic of the relationship, but is placed on me, as if I have "gotten too good for the family." From what I have seen in counseling, it is more often the case where the family of origin feels as if the original member has somehow "abandoned" them due to educating themselves.

FOLLOW-UP QUESTIONS

1. How do you feel as you read this reflection?
2. How do you identify your own social status? Is it similar to the social class of your family of origin?
3. How would you counsel a family member who states he or she feels guilt for reaching beyond the social status of his or her family of origin?

Self as Therapist

A therapist is called to believe in the family and to communicate that therapy sessions have the ability to help the family tap into their own potential to deal with their difficulties. A pragmatic approach to counseling is called for when working with families of lower social status, in which the counselor is down to earth, practical, hands on, and nonideological in order to deal with each family situation in a unique way. This involves constantly seeking to respect and understand their strengths, coping styles, difficulties, ability to advocate for themselves, cultural and ethnic connections, and access to formal and informal supports. The family members may not believe they are capable of meeting their own needs; therefore, the counselor's role is to convey a belief in the family, instilling pride, courage, self-esteem, and hope (Kaplan & Girard, 1994).

The counselor does not tell the family what they need to work on; rather, the family and therapist work together to solve their presented issue. A therapist who tries to prioritize a family's needs and dictate treatment goals may give a family the message of disempowerment by conveying that they are incapable of dealing with their problems. This is the exact opposite message counselors should give a family who is already receiving this message by society. Instead, therapists should work to empower families of lower social status by believing in their power to change and helping families believe in themselves. Therapists also provide families with a new perspective or outlook on the issues presented. Another empowerment tactic is to educate families about their options and to help them increase their own skills. A therapist can recognize and build on therapeutically useful strengths and resources. Empowerment serves as the driving force in the goal of family preservation, which strengthens families' coping skills and improves their ability to function effectively in the community (Kaplan & Girard, 1994).

It is important for therapists to recognize the inherent power differential between the client and a therapist and the added power that has when social class is layered into the relationship. Successful techniques that respect the lower social status family require finding a comfortable middle ground. Once such common technique is circular questioning, which allows the counselor to gain an understanding of the family through their own eyes. Circular questioning evens the power differential in the therapy room and allows the therapist time to suspend his or her own opinions and theories in the interest of learning how the clients make sense of the world and their situation (Kissman & Allen, 1993). Another aspect to address with families of lower social status is how the family has organized itself to meet its needs. This technique is especially helpful when dealing with a family where the social situation has changed considerably by a recent divorce or death of a family member that has perhaps led to the current economic situation.

Unconscious distancing from the poor overrides the better intentions that clearly exist among helping professionals, with the result that the poor are "disappeared" from many counselors' professional and personal worlds (L. Smith, 2005). The therapeutic relationship should be a safe place for a family of lower social status to talk about their challenges and to seek solace from the outside world. Regrettably, at times the therapist is a contributor to the stress that the working poor feel because the counselor subscribes to similar stereotypes as the society at large.

Differing worldviews and class-based experiences may get in the way of the therapist's ability to develop empathy for a client (Ballinger & Wright, 2007). Families who have a history of crisis often have their own agendas for therapy. The goals of clients from lower social status may include reducing pain, hiding secrets that could threaten the family, avoiding painful issues, remaining loyal to the family's rules, beliefs, and patterns of interaction, getting someone under control when they are out of control, and namely, utilizing all possible resources and energies to maintain a "no change" position (Kagan & Schlosberg, 1989). These goals are directly the opposite of most therapeutic goals; however, working with families to address the needs and hopes underlying these goals is needed, not simply dismissing them as invalid.

SELF-REFLECTION OPPORTUNITY 9.3

As an African American woman, growing up my family made sure I was cognizant of not only educational value in society but also what being educated meant to my culture. Education meant that we had a better chance at a better life, even if we were African American. I was also made aware of certain stressors that may be specific to my culture, and how they could impact social class. While my family's views are not universal, if they are expressed during my work (with families), they give me somewhat of an "insider's view" to what is going on with them.

FOLLOW-UP QUESTIONS

1. How does race affect one's opportunity to advance educationally and move upward in social status?
2. What are challenges that African American women endure that might impact "a chance at a better life"?
3. How does the description of this therapist's experiences relate to your own family of origin experiences?

Multigenerational Counseling

Family therapy in its truest form includes as many family members as possible to address an issue. Including three generations at a minimum is the rule of thumb given in many family therapy primers. Family therapists believe that a presented problem in an individual can be traced back to the family system itself. One's family of origin and immediate family are powerful influences, important contributors for information, and can be helpful consultants to the family therapist.

Case Study 9.3

My experience in family counseling started with my own therapy, with my parents and grandparents. It started as a problem that I was having in school, and the referral to a family therapist led to an experience that ultimately impacted my selection of career—although as a teenager I didn't want to get dragged into counseling and certainly not with my grandparents! I learned about myself more through the words of those people I cared about the most. I learned so much about what they wanted for me and why my issues in school and with my parents held so much meaning to them. It truly was a powerful experience, which I have carried with me through my entire adult life.

FOLLOW-UP QUESTIONS

1. What is your experience with family counseling that includes multiple generations?
2. What are challenges that a family therapist might encounter when conducting multigenerational counseling?
3. How can you broaden your view of extended family, multigenerational family, family of origin, and nontraditional family systems in order to allow for the variations that are bound to occur within the therapy setting?

Throughout this chapter, we have discussed various aspects of social class as they intersect with families, family structure, and effectively counseling families. Perhaps the one hope is that you have been able to broaden your view of family and allow yourself to think beyond traditional class identities when you work with families. While there are certainly characteristics, belief systems, and practices common to various social classes, taking a constructivist approach to working with families is essential. Challenge your own notions of what family means, what family looks like, and what family goals "should" be. And then work to understand the true story of each family that sits with you, understand their experience in our culture, and seek to find the strengths, solutions, and goals that are most meaningful to them.

RESOURCES

McAuliffe, Garrett. (2008). *Key practices in culturally alert counseling: A demonstration of skills* (DVD). This DVD, which accompanied McAuliffe's textbook (*Culturally Alert Counseling: A Comprehensive Introduction*), illustrates for the reader various perspectives on race, ethnicity, social inequality, social justice, and various cultural backgrounds to benefit the work and education of the counselor in today's world.

American Association for Marriage and Family Therapy. This is a great resource for all things related to family therapy. Be sure to check out their library of resources at www.aamft.org.

Minuchin Center for Family Therapy. Dr. Minuchin began his work with a strong commitment to marginalized families. That same commitment continues today and is evident throughout the resources available through his center. www.minuchincenter.org.

Minuchin, Salvador. (1974). *Families and family therapy.* Cambridge, MA: Harvard University Press.

Satir, Virginia. (1964). *Conjoint family therapy.* Palo Alto, CA: Science and Behavior Books.

10

Social Class and the Schools: Beyond Ruby Payne

Kathy Biles, Joyce Mphande-Finn, and Daniel Stroud

In this chapter, school counseling is discussed with respect to social class, education, achievement, and advocacy/action. With an understanding of these concepts, counselors can better assess and address—in culturally sensitive ways—the needs of all students.

Case Study 10.1

Several years ago, I and another counselor were asked to visit the classrooms of all fifth graders at a magnet school comprised primarily of lower socioeconomic status children as they were preparing to take achievement tests—from which the results would determine the school's next-year funding. We had the entire week—as no new curriculum was being introduced. Instead, the principal wanted everyone to be getting prepared and focused so as to excel. The other school counselor and I thought it best to use the first day of classroom visits as a sort of needs assessment, and to ask how the students were doing with all this "excitement" (a.k.a. pressure!).

That which students shared represented themes of concern and worry both for themselves and for their school. Specifically, some commented that they hope they make it to school on time that day, sleep the night before, don't have stomachaches during the test, can complete all the answers, and the test isn't too tough.

FRAMEWORK FOR DISCUSSION

Payne (2005) provides a working definition of poverty as the degree to which one does without resources. She lists resources as:

Financial: Having the money to purchase goods and services.

Emotional: Being able to choose and control emotional responses, particularly to negative situations, without engaging in self-destructive behavior. This is an internal resource and shows itself through stamina, perseverance, and choices.

Mental: Having the mental abilities and acquired skills (reading, writing, computing) to deal with daily life.

Spiritual: Believing in divine purpose and guidance.

Physical: Having physical health and mobility.

Support systems: Having friends, family, and backup resources available to access in times of need. These are external resources.

Relationships/role models: Having frequent access to adult(s) who are appropriate, who are *nurturing* to the child, and who do not engage in self-destructive behavior.

Knowledge of hidden rules: Knowing the unspoken cues and habits of a group (i.e., middle class).

Keep these resources in mind as you reflect on the questions below.

FOLLOW-UP QUESTIONS

1. What is your initial reaction to this scenario, and what does that say about assumptions and values that you possess?
2. What additional information would you need to accurately assess what these students need in order to do well on the test? How can you go about assessing?
3. With regard to Payne's resources, what might be explanations for the students' comments that they hope they made it on time, slept the night before, didn't have a stomachache, and the test was not too tough?
4. How will answering these questions impact your future work with students?

Education standards and education reform have long been researched and discussed in the literature. Since No Child Left Behind (NCLB, 2001) legislation was enacted, closing the achievement gap has been and is currently a goal of educators, counselors, parents, and politicians alike. As we further discuss the importance of more funding for education and better prepared teachers, the achievement gap widens among children of color and children living in poverty.

In order to work toward providing an equitable education for all children, we must begin to understand the underlying issues that contribute to an achievement gap among students. As professionals working with children and their families, we must be knowledgeable about classism and how it contributes to an achievement gap. For example, in 2004 there were 13 million children in the United States living in poverty, an increase of 12.8% from the number of children living in poverty in 2000. Today the number is closer to 17 million (Ametea & West-Olatunji, 2007).

There is no one definition of poverty. According to Amatea and West-Olatunji (2007) poverty is defined as "a condition that extends beyond the lack of income and goes hand in hand with a lack of power, humiliation, and a sense of exclusion" (p. 36). This definition extends Payne's definition of poverty—the extent to which an individual does without resources (Payne, 2008). As introduced in the case study above, Payne, in her book *A Framework for Understanding Poverty*, describes these resources: financial, emotional, mental, spiritual, physical, support systems, relationships/role models, and finally, knowledge of hidden rules. To add to these two definitions, the Census Bureau utilizes variations such as monthly or annual poverty and episodic or chronic and long-term poverty. These consider a monetary measurement of poverty in determining applicant classifications for census surveys.

In addition to defining poverty, we must have an understanding of the phrase "culture of poverty." The notion of a culture of poverty was coined by Oscar Lewis in his 1961 book *The Children of Sanchez* based on his ethnographic studies of small Mexican communities. Although his study looked at only a handful of communities, Lewis (1961) generalized his work by suggesting there was a universal culture of poverty. This paradigm still exists today (Gorski, 2008).

The culture of poverty described by Lewis theorizes that there is a system of values and behaviors for poor people such as poor motivation in educational settings, lesser work ethic, language problems, and a higher likelihood of alcohol and drug abuse. We can see a "culture of poverty" paradigm in Ruby Payne's "the hidden rules of poverty" (2005, p. 37). One of the major criticisms of this approach is the culture of poverty presents the notion that people in poverty *are* responsible for their situation due to *their* characteristics or own deficiencies (Gorski, 2008). It essentially blames the poor for their situation and fails to ascribe sufficient systemic influences.

While many educators have been taught about the hidden rules of poverty and the culture of poverty, there are those who have described the culture of poverty as a myth and instead advocate looking at the culture of poverty as stereotyping and classism (Davenport, Tolbert, Myers-Oliver, Brissett, & Roland, 2007; Gorski, 2008; Rogalsky, 2009). In learning theories about poverty and what people experience living in poverty, counselors, educators, and other professionals working with students and families in poverty must balance these theories with seeking an expanded view of social class, understanding the influence of social class, and the impact of classism.

SOCIAL CLASS

"Poverty with a view" is a saying in the area where the authors of this chapter work and live. A beautiful area of a state where snow-capped mountains meet rushing rivers and trails and outdoor sports abound, such as skiing, golfing, hiking, mountain biking, and fishing. Before the economic downturn, the area was one of the fastest-growing communities in the state. Additionally, this part of the state has seen an influx of retirees moving in because of perceived quality of life.

Yet many people are willing to live here, in spite of not making a living wage or making a wage that goes along with obtaining an advanced degree and work experience, because the area is so beautiful. While there are neighborhoods where the average family income is substantial, there are many more neighborhoods that are older and have mixed below to average family incomes. There are approximately five school districts within a 50-mile radius. Within each school district, the numerous elementary, middle, and high schools had realized some growth before the recent economic downturn. As may be the case with many school districts across the United States, there are schools within each district considered "high poverty" or Title 1 schools, while other schools within the same district are low-poverty schools, where the students come from middle and upper class families. Yet many of the schools in these districts have students from all socioeconomic levels.

As seems to be the trend, according to Burney and Beilke (2008), racial and economic diversity, as well as increased poverty, have become more dispersed throughout all geographic areas and locale classifications. In addition to this dispersed poverty, Burney and Beilke (2008) state, "No racial or ethnic group is immune from poverty nor do they experience poverty in universal ways" (p. 175).

The intersection of poverty and one's social class status can be fraught with classism. In order to address classism and eradicate educational inequities and the achievement gap for our students, we must define class, social status, class privilege, classism, and internalized classism. According to Adams, Bell, and Griffen (2007), class is defined as the relative social rank in terms of income, wealth, education, occupational status, and power. Thus, social status can be understood as the degree of honor or prestige attached to one's position in society.

Lareau (2003) observed families at different class levels and races to see how families and parenting styles differed and the impact of class on children's development. Lareau observed that middle class parents in suburban neighborhoods were more likely to control their children's activities outside school by enrolling them in multiple activities such as sports, clubs, and music lessons. These parents were engaged in what Lareau called *concerted cultivation*. This concerted cultivation seemed to lead the children to have a strong sense of entitlement. These children were more likely to question adults, talk to adults as equals, and also not know how to fill their time if it was not planned (Lareau, 2003).

During her observation, Lareau (2003) also found that parents from blue-collar and public housing neighborhoods do not focus on concerted cultivation. Rather, these parents engaged in providing the basic necessities, such as ensuring their children are fed, have clothes, and a home to live in. In contrast, children from lower class families were often left with extended family or friends after school and had more autonomy in choosing their activities. These children may have only one sport they play or formal activity throughout the school year, but generally they played with their cousins or neighbors outside or watched television after school. Lareau (2003) described this as parents and guardians facilitating the accomplishment of natural growth.

The difference in parenting styles, however, can result in families becoming victims to classism when our schools promote strategies of parenting and caring for children that align with concerted cultivation. For working class parents and parents in poverty, the cultural logic of child rearing is not aligned with the standards of the institution. While these parents want what is best for their children, the constraints of providing for their families' basic needs and navigating barriers such as living in unsafe neighborhoods, or ensuring their children are cared for after school because they are still working, are their focus (Lareau, 2003).

Thus, classism is described as the institutional, cultural, and individual set of practices and beliefs that assign differential value to people according to their socioeconomic class, and within an economic system that creates excessive inequality and causes basic human needs to go unmet. It is important to understand class privilege, which is defined as the many tangible or intangible unearned advantages of higher class status, such as personal contacts with employers, good childhood health care, inherited money, and speaking the same dialect and accent as people with institutional power (Adams et al., 2007).

Lastly, defining and understanding internalized classism may help change our worldview of a culture of poverty. Internalized classism is one's acceptance and justification of classism by working class and poor people. This acceptance and internalized feelings of inferiority to higher class people, hostility and blame toward other working class or poor people, and beliefs that classist institutions/policies are fair are all examples of internalized subordination. Adams et al. (2007) not only define internalized classism, but also describe how internalized classism leads to internalized subordination or internalized dominance.

> Feelings of superiority to people lower on the class spectrum than oneself, a sense of entitlement, rationalizations of classist policies and institutions on the part of middle class and people on the upper end of the class spectrum are examples of internalized domination. Both internalized subordination and internalized dominance are manifestations of internalized classism. (Adams et al., 2007, Appendix 13C)

Understanding classism, class status, and class privilege is the first step in working from a social justice framework. Identifying classism in the education setting, and the impact on our students, is the next step to achieving a more equitable education system and providing the education each student deserves, regardless of income level. Rather than considering the culture of poverty, we look at Payne's (2005) hidden rules or Lareau's (2003) paradigms on parenting, such as concerted cultivation and accomplishment of natural growth, and begin to address the educational setting when we observe institutional classism.

EDUCATION

Children from poverty are more likely to attend schools with the least qualified teachers. High poverty schools are defined by the Department of Education as having 76% or more of the students who are eligible for a free or reduced lunch program (National Center for Education Statistics, 2010). One reason for high-poverty schools having a difference in teacher quality may be due to the hiring rate of new teachers in underfunded schools, while more experienced teachers are working in low-poverty schools. New teachers in these schools have reported feeling unprepared to address the challenges and needs of their students. They also report working in dismal conditions and lacking resources and support (Amatea & West-Olatunji, 2007). There are often a larger number of teacher vacancies and classes conducted by substitute teachers or teachers who are not certified (Gorski, 2008).

In addition to differences in teacher preparation, we must be aware of differences in access to material resources and time students and parents in poverty have that we may not think about as it relates to their economically advantaged peers. While we may do a better job recognizing what students from poverty need in terms of material resources, such as paper, pens, and a book bag, we make assumptions about resources, such as time—or the lack thereof—when wanting parental involvement (Gorski, 2007).

Parents who live in poverty, and the blue-collar workers that Lareau (2003) observed, may not attend the parent–teacher conferences or other functions occurring during the school day. Do we make assumptions about these parents not caring for their children, or do we consider that these parents may work two or more jobs just to pay rent and feed their children? Many of these parents do not work for employers who allow time off for school meetings or doctor appointments. Many may not have transportation and rely on public transportation or riding with coworkers. Oftentimes these meetings and other school activities are held after school hours, but before the dinner hour.

CURRICULUM RIGOR

Teacher expectations and course rigor may be lower in high-poverty schools as well. For example, Adelman (1999, 2006) stated that one of the best predictors of postsecondary success is successfully completing mathematics courses beyond Algebra II and Advanced Placement courses during high school. He stated that students who successfully completed courses such as trigonometry or precalculus more than doubled the odds that a student with that level of math preparation would eventually graduate if he or she went to college. Yet schools with high poverty and a higher minority student population are less likely to offer these rigorous or Advanced Placement courses (Burney & Beilke, 2008). Therefore, students who do have their sights on college may not be challenged or encouraged to seek admission to a four-year institution. Schmidt (2010) discovered that students from the bottom half or fourth of the income distribution have accounted for a growing share of enrollments at community colleges or noncompetitive four-year colleges, while students from the wealthiest fourth of society are the growing share in enrollments in more selective institutions.

INTERNET AND THE DIGITAL DIVIDE

Schools with a higher poverty student population have limited computer and Internet access, larger class sizes or a higher student-to-teacher ratio, a less vigorous curriculum, and facilities tend to be run down (Gorski, 2008). Research conducted by the Pew Research Center (Fox, 2011) indicates those with limited income and education are more likely not to use the Internet or have an understanding of how to use a computer. Increased Internet use is tied to economic status and education, thereby increasing the digital divide. The Pew Research Center (Fox, 2011) also found 95% of upper income households use the Internet, while 48% of those without a high school diploma do not. About half of nonusers identify cost and lack of computer skills as primary barriers (Narcisse, 2010).

When people do not have Internet access at home or through school or a job, they often rely on public libraries to access the Internet or use a computer. With libraries limited hours and limited time allotted on public computers, the nearly 19 million people living in poverty who use public libraries computers still have limited access to health, education, and employment information (Narcisse, 2010). While more and more information is readily available online, people in poverty's access to the Internet is limited, and the digital divide becomes even wider.

Another consequence of limited computer and Internet access for students and families living in poverty is a lack of computer literacy. Robinson found that the quality of Internet access, the freedom to use the Internet without time and equipment constraints, and opportunities to develop information-seeking skills have significant impact on computer literacy levels (Narcisse, 2010). When low-income students did their work in the short time allowed in schools or public libraries, they did not do as much Internet surfing to find the information or resources necessary for their schoolwork. This limited access also contributes to low-income students feeling emotional stress when trying to complete homework assignments.

In summary, in rural and urban areas across the United States schools can be identified as high-poverty or low-poverty schools. There are many schools where the student population is a mix of socioeconomic levels. Classism may be more subtle in these schools, and lower student achievement may be attributed to student deficiencies rather than a system issue or bias. Overall, whether students living in poverty attend a school that has a mix of students from various social class backgrounds or attend a high-poverty school, and in spite of the lack of resources, funding, quality instruction, or barriers that students face, we approach student learning from a deficit model.

ACHIEVEMENT

Though touched upon earlier, the impact of poverty on education is worth exploring further in terms of an achievement gap. According to Farkas (2003), there are three potential causes for an educational achievement gap. These potential causes can be identified across cultures and include socioeconomic status, discrimination, and educational opportunities—including adequate teachers and student effort. As mentioned previously in this chapter, low socioeconomic status may be a contributing factor to educational achievement gaps for several reasons. One reason may be the limited amount of resources available to enhance learning opportunities compared to those of a higher economic status. Another consideration may be that some parents of these youth may have limited educational skills and abilities, thereby decreasing their ability to focus on preparing their children for school and supporting them throughout the process (Farkas, 2003).

Discrimination may occur in a variety of ways, including teachers and administrators not providing ethnic minorities with the same quality of teaching as those who are White or Asian, or teachers may isolate lower-skilled individuals into "ability" groups, decreasing the extent of knowledge able to be gained (Farkas, 2003). Lastly, educational opportunities can induce educational gaps because of a separation between abilities and skills for certain groups of individuals. All of this can combine to decrease the amount of effort a child puts into learning and a lack of confidence in his or her ability to perform differently (Farkas, 2003).

"President Obama has said that by 2020, he wants the United States to have a higher proportion of students with college credentials than any other nation" (Schmidt, 2010, p. 3). As educators, parents, counselors, and other professionals hear the president's charge for college and career readiness, we must take a look at the role of achievement and the achievement gap, in order to act effectively.

Hence, we now shift our focus to achievement, specifically as it relates to classism. Burney and Beilke (2008) examined poverty's impact on high achievement as it related to the field of gifted education. They discovered that it is nearly impossible to identify potentially high-achieving students who are living in poverty based on the current system of identifying students for gifted programs. They define *high achieving* as "a level of performance that is higher than one would expect for students of the same age, grade, or experience; and proficiency is demonstrated by successfully mastering content (instructional) material beyond what is considered to be grade-level curriculum" (Burney & Beilke, 2008, p. 300).

States have developed their own curriculum standards for what students are required to know and learn. As students are tested to determine if they meet these standards, most tests used for this are not designed to measure achievement above grade-level standards. Therefore, when states establish their gifted and talented programs, they look for students who demonstrate high achievement capability in areas such as intellectual, creative, artistic, or leadership capacity. They may look for students who excel in one academic subject and who need services or activities to challenge and develop these abilities (Burney & Beilke, 2008).

There are several factors that stand out in the absence of identifying students in poverty who are also high achieving. First, students in poverty have limited access to programs outside of school that provide lessons and enrichment opportunities that would build their self-efficacy and confidence in their ability to learn new things. As mentioned in the beginning of the chapter, parents classified as blue color or at the poverty level rely on the accomplishment of natural growth. Additionally, after-school activities that would otherwise enrich students' high-achieving capability often charge fees for registration and participation (Burney & Beilke, 2008; Lareau, 2003), making such opportunities all but impossible for those without sufficient means. Finally, an additional factor that contributes to the lack of students in poverty being identified as high achieving is the issue of more students living in poverty being misidentified for special education (Gorski, 2007; Holcomb-McCoy, 2007).

ADVOCACY/ACTION

An advocate is defined as one who pleads the cause of another or one who defends or maintains a cause (Merriam-Webster, 1999). Kiselica and Robinson (2001) use the term *advocacy counseling* to describe the type of counseling whereby counselors go beyond providing traditional, direct services by also engaging in "indirect forms of helping that involve influencing the people and institutions that affect clients' lives" (p. 387). Earle (1990) describes a counselor/advocate as one who possesses a nonjudgmental attitude, patience, and persistence, along with a genuine belief that change can be achieved for a particular student, client, group, or sociocultural issue, and the capacity to negotiate and communicate effectively. Trusty and Brown (2005) highlight, in more broad terms, that according to the American School Counselor Association (ASCA), advocacy is a broad and multifaceted process. In particular, the ASCA national model states, "Advocating for the academic success of every student is a key role of school counselors and places them as leaders in promoting school reform" (ASCA, 2003, p. 24). The national model's position is that school counselors' advocacy efforts are aimed at (1) eliminating barriers impeding students' development, (2) creating opportunities to learn for all students, (3) ensuring access to a quality school curriculum, (4) collaborating with others within and outside the school to help students meet their needs, and (5) promoting positive, systemic change in schools.

The Transforming School Counseling Initiative (TSCI), in collaboration with the Education Trust, in 1996, began to examine innovative roles for school counselors (Paisley & Hayes, 2002). This resulted in the TSCI's assertion that advocacy must be a critical counseling role, especially as it relates to the collection of data to highlight educational disparities. According to Lee (2001), school counselors have both a moral and ethical responsibility to advocate for students and serve as agents for social and political change. The need for school counselors to be advocates for social justice seems to be especially important for students in poverty and students of color who attend schools that accept the false belief that these students cannot achieve at a high level (Bemak & Chung, 2005). These writings are supported by the endorsement of the advocacy competencies in 2003 by the ACA Governing Council, which signify the increased role of social justice advocacy in the field, and the importance of preparing counselors to be social justice advocates (Ratts, DeKruyf, & Chen-Hayes, 2007). They add that social justice advocacy is warranted to right injustices, increase access, and improve educational outcomes for all students. To this end, it is believed that professional school counselors can serve as agents for social change by using the American Counseling Association's (ACA) advocacy competencies as a framework for executing social justice advocacy strategies (Ratts, 2006).

School counselor advocates are encouraged to address a range of educational inequities and differences in academic achievement that may be grounded in issues of race/ethnicity, gender, class, disability status, and sexual orientation, and may prevent many students from maximizing their academic, social, and personal potential (Cox & Lee, 2007). Perhaps Menacker (1976) captures this idea by offering that sometimes it is the system, not the student, that needs adjusting, suggesting that school counselors need to go beyond helping individuals adjust to the system by advocating for the system to adjust to the students.

Increased attention has been extended to inequities in schools because historically students of color and those from families with low income have experienced a significantly lower rate of academic achievement than their White middle class peers (Gordon, 2006; Ratts et al., 2007). It is essential that culturally sensitive school counseling interventions be used to help empower students from diverse groups to overcome the dominant culture's negative views of their cultural characteristics. Instead, these cultural characteristics can be identified and used as strengths (Harley, 2009). It follows then that school counselors—the professionals typically charged with addressing the psychosocial needs of students and families (Schmidt, 2003)—will be in a better position to advocate for students.

IMPLICATIONS

In this chapter, the literature review of children living in poverty presents a profound challenge to today's educators and counseling professionals. These marginalized children are significantly more likely than children from middle class backgrounds to report increased levels of anxiety and depression, a greater incidence of behavioral difficulties, and a lower level of positive engagement in school (Black & Krishnakumar, 1998; Caughy, O'Campo, & Muntaner, 2003; Samaan, 2000). The hope is that school counselors and teachers will serve students well by utilizing interventions that specifically address past and current effects of classism in the schools in pursuit of equality for all students.

Amatea and West-Olatunji (2007) suggest that school counselors bring special skills to the effort of educating low-income children. Their review of literature on poverty and social class as correlates of student success, teacher expectations, and parent involvement provides a rationale for school counselors expanding their leadership roles in high-poverty schools by (1) serving as cultural broker among students, their families, and school staff; (2) partnering with staff to design more culturally responsive instruction; and (3) developing a more family-centric school environment. Research seems to support the role of professional school counselors to empower and support students from lower class backgrounds and to promote equity in schools.

Schellenberg (2008) believes that teachers are more successful with diverse learners when they have high levels of awareness and understanding about the cultural factors that influence academic achievement. So, what does this mean for professional school counselors and teachers? One answer is to promote aligning school counseling programs with academic achievement missions. This also allows school counselors to exercise the role of educational specialist—explicitly reinforcing core academic standards—while simultaneously attending to the role of mental health specialist, addressing the personal, social, emotional, and career development needs of students (Schellenberg, 2008). The importance of understanding the significant impact of classism and poverty in schools is necessary for both teachers and counselors. This is supported by the notion that professional school counselors can train faculty on the effective use of standards in a way that incorporates students accessing their cultural knowledge and strengths (Manning & Baruth, 2004).

School counselors and teachers, who are in leadership capacities, may want to formulate a vision or professional statements that help students from poverty and lack of wealth feel empowered. It is clear that professional school counselors are uniquely trained and positioned to identify and alleviate the cognitive, emotional, social, and behavioral barriers to student success and the school-wide environmental conditions that interfere with academic achievement (Galassi & Akos, 2004; Hines & Fields, 2004). Efforts must increase to change the environment in which students from different socioeconomic backgrounds can have positive learning and goal attainment, while they come to terms with the challenges they experience in their everyday lives. Culturally sensitive school counseling interventions can help empower students from diverse groups to overcome the dominant culture's negative views of their cultural characteristics and embrace and utilize their cultural attributes (Harley, 2009).

Finally, Schellenberg (2008) suggests rather than assumes a stance of cultural blindness; school counselors systemically identify and blend specific core academic standards with school counseling standards in a culturally sensitive fashion to produce integrated lessons that assist students across curricula. This fosters an encouraging and safe environment for student learning. It is believed that culture, seen as encompassing a constellation of factors (e.g., gender, ability status, race, ethnicity, sexual orientation, socioeconomic status, spirituality), is perhaps the most powerful force in forming behaviors, attitudes, strengths, beliefs, and values (Delpit, 1995; Harris, Thoresen, & Lopez, 2007; Lindsey, Roberts, & CampbellJones, 2005). Research findings inform it is beneficial for the counselor to initiate discussion about culture and cultural strengths (Erickson, 2005; Harley, 2009). Moreover, it is critical that professional counselors and teachers assist in shifting the focus of attention to the needs of students who come from poverty and the lower class and encourage a strength-based versus deficit-based pursuit of meeting these needs.

CONCLUSION

Educators, counselors, and administrators, to a degree, have been addressing the issue of poverty and its impact on students' education from a perspective influenced by Ruby Payne's *A Framework for Understanding Poverty* and hidden rules. Now is the time to extend this framework, by considering the possibility that classism is what keeps us marred in a cycle of poverty and impeded student achievement. A first step toward effective practice is to become aware of education policies, curriculum design, and educator training, as well as an understanding of student and family expectations.

In increasing your understanding, you become well positioned to advocate for children. Advocacy is a key component of creating change and eliminating education inequities. School counselors, along with all educators, are encouraged to influence systemic change with regard to barriers to academic achievement that may be grounded in issues of race/ethnicity, gender, class, disability status, and sexual orientation and may prevent many students from maximizing their academic, social, and personal potential (Cox & Lee, 2007). Advocacy can be as basic as talking with a teacher or administrator when you hear that homework is expected to be typed and have references from the Internet or to speaking up when schools make a change in policy that may only address the needs of students from middle and upper class families. Advocacy for high expectations and standards of all students to ensure every student is college ready may mean volunteering yourself or seeking out a volunteer tutor for students whose parents may not be able to afford one. Advocacy, in its simplest form, means tapping into your strengths and using those strengths for the benefit of others.

Lastly, this chapter has only focused upon the tip of the iceberg, as far as the impact of poverty and classism in education. The authors hope you further your awareness of this issue through continued readings, such as those listed at the end of this chapter, as well as immersion opportunities and discussions with education professionals regarding how well-intentioned policies and programs may inadvertently perpetuate classism in our schools.

RESOURCES

On Social Class

Lareau, A. (2003). *Unequal childhoods: Class, race, and family life.* Berkley and Los Angeles: University of California Press.

Noguera, P. (2008). *The trouble with black boys: And other reflections on race, equity, and the future of public education.* San Francisco: Jossey-Bass.

On Education

Burney, V., & Beilke, J. R. (2008). The constraints of poverty on high achievement. *Journal for the Education of the Gifted, 31*(3), 295–321.

On Achievement

Farkas, G. (2003). Racial disparities and discrimination in education: What do we know, how do we know it, and what do we need to know? *Teachers College Record, 105*(6), 1119–1146.

On Advocacy/Action

Dixon, A. L., Tucker, C., & Clark, M. (2010). Integrating social justice advocacy with national standards of practice: Implications for school counselor education. *Counselor Education and Supervision, 50,* 103–115.

On Culturally Sensitive Interventions

Wolfe, P. S., Boone, R. S., & Barrera, M. (1997). Developing culturally sensitive transition plans: A reflective process. *Journal for Vocational Special Needs Education, 20,* 30–33.

III

11

Exploring Classism and Internalized Classism

Lyndon Abrams and Peggy L. Ceballos

The idea that competent services be extended to all is a central tenet of socially just counseling practice. Recently there has been intensification in the calls for all helping professionals to better serve people who live in poverty and are subject to its impact (Liu, Soleck, et al., 2004). While these calls have persisted, the counseling community has not responded with a concerted effort to fully meet the needs of this vulnerable population. A number of causal factors have been identified for this void. Some include classism (L. Smith, 2005), inadequate definitions of poverty (Liu, Soleck, et al., 2004), and unclear delineations of who is impoverished (Liu & Arguello, 2006). Laura Smith (2005) cited unexamined classism on the part of mental health providers as a particular hindrance to impoverished people receiving fully competent services. In this chapter, the concept of classism is explored and the seminal work of Allport (1954, 1979) is utilized to provide a theoretical framework for understanding the effects of classism on impoverished clients. We then utilize the components of marginalized identity development as a frame to examine internalized classism among individuals living in poverty. The chapter concludes with classism self-reflection activities, case vignettes, practical clinical applications, and resources.

CLASSISM

An old baseball adage of questionable origin suggests that some are born on third base and believe they hit a triple. Privilege, or more precisely unearned privilege, has the effect of creating in some a belief of personal superiority to others based on status without recognition of any unearned advantages that they may have received in obtaining that status. Collins and Yeskel (2005) explained the systematic oppression of impoverished people by well-resourced, privileged groups. Within this context, classism is defined as "a set of personal and systemic assumptions, beliefs, attitudes, and practices that often discriminate against persons according to their socio-economic status. It includes differential treatment based on social class, or perceived social class" (Elementary Teachers Federations of Ontario, 2009, p. 2). Classism is simply the behavioral and perceptual arm of unearned class privilege (Lott, 2002), and it may be blatant, covert, or subtle.

The blatant classist, comparable to the blatant or overt racist, communicates classist dogma willfully and directly just as a blatant racist might transmit racist beliefs or feelings. Covert classists may have similar internal processes but seek to propagate the classist thoughts without clearly revealing their intentions (Smith & Shin, 2008). These first two types of classism, while harmful, pale in comparison to subtle classism, which is often perpetuated unconsciously by well-meaning individuals who seek to be supportive and encouraging of impoverished people. The danger with subtle classism is that it often operates outside of the detection of the sender or receiver. Subtle classism is the type of classism most likely to impact helping professionals in their clinical work.

Practitioners engaging in subtle classism may make sweeping generalizations like: If poor people would only do X, then they, too, could rise above their circumstances. Often this sentiment is expressed by those who have little insight or appreciation of the accuracy of such a statement and who do not recognize their own socioeconomic privilege. Helping professionals working from this framework may be blind to their own class encapsulation, which in turn limits their appreciation of the worldview of the impoverished client. Their attempts to change the seemed errant behavior and thinking of the poor person serves to create estrangement in the therapeutic process. In the therapeutic relationship, this may take the form of the client not trusting the counselor, becoming passive and less verbal, or exiting the counseling relationship entirely. The different types of classism create chasms between groups like those Allport (1954, 1979) described in the classic text *The Nature of Prejudice*.

Allport (1954, 1979) suggested that oppression is carried out through behaviors that range on a continuum from subtle to more harsh, including: (1) antilocution, which is to make verbal remarks against, (2) avoidance, (3) discrimination, (4) physical attack, and (5) extermination. These behaviors are geared at separating and maintaining distance between the individual and the oppressed group—in this case poor people. Historically we have seen this pattern of behaviors used against oppressed groups (e.g., the Holocaust, Manifest Destiny, and tribal atrocities in the Sudan). While we are not likely to see this continuum carried out fully in the counseling context, the underutilization of counseling services by impoverished clients seems to signal that the counseling profession may have inadvertently eliminated poor clients from service venues. In order to end this form of classism within the counseling field, counselors must become aware of their classist behaviors and understand the impact that classism has on impoverished clients.

EFFECTS OF CLASSISM ON IMPOVERISHED CLIENTS

Perhaps one of the most damaging results of classist behavior is the toll it takes on the collective psyche of those subjected to it. Allport (1954, 1979) pointed us toward a conceptual framework that helps us to categorize how poor people may respond to classist oppression. In a group of behaviors Allport labels "traits due to victimization" (p. 142) he outlines a set of responses that may result from group oppression. These behaviors or traits include: (1) obsessive concern with group membership, (2) increased group identification with other poor people, (3) disidentification from other poor people, (4) enhanced status striving, (5) prejudice toward other oppressed and marginalized groups, (6) sympathy toward other groups, and (7) militancy. Such behaviors are adopted by oppressed groups as ego defense mechanisms. Understanding these responses can aid helping professionals in appreciating the worldview and behaviors of impoverished clients.

Obsessive concern about membership in the impoverished group may cause impoverished clients to be hypersensitive to stereotypes and discrimination by privileged groups. For example, the performance of African American students is negatively affected by stereotyped threats (Steele & Aronson, 1995). According to Steele and Aronson, when African American students are reminded of their race during or prior to the completion of a task that African Americans are stereotyped to be less skilled at, their performance decreases. Further, Allport (1954, 1979) described the thinking process resulting from obsessive concern: "We've been hurt so often that we have learned to protect ourselves in advance by trusting no member of the group that so frequently inflicts injury" (p. 145). This type of response by impoverished clients has a direct effect on the counseling relationship, reminding practitioners of the importance of establishing trusting therapeutic relationships characterized by unconditional acceptance. The increase of within-group identification and disidentification from one's group are also methods used to turn away from oppressive forces (Allport).

With increased group identification the poor individual seeks to identify with others of similar economic standing and reject relations with individuals of higher economic standing. Conversely, disidentification leads impoverished clients to not wanting to be identified with other poor people. An illustration of this behavior actualized is the impoverished individual who expends resources on material trappings and activities geared to give the appearance that one is of a higher economic class. Another example of this trait might be the attempt to simply hide one's socioeconomic background. In extreme cases, this disidentification with one's group leads to self-hate by internalizing and agreeing with negative stereotypes the privileged group has created (Allport, 1954, 1979). Such response has a detrimental effect on the socioemotional well-being of impoverished clients. In some cases, disidentification leads to enhanced striving, a need for compensating for one's "handicap" (Allport, 1954, 1979, p. 156), or characteristics that have been stereotyped as negative by members of the privileged group.

Enhanced striving is the increased efforts by the marginalized poor person to better fit in with more economically wealthy people. Allport (1954, 1979) explained that individuals who respond in this manner assume that "to redouble one's effort is a healthy response to an obstacle" (p. 156). Enhanced striving occurs under the notion that working harder will allow for success within the system. This belief assumes that the system is otherwise equal and not set against the poor person. Increased effort with no payoff, however, may lead to a lack of belief and trust in the system and a disengagement from effort. In counseling, operating with this belief without an appreciation of the greater context can cause great damage to clients, as it perpetuates the belief that there is something wrong with them and increases feelings of helplessness. This framework fails to recognize oppression by denying that factors out of clients' control play a role in their current situations. Other responses to classism may lead impoverished clients to engage in prejudice or sympathy toward other groups.

Living under oppressed conditions affects the relationships between members of oppressed groups (Allport, 1954, 1979). Impoverished clients may engage in discrimination toward members of other poor minority groups. Allport explained that this behavior may be due to one's need to regain power taken away by the privileged group. Because classism deprives individuals living in poverty from power and status, a way to reclaim a sense of control is to exercise power over others who are seen as weaker. An example is the prejudice sometimes found between African Americans and Latinos of low socioeconomic status. On the other hand, some impoverished clients react by becoming sympathetic toward other groups who live in poverty. Using this framework, it would not be uncommon to see impoverished Caucasian individuals who are sympathetic to the social standing of African Americans. These types of responses become part of impoverished clients' perceptions and behaviors that ultimately affect their social and emotional well-being. For example, these responses guide clients' ability or manner in which they relate to coworkers from other impoverished minority groups.

The last type of response to classism to be discussed in this chapter is militancy. Allport (1954, 1979) suggested that some oppressed individuals will simply act out against oppression. This behavior may or may not be violent in nature. In some cases volatile acts on the part of some may prompt less intensive, less violent, but effective actions or protest and attempts for redress by others. This type of response is characteristic of the client who is aware of classism and not only rejects it, but becomes an activist to fight against it. This response, while not violent, can be very positive for impoverished clients, as it empowers them. Nonviolent militancy gives people living in poverty a way to fight helplessness without denying oppressive factors. The before-mentioned responses do not happen exclusive of each other. An impoverished client may display various responses simultaneously.

Understanding how individuals may respond to classism gives rise to an increased appreciation of the worldview of the impoverished person. Without such understanding, clients' behaviors may seem baseless and incongruous. Thus, counselors' ability to comprehend clients' behaviors within the context of responses to oppression and classism aids in the development of basic therapeutic conditions such as empathy and positive regard. It seems essential to understand why one might utilize limited financial resources needed for physical survival for material possessions that only give the appearance of greater wealth. Counselors and other helping professionals who are able to conceptualize such behavior as the client's response to the psychological pain of being perceived as being less than by members of the privileged group can develop a nonjudgmental therapeutic relationship. In addition, empathy rises when one is able to perceive how such a sacrifice, in the mind of the oppressed, becomes not optional but necessary. Practitioners must become familiar with impoverished clients' internal need for societal acceptance and anticipate that this may evolve over time in the impoverished clients we serve. In addition to gaining knowledge of impoverished clients' responses to classism, it is pivotal for those in the helping professions to understand how clients internalize classism over time.

INTERNALIZED CLASSISM AND ITS PROGRESSION OVER TIME

Allport's (1954, 1979) framework for oppression and oppressive traits considers individuals at one point in time. Marginalized identity development models provide a framework for considering how individuals from historically oppressed groups function in society and respond over time to oppression (Sue & Sue, 2008). These models began with Black racial identity models (Cross, 1971, 1995) and have been expanded to conceptualize the identity of women (Downing & Roush, 1985), sexual minorities (Cass, 1979; McCarn & Fassinger, 1996), as well as other historically oppressed groups (Sue & Sue, 2008). Identity development in general terms is the process of coming to view one's own reference group as a viable self-identification group (E. Smith, 1989). For members of marginalized groups this developmental process is a more complex progression. Similar to Allport, Erikson (1968) suggested that members of marginalized or historically oppressed groups experience oppression and may internalize it over time. Healthy development for these individuals involves resisting this oppression and developing a self-identity that is not based on the stereotypical oppression that is often thrust upon the marginalized group members.

Helms and Cook (1999) identified the underlying assumptions that are associated with the varying models of racial and ethnic identity. These assumptions seem applicable to our current consideration of individuals living in poverty and include the notions that: (1) we live in a world where marginalization has benefited majority, or nonmarginalized, groups at the exclusion of minority or marginalized groups; (2) individuals within these marginalized groups internalize this oppression, and as a result, they tend to develop negative views of self; and (3) shifts from this internalized negativity result from an event that is strong and powerful enough to create cognitive dissonance.

Rowe, Bennett, and Atkinson (1994) pointed up the common stage progression for marginalized identity development models. In the first stage of these models individuals begin with a negative view of self resulting from the stereotyping by the more powerful majority group. Clients who live in poverty find many oppressive messages of a classist nature in their daily lives. These oppressive messages often occur without the knowledge or the will of the oppressor and can be present in counseling when the counselor is not aware of his or her own classism. Laura Smith (2005) identified classist barriers to working with the poor that involved middle and upper class helpers who superimposed their class values on impoverished clients. This results in impoverished clients not being effectively served. An example of this is the notion that individuals who live in poverty are so concerned with day-to-day existence that they are unable to benefit from traditional counseling services. When already disenfranchised clients receive a message of this nature they are likely to receive and internalize it by drawing negative conclusions about self. This notion is contrary to the development of a positive therapeutic alliance and contributes to the oppression of the client.

The second stage of these models results from dissonance where the individual questions internalized assumptions from the previous stage (Rowe et al., 1994). This might occur when the client begins to question why a helping professional seems to patronize rather than confer and discuss the individual's presenting concerns. That client may come to the conclusion that the problem with the exchange does not reside within her but within a system that has predetermined the level and type of care she needs. This growing awareness may result in little trust in the therapist and in the therapeutic process. Some would argue that this second stage could best be conceptualized as a transition rather than an actual stage (Helms, 1990). In the two final stages, the individual continues to move toward greater appreciation of self and others with some important caveats.

In stage three of these models the individual moves toward embracing cultural factors associated with self (Rowe et al., 1994). A complication of this stage is that these cultural factors are often informed by the prevailing stereotypes that the marginalized individual has been exposed to up to this point. In the fourth and final stage, the individual moves toward greater acceptance of self and others as a result of having garnered and integrated a more realistic view particularly of self (Rowe et al., 1994). It is central for helping professionals to understand how individuals progress through a classist marginalized identity development process. Such understanding gives rise to an appreciation of (1) the client's worldview, (2) the way that a client may view a culturally different helper, and (3) the way a client may view self. In order to provide responsive therapeutic services for impoverished clients, practitioners not only need to understand classism and its effects on clients' socioemotional well-being, but they must also examine their own classism.

IMPORTANCE OF SELF-EXAMINATION

Despite the advances in multicultural training for mental health professionals in addressing biases, little attention has been given to classism (L. Smith, 2005; Liu, Soleck, et al., 2004; Toporek & Pope-Davis, 2005). In fact, mental health professionals "know little more about the therapeutic experiences of poor people today than they did decades ago" (L. Smith, 2005, p. 687). The importance of engaging in self-reflection regarding issues of classism cannot be overstated. Without such reflection, therapists risk being unaware of oppressive factors that have a direct influence on clients' mental health.

According Sue and Sue (2008) clients who do not mirror the middle class values engraved in traditional therapy are at risk for not receiving appropriate treatment. Oftentimes, lack of awareness regarding classism leads therapists to engage in a process that unintentionally works to adapt their clients to poverty (Waldegrave, 2005) while allowing clients to internalize self-blame for problems that are largely caused by external factors (Toporek & Pope-Davis, 2005). On the other side of the spectrum, therapists who are unaware of their biases toward high class clients also risk engaging in a therapeutic process led by unrecognized prejudices toward the client. In either case, therapists' lack of knowledge of their own biases and prejudices in regards to classism is detrimental to clients. Within this framework, one can easily see the inherent importance of engaging in opportunities for self-reflection.

The following exercises are developed with the intention of increasing one's awareness regarding classism through self-introspection. As with all multicultural issues, uncovering one's prejudices and biases toward classism is a lifelong journey that can only be embraced through commitment and self-determination. Experiencing feelings of anger, guilt, and shame, among others, is common when examining one's prejudices and privileges (L. Smith, 2005). However, it is such a psychological process that allows us to internalize learning and translate learning into actions—thus the importance of not denying one from such process. The exercises proposed in this chapter are adapted to be used individually; however, these exercises can also be used in groups. Additionally, when doing these exercises alone, the authors of this chapter highly encourage readers to process their journey with others who can identify with the process. Finding people who can provide emotional support and who can help to process one's journey is essential.

SELF-REFLECTION OPPORTUNITY 11.1

EXAMINING ONE'S DEFINITION OF CLASSISM

This exercise was adapted from Gorski (2010) and is designed to help readers engage in understanding their own definition of classism.

We all grow up assimilating different messages from our family of origin, society, and the media, among others. It is essential to find how these messages have shaped our concept of classism and our prejudices against others who belong to a different social class. Following are the guidelines:

1. Write down your own concept of classism. Make sure to include everything that comes to mind. Do not stop yourself from writing incomplete thoughts or just words. The following questions can help you get started: (a) What comes to mind when you think of poor people, middle class people, and high class people? (b) What qualities do you associate with different social classes (poor, middle, and high)? (c) What negative and positive stereotypes do you have about people in different social classes? (d) What messages did you get growing up about different social classes? Make sure you allow yourself enough time to truly reflect on these questions and to write down all your thoughts and feelings.
2. The next step is to divide what you wrote into categories. For this part of the exercise, we are adapting Nitza Hidalgo's (1993) "three levels of culture." On a separate piece of paper, write down the following subtitles: "concrete," "behavioral," and "symbolic." Based on what you wrote, under the subtitle "concrete" write down everything in your original list that is related to physical characteristics you associated with people from different social classes (e.g., people in poverty wear old, cheap, and flashy clothes). Under the subtitle "behavioral," write down everything in your original list that is related to behaviors you associated with people from different social classes (e.g., people in middle class buy expensive cars to show off). Under the subtitle "symbolic," write down everything in your original list that is related to values and beliefs you associated with people from different social classes (e.g., people in the upper class value money and material things).

3. Look at your categories. Which statements in these categories are stereotypes you have assimilated growing up? Are any of the characteristics you wrote about people in various social classes based on facts? When you meet somebody, which of the characteristics do you use to form a first impression about their social class? Is your view of your own social class consistent with how you want to be viewed and understood by others?
4. This activity should be a starting point to become aware of your own stereotypes toward people in different social classes. Following the activity, make an effort to be self-aware of what you wrote throughout the next week as you go on with your daily tasks. Be aware of what comes to mind when you see someone who seems to be from a specific social class. Are you now more aware of your own stereotypes toward others?

SELF-REFLECTION OPPORTUNITY 11.2

EXAMINING ONE'S EXPERIENCE WITH CLASSISM

The following exercise is intended for the reader to become self-aware of how classism has played a role in one's own life. All of us have been exposed to classism and experienced classism growing up. This exercise builds on the first exercise by allowing the reader to get in touch with his or her own experience regarding classism.

1. Close your eyes, go back to childhood, and try to remember the first time you became aware of class differences. Perhaps this was a time when you were not able to buy what other kids had or a time when you felt embarrassed to invite classmates to your house because your living conditions were different. The following prompts can help you get in touch with your past experiences with classism:
   a. The first time you felt stereotyped because of your social class
   b. The first time you felt excluded because of your social class
   c. The first time you felt included because of your social class
   d. The first time you stereotyped someone else because of his or her social class

As you are thinking about these prompts, pay attention to the feelings you are experiencing. You may want to write down these feelings as you start remembering each incident. Once you have finished becoming aware of your own experiences with classism, think how these experiences have influenced who you are today (e.g., your belief system, your behaviors, your feelings toward people from different social classes).

SELF-REFLECTION OPPORTUNITY 11.3

EXAMINING ONE'S PRIVILEGES

Examining one's privileges is an essential part of multicultural awareness (Sue & Sue, 2008). In the same manner in which we examine White privilege and male privilege, we need to examine class privilege. L. Smith (2005) stated that part of understanding classism is identifying specific social privileges people from the middle and upper classes enjoy as compared to people in poverty. As helping professionals, we need to engage in a self-reflecting process that allows us to face our own unearned privileges.

1. Think about the financial resources you were offered growing up. We recommend writing down the answers to the following questions:
   a. What kind of activities were you able to enjoy growing up? (e.g., Did your family have enough money for you to go to swimming lessons/ballet/piano? Did you grow up in a family that did not have financial resources for you to be involved in extracurricular activities?)
   b. What type of school did you go to? (e.g., Did the school have resources? Were the class sizes small? Was the building clean? Were the facilities new?)
   c. What type of freedom did your caregivers enjoy because of their work? (e.g., Were your caregivers able to miss a day of work to have a teacher conference? Were they able to work only one job? Were they able to come home and spend time with you during the evenings?)

d. How was your neighborhood? (e.g., Was the neighborhood safe? What type of role models were you exposed to growing up in the type of neighborhoods you lived in? Were these role models professionals like doctors and engineers?)
e. What type of material things did you own? (e.g., Were you able to buy the latest fashion when you were a teenager? Were you able to have a car? What other things did you own?)
f. Was your family able to afford health care insurance?

These questions can help you get started, but we encourage you to think of other types of experiences growing up that were tied to your family's finances.

2. Once you have reflected to what extent your financial resources allowed you to afford things, activities, places, and so on, read the "The Invisibility of Upper Class Privilege" (Women's Theological Center, 1997). This paper can be found at http://www.thewtc.org/Invisibility_of_Class_Privilege.pdf, and think about which of these privileges you had growing up and which ones you have now.

SELF-REFLECTION OPPORTUNITY 11.4

MAKING A COMMITMENT

Advances in multicultural awareness have been made thanks to activists who were willing to stand for what is right even when no one else was willing to listen. Based on what you have experienced through engaging in these exercises, what commitments are you ready to make at this point? Write down three specific behaviors you are ready to engage in to end classism. These behaviors can be anything you feel ready to do. Not everyone is ready to start by becoming an activist; thus, do not write behaviors that are not realistic for you in your current situation. Instead, write behaviors you know you can start engaging in today. Keep in mind that no commitment is too small or insignificant.

Case Study 11.1

Emilio is a 24-year-old man from Ecuador. He came to the United States after graduating from high school. He has a student visa and is currently working toward his bachelor's degree in business administration. He states that he comes from a middle class background and that back in his country he enjoyed having enough money to go out to "nice" places and even had friends from the upper class society, which allowed him to socialize in private clubs. According to Emilio, his parents, although not rich, were able to buy him clothes and material things that allowed him to keep up with his friends from the upper class. After arriving in the United States, Emilio's financial situation changed. He explains that his family sends him enough money to pay tuition and housing, but not enough for his daily expenses, such as food and transportation. Emilio says this is due to his father having to buy dollars, which nearly doubles the amount of money he has to give to Emilio. For Emilio, finishing his degree in the United States is extremely important. Thus, he accepted a job at a local restaurant washing dishes and cleaning the establishment. Emilio came to counseling because he recently started dating a Latina student who comes from an upper class family, but he has not told her about his job. He says he is afraid that telling her and her family about his job will make him "not good enough for her." Throughout the course of his first session, he talks about feeling inferior when he compares himself to classmates. He also says he is embarrassed about his new job and at times he has thought about going back to his country. However, he has a 4.0 GPA and his family has "sacrificed a lot" for him to be here; thus, he feels a responsibility to finish his degree.

FOLLOW-UP QUESTIONS

1. What are some of the prejudices that Emilio has grown up with regarding classism?
2. How are these prejudices affecting his present situation?
3. What are some prejudices that Emilio may be experiencing as a Latino international student in the United States?
4. With an understanding of Latino culture in mind, think of how gender roles and family values are interjecting with classism in Emilio's case.
5. What are your own thoughts and feelings about the situation? What are some of the prejudices you bring in as Emilio's counselor?

Case Study 11.2

Bryce is a 17-year-old African American male. He goes to the high school counselor because his ex-girlfriend (14 years old) just told him she is 3 months pregnant. Bryce recently accepted a full scholarship to play football at a university out of state. He states that his family is very proud of him, as he will be the first one to go to college. Bryce's family history reveals that his parents are lower middle class; money is tight, but good enough to support Bryce and his two younger brothers. Bryce's parents want the baby to be given up for adoption and for Bryce to go on with his plans to attend college out of state. Bryce's ex-girlfriend comes from a family that lives in poverty. Her parents work two jobs each and barely make it, supporting a family of five. Bryce discloses that his ex-girlfriend's family wants for Bryce to "be a man" by staying to support the baby. Bryce discloses he is unsure if he should go through with his plans of going to college or if he should postpone college to get a job to support the baby and his ex-girlfriend. He states he does not want to end up living in poverty by not going to college, but at the same time, he would feel "terrible" not taking complete responsibility for his baby. He is hoping that the school counselor can help him sort out his feelings and make the "right decision."

FOLLOW-UP QUESTIONS

1. As you conceptualize this case, how are the two different social classes between Bryce and his ex-girlfriend influencing the situation? Would the situation be different if both families were from the same social class?
2. What are your own biases regarding what Bryce should do? Where do these biases come from? Think about your own belief system and how it influences what you think is "best" for Bryce.
3. If you were the school counselor, how would you help Bryce?

Case Study 11.3

Sandy is a counseling intern working at a homeless shelter where she has been assigned to work with a 17-year-old client named Deja. Deja lives at the shelter with her mother, Denise, who is involved with the shelter's retraining program for displaced textile workers. Despite recent transiency, Deja has developed an excellent academic record. She is a senior preparing to graduate and go to college in the upcoming fall. She has earned scholarships that will allow her to attend her first college choice, a private school with a highly respected premed program. She will need to borrow about $3,000 per year in student loans. Sandy is encouraged that the prestigious woman's college (also Sandy's alma mater) that Deja wishes to attend has done so much to facilitate Deja's attendance. Denise fears credit debt of any type and is flatly against Deja taking out a loan of any sort. Her preference would be that Deja attend community college, remain at the shelter in the short term, and work part-time. Sandy views Denise's reluctance to encourage Deja to take the student loans as acts of sabotage against the daughter. To circumvent this she has approached her on-site supervisor Margie, who grew up with limited economic means. Sandy asks Margie to ally with her to help her convince the mother of the importance of her support with the loan request. Margie is taken aback by this request.

FOLLOW-UP QUESTIONS

1. What are some class-bound values that Sandy might need to guard against in conceptualizing this case?
2. What would you do if you were Margie and were approached by Sandy with the request above?
3. What are the essential differences between Denise's and Sandy's worldviews?

PRACTICAL APPLICATIONS

To provide culturally responsive services, mental health providers must integrate class and classism as relevant constructs in the conceptualization of clients' presenting issues (Liu & Pope-Davis, 2004; Waldegrave, 2005). Failing to consider the effects of classism on clients carries the risk of becoming part of the oppressive system clients in poverty experience in their daily lives (Toporek & Pope-Davis, 2005). In response, several scholars have advocated for the need to be proactive in addressing classism and its link to clients' socioemotional problems (L. Smith, 2005; Liu, Soleck, et al., 2004). Liu and Arguello (2006) emphasized the need to look at class and classism as an "intrapsychic process" by examining how classism is affecting clients' perceptions, feelings, and situations they face when coming for therapy.

Helping professionals can use Allport's (1954, 1979) framework as well as proposed models of racial identity (Rowe et al., 1994) as guidelines for understanding the experience and worldview of impoverished clients. Gaining such understanding becomes essential to form a nonjudgmental therapeutic relationship characterized by empathy and positive regard. Following are suggestions on specific practical applications clinicians can follow to ensure they address classism throughout therapy.

Engaging in Self-Awareness

The first step to become responsive to the effects of classism on clients begins with oneself. The need to explore our own biases/prejudices as well as our ability to see our privileges has been emphasized in the multicultural literature (Sue & Sue, 2008; Waldegrave, 2005). Smith, Foley, and Chaney (2008) explained that even counselors who see themselves as wanting to work with people in poverty need to carefully reflect on their desire and motivations for wanting to "help the needy" (p. 86). Not examining our own classism could result in being condescending instead of empathetic, and could ultimately lead to perpetrating negative stereotypes toward people who are oppressed by poverty.

Gorski (2008) exemplifies the danger of being unaware of one's prejudices when referring to Payne's work *A Framework for Understanding Poverty* (2005). In his article, the author provided a critical analysis of how Payne's work has furthered negative stereotypes toward people living in poverty. Gorski's (2008) article reminds the readers of the importance of critically analyzing how one perceives and feels about people living in poverty and emphasizes the need to critically look at our motives. Thus, the first step for any counselor is to engage in a self-awareness process. We must ask ourselves the difficult questions: How do I *truly* perceive people who live in poverty? Do I believe *any* of the stereotypes toward people living in poverty? What are my *true* intentions when counseling people living in poverty? Do I respect their decisions? Or is it my hope to lead them to make decisions that are congruent with what I would do in their situations? How do I filter what I hear about classism? Am I aware of my biases when conceptualizing cases?

Harry and Klingner (2007) stated, "Language in itself is not the problem. What is problematic is the belief system that this language represents" (p. 16). Oftentimes, our unconscious feelings and perceptions toward people living in poverty are represented in the way we express and behave. For example, children who live in poverty are overrepresented in special education and usually labeled as "disabled" without any consideration to how external factors have an influence on children's ability to learn in school (Harry & Klingner, 2007). Similarly, we fail to consider the effects of the inequalities that children in poor schools face on a daily basis (e.g., less qualified teachers, fewer resources) (Education Trust, 2005).

In therapy, Waldegrave (2005) reminded readers of how families who live in poverty are constantly being viewed as "dysfunctional" (p. 274). The author stated that such a negative view in combination with the sense of culpability these families internalize from classism in our society becomes a self-fulfilling cycle. In addition, such a negative view deprives helping professionals from looking at strengths (Waldegrave). In light of the risks associated with not being aware of one's classism, answering the questions above with complete honestly becomes essential. Looking at how we have contributed to classism through our prejudices and behaviors can be quite difficult, yet it is the only way we can avoid working from a deficit model.

Avoid the Deficit Model

A deficit model views clients' problems as rooted within themselves and their community. This model is based on negative beliefs regarding "the ability, aspirations, and work ethic of systematically marginalized peoples" (Irizarry, 2009, para. 2). Bohn (2007) explained this phenomenon by calling attention to the lack of consideration given to examining institutionalized classism. Instead of looking at inequalities, people working from a deficit model look at individuals as being at fault for their circumstances (Bohn). Approaching therapy from a deficit model leads to ignoring external factors that have a direct effect on clients' life situations and results in an ineffective therapeutic process (Waldegrave, 2005). In fact, counseling from this framework can perpetuate enhanced striving, one of the self-detrimental ways in which impoverished people may respond to classism.

To avoid a deficit model perspective, mental health professionals must conceptualize clients' cases with special attention to external events that are oftentimes the roots of socioemotional problems. Advocacy should be at the forefront when helping clients who live in poverty, and services should be comprehensive. Working with people who live in poverty requires finding community resources that can help fulfill basic needs, such as housing and food, while providing them with a therapeutic process characterized by empathy and understanding. Additionally, practitioners should work to replace the deficit model with a strengths-based model.

Strengths-based interventions seek to enhance clients' resiliency and protective factors as a means to reduce social-emotional problems (Galassi & Akos, 2007). Recognizing clients' strengths serves to replace clients' self-blaming or internalized classism with a sense of competence. This can be achieved by allowing the client to gain awareness of his or her inner resources and assets. Mental health professionals must intentionally seek to identify clients' strengths in an effort to: (1) allow clients to become self-aware of behaviors that have allowed them to be resilient, and (2) build on those strengths as a way to contradict self-blame created by classism. It is important to empower clients who live in poverty by building on their survival skills. Thus, case conceptualization should include an understanding of clients' resiliency factors and therapeutic goals should build upon clients' strengths. In order to avoid a deficit model and work from a strengths-based approach, counselors must be ready to enter clients' worldviews. Listening and understanding clients' experiences is essential to mitigate the effects of classism on clients.

Understanding Clients' Worldviews and Conceptual Framework

Liu and Arguello (2006) emphasized the need for mental health professionals to understand clients' worldviews, including clients' experiences of classism and the stresses clients face due to their social class. Such understanding cannot occur without complete empathy on the therapist's part. One of the barriers Laura Smith (2009) identified to counseling clients living in poverty is the belief that these clients' daily problems are so overwhelming that there is little therapy can do for them. The author explained that this belief is classist and deprives clients living in poverty from receiving the same quality of therapeutic services as clients from the middle and upper class. While it is true that helping clients living in poverty find resources to satisfy their basic needs is an essential part of counseling, this reality should not take away from rendering a therapeutic process characterized by active listening and therapeutic core conditions.

Understanding clients' worldviews requires listening to clients' stories to become aware of how they have internalized classism. Irrational beliefs regarding their social class as well as behaviors they must engage in to maintain or attain a different social status must be challenged during counseling (Liu & Arguello, 2006). Because classism is interrelated with other "isms" (e.g., racism, heterosexism), mental health professionals must identify how these other means of oppression contribute to clients' socioemotional problems. Liu and Ali (2005) recommended for therapists to look at how clients have been affected by sociopolitical factors such as inequality, sociohistorical factors such as erroneous histories of racial groups, and sociostructural factors such as the educational system. All three components must be part of understanding clients' worldviews and current socioemotional problems.

RESOURCES

The documentary *People Like Us*, a film by Louis Alvarez and Andrew Kolker (2001), offers a look into how social class works in the United States. Information regarding the film as well as activities and other resources related to the film can be found at the companion website: http://www.pbs.org/peoplelikeus/.

The website *Critical Multicultural Pavilion* by Gorski (2010) (http://www.edchange.org/multicultural/index.html) offers many activities and resources to advance multicultural awareness. One of the links on this website (http://www.edchange.org/multicultural/arts/class_songs.html) takes users to a list of songs about classism and poverty. Many of these songs can be used as a way to explore the concept of classism as well as to empathize with the experiences of people living in poverty.

A classic of modern American literature, *To Kill a Mockingbird* by Harper Lee (1960) contains many issues related to classism and its link to race. Reading this novel from the lens of classism helps readers get a deeper understanding of the issue. In addition, because this novel was written based on the author's experiences and on an event that took place close to hometown in 1936 (Wikipedia, 2011), it provides a historical context regarding classism. Readers are encouraged to read the book to: (1) pick up themes of classism, including prejudices based on social class; (2) think of the historical context of classism and its link to today's statistics showing minority groups are overrepresented in poverty; and (3) think of characters' worldviews as they relate to classism.

A Question of Class is an exercise from the Teaching Tolerance project of the Southern Poverty Law Center (http://www.tolerance.org/activity/question-class). It is geared to help students consider classism as it exists in contemporary political situations. The exercise was envisioned for the high school student but can be easily adapted for the adult learner.

Community Action Poverty Simulation. The Missouri Association for Community Action (http://www.communityaction.org/Poverty%20Simulation.aspx) has developed a poverty simulation program that allows participants to simulate life from the perspective of an individual living at or below the poverty line. This 3-hour activity is designed for large groups of about 50 to 80 participants, along with approximately 16 to 20 facilitators.

12

The CARE Model for Working With People Living in Poverty

Louisa L. Foss and Margaret M. Generali

In many ways all counseling clients have similar, basic needs. Life challenges or mental illness can overwhelm anyone, regardless of socioeconomic status or class. Common presenting concerns include a sense of isolation, feelings of intense anger or irritability, sadness or anxiety, or a futility in living. However, for those living in poverty there are additional issues that may impede successful help seeking and recovery. People living in poverty may wrestle with basic survival needs, such as food security, stable living conditions, or safe and adequate child care (Campbell, Richie, & Hargrove, 2003). In this way, one may spend the majority of one's time seeking basic needs low on the Maslow hierarchy rather than attending to mental health concerns (Maslow, 1943).

Amid the moment-by-moment struggles, people living in poverty in the United States experience more marginalization and stigmatization than nearly any other group (Gilens, 1995). Stigma is linked to stereotypes and prejudicial beliefs that impose disgrace on an individual presumed deserving of rejection or exclusion (Lewis & Elder, 2010). Poverty can create very visible differences, such as poorly fitting clothing, failure to have regular haircuts, or dental problems that indeed may lead to different treatment by others in the client's world (Wilton, 2004). Instead of compassion, others, including mental health professionals, tend to cast blame. For example, a statement such as "Why don't they just take better care of their teeth?" fails to address the high cost of regular dental care. Or those with warm, clean, private bathing spaces or easily accessible and safe laundry facilities may wonder why anyone living in the United States could have poor hygiene. The frequent assumption is that the individual must surely be responsible for his or her station in life. Perhaps he or she is lazy, stupid, or otherwise morally damaged. Most insidiously, a person living in poverty may also internalize these beliefs, resulting in shame, embarrassment, and overall negative self-esteem (Mickelson & Williams, 2008). In addition to the stigma of poverty, those who are poor tend to belong to multiple stigmatized groups, such as racial, ethnic, religious, or ability status (W. R. Williams, 2009). The daily effects of stigma and classism often narrow life choices or options for healthy living, making healing ever more complicated.

People living in poverty are at higher risk for mental health problems compared to those in privileged or more empowered groups (Belle & Doucet, 2003; Costello, Compton, Keeler, & Angold, 2003; Kessler et al., 2008; Wadsworth & Santiago, 2008). Though we must be cautious to recognize that correlation is not causation, it is not difficult to imagine that poverty could promote psychological stress or dysfunction (Lustig & Strauser, 2007). Indeed, those living in poverty may be twice as likely to develop psychological distress than their middle or upper-middle class counterparts (Bruce, Takeuchi, & Leaf, 1991). Life may be characterized by ongoing anxiety about protecting one's self and loved ones. The fear of eviction may be constant for some families living in poverty. Obviously, having a stable and consistent living environment is important to mental health, as it provides a greater sense of control and ability to protect one's privacy (Borg, Sells, Topor, Mezzina, Marin, & Davidson, 2005). Debt and financial problems appear to be correlated with mental illness as well as symptoms of generalized anxiety, posttraumatic stress, social phobia, depression, and dysthymia (Jenkins et al., 2008; Van Dorn et al., 2010). It is possible that poverty brings on more severe symptom presentations, often requiring higher rates of psychiatric hospitalizations (Fortney, Xu, & Dong, 2009).

Exposure to poverty may be particularly harmful to children, placing them at risk for a variety of negative mental health outcomes over the life span (Barnett, 2008; Van Dorn et al., 2010). Children in poverty are more likely to experience a number of psychological disorders, such as depression, anxiety, oppositional defiant and conduct disorders, and attention-deficit hyperactivity disorder (Costello et al., 2003). Conduct disorder and related symptoms appear to be most clearly linked to socioeconomic disadvantage, and indeed these behavioral symptoms appear to remit when family socioeconomic status improves (Costello et al., 2003; Ford, Goodman, & Meltzer, 2004). Child abuse and neglect also tend to be more prominent among those living in poverty, an important correlate of a myriad of both child and adult psychological problems (Sedlak et al., 2010).

An effective approach to treatment views these poverty-related barriers as intertwined with more traditional therapeutic issues, and therefore integrates these needs into the counseling treatment plan. Basic survival needs are actively addressed while simultaneously supporting the client through his or her emotional, behavioral, or cognitive healing. However, this approach sounds misleadingly simple. Many variables contribute to a counseling world that often fails to adequately meet the needs of clients living in poverty (Grimes & McElwain, 2008). Traditional counseling models are often provided on a "one size fits all" basis, which imposes middle class experiences and values on everyone (G. Gonzalez, 2005; Javier & Herron, 2002). In this way, middle class practitioners may miss important systemic factors that may severely impact the client's wellness, such as unemployment and housing (Grimes & McElwain, 2008).

While the broader mental health community is beginning to see the needs of those living in poverty, it is apparent that a practical approach to counseling people living in poverty would be highly beneficial in providing tools for new and seasoned practitioners and provide a foundation for future clinical interventions. The approach should promote a humanistic, developmental perspective that fosters hope in the inherent strength and potential of individuals regardless of their circumstance in life (Fitzsimons & Fuller, 2002). It should also address multiple systems at the individual, group, and community levels of poor clients' lives and provide specific suggestions for dealing with unique needs of these persons (Black & Krishnakumar, 1998). To this end, we propose the CARE Model, a social justice and humanistic approach to better assist clients living in poverty (Foss, Generali, & Kress, 2011). The CARE Model has four basic elements: *cultivate* a caring relationship with the client living in poverty, *acknowledge* the realities of living in poverty, *remove* barriers that stand in the way of client healing, and *expand* the client's already existing strengths.

SELF-REFLECTION OPPORTUNITY 12.1

A person living in poverty often presents with a chaotic or unpredictable living situation. One may need to work multiple jobs, rushing to meet personal and family needs, while also working long and often inconvenient hours. Because of these and other similar demands, children may not receive the time and nurturing they need to be healthy and successful. There is simply no time for involvement in the school and community, transportation to enrichment activities, or help with homework. If a child begins to struggle academically or behaviorally, parents may lack the financial resources to get them the help they need, such as tutoring or participation in positive community activities. In this way, poverty impacts nearly every aspect of family life, resulting in complex systems of need and layers of obstacles. These multiple levels of need can feel confusing or overwhelming for both new and seasoned mental health clinicians.

FOLLOW-UP QUESTIONS

1. Consider for a moment, what aspects of a person's life does poverty impact? How might you as a practitioner prioritize these multiple needs?
2. How do your values, early life experiences, or current socioeconomic situation impact these clinical choices?
3. How might your unique experiences translate into power differences within the therapeutic relationship?

CULTIVATE RELATIONSHIP

The first stage of the CARE Model involves the cultivation of a therapeutic relationship with the client. It is essentially the counselor's view of the client living in poverty. The importance of the counseling relationship is well established and universally accepted. Indeed, Frank and Frank (1991) suggest that the relationship with the client is of utmost importance, far more critical than techniques. In recent years, the common factors movement has lent support to the critical nature of the therapeutic alliance (Halperin, Weitzman, & Otto, 2010). A counselor's understanding and caring helps shatter the isolation and loneliness experienced during times of suffering and can begin to build a bridge toward hope. The relationship creates a space for collaborative goal setting, a critical step toward a successful counseling outcome with people of diversity (Vasquez, 2007).

The therapeutic relationship is even more critical for a person living in poverty (Ware, Tugenberg, & Dickey, 2004). Consider the impact that stigma, prejudice, and marginalization has had on the client's perception of others, including mental health professionals. The client may have been ignored, discounted, or otherwise negatively judged by the "system" (Schnitzer, 1996). With this kind of relationship history, a client may approach a counselor with justified suspicion, distrust, and doubt. If a client cannot trust the counselor early on in counseling, there may be a heightened risk of premature termination (Stevens, Kelleher, Ward-Estes, & Hayes, 2006). Because of this, the clinical intake should be adapted to address the unique challenges of poverty and make early treatment goals more relevant to the client's key concerns. This adaptation requires the counselor to release one's own middle class therapy agenda, and instead attend to the client's most pressing survival needs as appropriate.

No matter how well intentioned, counselors are not immune to replicating harmful stereotypes about people living in poverty. None of us can be separated out from our society. We are all highly likely to hold conscious or unconscious negative stereotypes about the poor (Smith, Chambers, & Bratini, 2009). Counselors are obligated to explore their own socioeconomic baggage and beliefs about poverty. If they do not do so, they risk negative consequences such as repetition of patterns of oppression and blame. An exploration into causal factors often reveals a great deal. According to Feagin (1972), explanatory frameworks fall into three categories. The individual is poor because of his or her own individual characteristics, because of the larger societal system, or because of luck or chance. Consider, for example, what do you believe causes poverty? Do poor people tend to be lazier or maintain less rigid moral standards? Do they tend to be unreliable, irresponsible, or disorganized? If your answer is yes to any of these questions, then you have taken a deficiency-based perspective, squarely placing responsibility on the character of the client (Amatea & West-Olatunji, 2007; Hirshberg & Ford, 2001).

On the other hand, some counselors may perceive poor clients as victims at the hands of society (Vasquez, 2007). In this view, structural forces are to blame for all of the client's difficulties. The biggest problem with this perspective is that poor clients may then assume a victim status and deny any personal responsibility for making change in their lives, instead waiting to be rescued (Boyd-Franklin, 2003). Rigid adherence to this rather patronizing approach may rob the client of his or her power and thereby perpetuates macro-level power differences within the micro-system of the counseling relationship. Another risk is that there may be an overemphasis on the challenges of poverty, such as housing and immediately pressing financial needs, resulting in a failure to adequately address mental health issues (Grimes & McElwain, 2008; L. Smith, 2010). This may be particularly true when clients naturally prefer to avoid painful work in counseling and instead focus on external stressors.

The clinical intake is a particularly crucial time for establishing a strong therapeutic alliance. For those living in poverty, it is important to assess for functioning in multiple life domains, emphasizing the complicated systems at play (Wilton, 2004). For example, a counselor may remark about how impressive it is that the client was able to overcome a number of obstacles just to attend the counseling session. In addition, Ackerman and Hilsenroth (2003) indicated that practitioner characteristics such as flexibility, honesty, confidence, and openness are particularly important for working with diverse peoples at all stages of therapy. Highlighting past successes in counseling, facilitating affective expression, and providing accurate interpretations may promote a strong therapeutic alliance.

Nonclinical connections such as practitioner efforts to find common ground or highlight similarities between the counselor and client may be particularly helpful for low-income clients (Ware et al., 2004). This may be effective because some diverse clients may feel less comfort with an authoritative or power-oriented stance (Vasquez, 2007). At the same time, a directive stance may be more successful when clients are in crisis (Day, 2008). In this way choosing one's approach to the delicate balance of power in session depends on the current needs of the client, strength of therapeutic alliance, and stage of therapy.

In addition, a study by Ware et al. (2004) suggests that the therapeutic relationship with low-income clients is strengthened when practitioners give "extra things" to their clients, such as coffee, jokes, or greetings (p. 556). More importantly, clients wanted to feel known and to feel like "somebody" (p. 557). Practitioners were able to accomplish these ends by allowing clients to talk freely while offering a deep level of empathy. The researchers found that low-income clients felt more connected to their practitioner when they had significant input into treatment decisions. In practice, this means making a clear effort to consistently regard the client with respect and partner with him or her in the change process.

Case Study 12.1

Robert is a counselor with about 2 years of experience in a public mental health agency in a midsized Midwestern city. He recently began working with Laura, a 38-year-old Caucasian woman with three children ages 20, 6, and 2. Laura was laid off from her job as a laborer with a local construction company about 3 years ago and has been unable to find consistent work since. Most of her adult life, Laura has been able to make ends meet, but barely. Her father died when Laura was 5, and Laura's mother scraped to get by. Laura's mother is disabled and has since moved in with Laura and her children. Even more stressful, Laura's 20-year-old daughter is due to give birth in a few months. Laura reports feeling anxious about being able to keep her home and perform as a good mother to her children. She appears to have agoraphobia with panic attacks.

During the first session, Robert proceeds to inquire extensively about Laura's attempts to find employment since being laid off. Laura explains that every time she has landed a job, there has been some crisis at home that required her immediate attention (parenting her 6-year-old with behavioral problems, caregiving for her mother, intervening with creditors). He also questions Laura several times about the whereabouts of the father of her children. At the end of the session, Robert lectures Laura about how she is going to have to "prioritize" and take counseling seriously, unlike the jobs she briefly worked over the past few years.

FOLLOW-UP QUESTIONS

1. One can assume that Robert intends to help his client. Describe his good intentions.
2. How might you characterize Robert's general knowledge or attitudes about people living in poverty?
3. How might Laura think or feel following this session?
4. What should Robert have done differently?

ACKNOWLEDGE REALITIES

The next stage of the CARE Model reminds practitioners to recognize and acknowledge the realities faced by clients living in poverty. It essentially involves how the client's problems are viewed. In spite of the grueling and often chronic nature of problems associated with poverty, it appears that counselors are unlikely to bring up financial issues as a relevant factor (Dakin & Wampler, 2008). It is inevitable that this veil of socioeconomic silence impacts the counseling process, through either poor training, preparation, and knowledge of practitioners, or through the unspoken judgment and accompanying isolation that is communicated to the client during the counseling process. However, it is critical that counselors speak of these issues, as they may heavily impact health and well-being. This is particularly important for the counseling process because clients living in poverty may prematurely terminate or generally underutilize counseling services, especially if they feel misunderstood or otherwise discounted (Coiro, 2001; G. Gonzalez, 2005).

The challenges of living in poverty are legion. Clients in poverty may constantly worry over their ability to purchase food and items needed for daily living. Payment for utilities and rent can become a serious concern, especially when living on the edge of homelessness. Limited transportation may make it difficult to stay connected with important others, get to work on time, or attend medical or professional appointments. Unstable or nonexistent employment may serve to demoralize a client who is striving toward self-sufficiency. Further, community crime and overcrowding may make it difficult to have adequate sleep, recreation, or privacy. For children, unsafe or ineffective schools may seriously limit academic performance and future vocational or professional achievement (Bienvenu & Ramsey, 2006; Black & Krishnakumar, 1998). Limited public play spaces and environmental hazards may expose children to harmful influences, including the potential for abuse or victimization (Evans, 2004). Families living in poverty are more likely to express concern about crime and juvenile delinquency (Evans, 2004; Hay, Fortson, Hollist, Altheimer, & Schaible, 2007). Indeed, this is a realistic concern when one considers scarce employment opportunities and high incidence of crime in impoverished settings. In some cases, generational poverty may make it virtually impossible for clients to seek help and support from family members or important others.

Though we should be careful not to infer causation, poverty appears to be linked to poorer psychological well-being (Robbins, Dollard, Armstrong, Kutash, & Vergon, 2008). Adults in poverty appear to experience higher incidences of depression and stress-related conditions (Belle & Doucet, 2003). Financial stress may be related to marital dissatisfaction, family conflict, or domestic violence (Bassuk, Dawson, & Huntington, 2006; Dakin & Wampler, 2008). In addition, those who are classified as poor are more likely to have survived a trauma, often multiple traumas at multiple developmental stages (Bassuk et al., 1996).

Parents and other caregivers suffer under many burdens and as such are less able to provide critical caregiving functions (Robbins et al., 2008). Indeed, unstable or chaotic home environments, oppositional defiant behavior, and attention-deficit hyperactivity disorder appear to be more common among children living in poverty (Costello et al., 2003). Parents may experience guilt for being unable to adequately supervise their children or help with homework. Meanwhile, children and adolescents themselves may feel that there is little use in trying when there are so few life opportunities available to those without financial means. In this cycle, it is logical that some impoverished adolescents would turn to criminal activity to find camaraderie as well as economic opportunity.

In order to adequately acknowledge these realities, counselors must possess awareness of their own personal beliefs, biases, and issues regarding financial privilege (L. Smith, 2010). Classism must be clearly identified as a form of oppression through which society's institutions, attitudes, policies, procedures, and economic structures continue to hold the poor and working class in a disadvantaged position in our society (L. Smith, 2009). However, as a last taboo, financial privilege is rarely discussed or explored in the professional context, including counselor education, supervision, or continuing education (Brown, 2002; L. Smith 2009). As a result, most counselors have not been encouraged to explore their own personal financial privilege issues as a part of their preparation, and so operate with a blind spot in the counseling room. Recognition of one's own invisible privilege usually results in a radical paradigm shift. For example, one's accomplishments as a person of financial privilege may dim in light of all of the help and support that was granted along the way, support that others in lower socioeconomic positions may not have received. This poverty blind spot can severely impair the counselor's ability to empathically connect with a client and effectively meet his or her needs. Further, the blind spot frequently extends to the entire mental health treatment system, which fails to build structures that meet the unique needs of the poor. Without a basic consciousness raising regarding the plight of poor clients, the larger field of professional counseling cannot hope to develop and expand theory, research, or best practice guidelines.

SELF-REFLECTION OPPORTUNITY 12.2

Although counselors in training are provided with the skills, knowledge, and experience to provide counseling services to an array of client populations within a variety of settings, working with people living in poverty requires further reflection, particularly for new counselors or counselors in training. Personal experiences of sympathy, condescendence, or judgment may surface as a result of bias or overidentification. People from a middle class background may not know what the realities are, particularly if they have not been exposed to poverty. It is natural to attempt to make sense of poverty based on your own personal messages about people living in poverty. Use the following questions to personally reflect on messages that you have learned over the course of your life.

FOLLOW-UP QUESTIONS

1. Have you been exposed to poverty, or do you know anyone who has lived in poverty?
2. Have you ever struggled financially with getting your basic needs met?

3. Can you identify some other realities inherent in living in poverty that have not yet been mentioned?
4. How is your life situation different from someone living in poverty?
5. How can the pain of one's history struggling with socioeconomic disadvantage or poverty influence his or her work in both positive and negative ways?

The acknowledgment of realities becomes most critical when moving toward problem identification and goal setting. The counselor ought to consider first what the client views as the top therapy priority. Similar to all counseling groups, the client living in poverty must view the treatment goals as relevant to her life situation. If the counselor imposes treatment goals that are laden with middle class, socioeconomically advantaged ideas, then the client is at high risk for premature termination (Stevens et al., 2006). For example, a client who is in danger of losing his or her job will feel invalidated if a counselor insists on leaving employment concerns out of the treatment plan. This is not to say that deeper, existential concerns cannot be a part of the client's treatment. On the contrary, meaning making and insight can be a critical part of surviving and later thriving through a crisis situation. However, basic needs should be held as first priorities, as determined by the client. Once acute crises are identified and addressed, it will be possible to begin to address longer-term issues, including the promotion of positive coping, health, and recovery.

Case Study 12.2

Michelle is a relatively new counselor with 5 years of professional experience. She has recently changed jobs from her position at a private therapy office to a town social service agency. She is unaccustomed to this population but really wants to work with what she sees as "disadvantaged" clients. Juliette is a 15-year-old high school freshman who lives with her mother, stepfather, and older brother in a rural town. Her biological father has not had contact with her since she was an infant. Juliette has been referred to the town's social service department on a recommendation of her school counselor due to issues of neglect and truancy. Money is a major issue for this family. Both of Juliette's parents are currently relying on disability benefits. Her stepfather suffers from early stages of multiple sclerosis and has been unable to return to work in the local garage since his last medical episode. Juliette's mother suffers from anxiety and is most recently experiencing an incapacitating bout of depression. She is being treated for this condition and takes prescribed medications as needed. Juliette's older brother attended the local community college but recently dropped out for financial reasons.

Juliette is suffering from poor nutrition, dental problems, chronic pain, and a learning disability. Juliette's school counselor has made several referrals to child protective services but has not seen results. He is especially concerned about Juliette's nutrition and loss of weight.

Michelle is immediately struck by Juliette's physical appearance. She is slight and frail, her teeth have obviously not been brushed, and her body odor is offensive. Michelle struggles to listen to Juliette's reported concern about a recent breakup with her boyfriend and problems with her parents, instead remaining fixed on the obvious physical difficulties. Michelle decides that Juliette's hygiene will be her first area of concern and begins formulating goals to address this. Juliette responds to these goals with resistance, telling Michelle that she has no hot water and does not know how to meet these goals. Juliette says that if she could be with her boyfriend again, her life would be so much better.

FOLLOW-UP QUESTIONS

1. Michelle and Juliette clearly have different treatment priorities. As Juliette's counselor, how might you negotiate these differences?
2. If in this situation, how could you manage your intolerance for her hygiene problems?
3. As counselor, what responsibility might you have for helping Juliette receive medical services, including attention to her nutritional needs?

REMOVE BARRIERS

As previously noted, there are multiple barriers to treating people living in poverty, both structural and attitudinal (Mendez, Carpenter, LaForett, & Cohen, 2009). Structural barriers are defined as those factors in the client's environment that restrict his or her access to mental health counseling. For example, they might include limitations in transportation or ability to pay. In contrast, attitudinal barriers involve a client's belief about the effectiveness of treatment or his or her general willingness to participate in the counseling process (Kazdin & Wassell, 2000). Structural barriers ought to be addressed first in order to implement strategies to help the client simply attend a counseling session (G. Gonzalez, 2005; Perese, 2007).

In general, structural modifications might include the provision of flexible service hours, such as weekend openings, to help the working poor attend even when they must adhere to an inflexible work schedule. Drop-in hours may also allow clients to attend at convenient times when they are able to acquire transportation or child care. Child care services can also be offered on-site at the counseling agency, an arrangement that works easily when group counseling services are offered.

Although practitioners may be less inclined to provide home-based counseling services due to safety concerns, environmental distractions, and boundary concerns, home-based psychotherapy appears to result in higher attendance and treatment engagement (Mattek, Jorgenson, & Fox, 2010; Slesnick & Prestopnik, 2004). Mobile services involve vans or recreational vehicles traveling to neighborhoods to provide counseling and psychiatric services (Caldwell, 2009). Mobile units have been especially helpful in providing counseling services to the homeless and those in acute psychiatrics. Finally, collaboration with community groups such as religious or cultural organizations may provide numerous opportunities for sponsoring on-site treatment (Mendez et al., 2009).

As indicated above, clients in poverty face numerous systemic barriers to change. For the poor, some needs, such as food or shelter, extend well beyond the 50-minute clinical hour. Practitioners may be unaware of the need to step out of the traditional talk therapy role and into more client-centered roles as advocates within complicated systems, including public assistance and educational settings. Mental health professionals tend to be influenced by silo thinking or a strict adherence to traditional professional roles and their accompanying tasks. Caldwell (2009) blames this pattern on "professional narcissism," or the tendency to perceive oneself as too important to deal with trivialities in the lives of the poor (p. 289). They may look only toward historical definitions of counseling and avoid or devalue flexible definitions of treatment that include systems-oriented interventions. For example, a counselor may help a client to generate ideas for stretching or increasing income as a legitimate part of the larger therapy treatment plan (Ware & Goldfinger, 1997). Some clinicians may consider such work outside the scope of practice of the professional counselor. But it is these artificial dichotomies that often make social services inefficient. Counselors should be willing to flexibly tailor treatment to immediate client needs, even if that means engaging in some case management–type activities while also providing psychotherapy.

Oftentimes poor clients need immediate attention for a problem of daily existence or personal protection, but it is difficult to overcome the bureaucratic and complicated procedures that plague many social services. A professional counselor ought to possess the institutional knowledge and professional savvy that is required to successfully navigate various social systems (Boyd-Franklin, 2003). Ethically sound intervention with people living in poverty utilizes client advocacy as a key component (ACA, 2003; Liu & Estrada-Hernandez, 2010). A crisis intervention approach proposed by Westefeld and Heckman-Stone (2003) is particularly useful for addressing the needs of people living in poverty. This cognitive-behavioral model draws on cultural competence and social justice concepts to present a series of strategies for working with those in crisis: build rapport, encourage empowerment, build on clients' assets, and collaborate to continuously evaluate goal attainment (Westefeld and Heckman-Stone, 2003). Using these concepts, counselors can help clients connect with critical social services or with other mental health professionals who can provide critical linkages in times of acute stress. In some cases, such advocacy can occur by making telephone calls or writing letters to outside providers. In other situations, it can be as simple as advocating for a client within one's own agency or institution. For example, a counselor may help internal agency personnel understand that the client's level of care status should be elevated in order to qualify for case management services, or the counselor may work closely with the business office to help solve a problem with payment.

In addition, the American Counseling Association advocacy competencies call for advocacy from a larger ecosystemic perspective, at the community and public arena levels (Lewis et al., 2002). In general, the counselor uses his or her own professional privilege to promote social justice at higher levels of impact (Manis, Brown, & Paylo, 2009). At the community level, a counselor might advocate for policies or resources that improve the poor living in a particular community or collaborate with other power brokers across professional boundaries (Scott, 2010). At the public policy level, a counselor maintains an awareness of public policy trends that may require political action.

Case Study 12.3

Lucas is a 15-year-old high school freshman of Puerto Rican descent attending a comprehensive urban school. His school counselor, Donna, is completing her first year within this position. She has spent the majority of her time concentrating on her freshman class, as they are at highest risk for school dropout. Lucas is struggling academically and actively seeks out services from Donna. He is interpersonally skilled and well liked by teachers and peers. Lucas lives in the local housing project with his mother, sister, and two brothers. His family is very supportive, but his mother speaks limited English. Lucas has taught Donna much about his community and the difficulties faced by students in his neighborhood. Donna works with Lucas individually and in small group settings. She has been focused on Lucas's academic transition to high school and has noticed progress. One Monday morning, Donna is notified that Lucas is out of school due to his arrest at a police raid at the local convenience store. Donna knows enough about Lucas and his character to know that he is an innocent victim of his neighborhood once again.

FOLLOW-UP QUESTIONS

1. What ethical issues can you identify in this scenario?
2. In what ways would you as a counselor advocate for this student?
3. Where, besides the school setting, would you anticipate advocacy to occur?

EXPAND ON STRENGTHS

The fourth stage of the CARE Model is focused on identifying and expanding the client's already existing strengths. In this component, we focus on resilience and empowerment to build forward momentum. In essence, resilience theory helps counselors to identify what is functional in the client's dysfunctional world. Indeed, it is easy to see that life in poverty requires the creative use of resources that other, more privileged people would not readily possess. Coping skills commonly known as "street smarts" can mean survival through a cold winter without heat or safe passage through a crime-ridden, impoverished neighborhood. This form of primary coping can require problem solving, emotional regulation, and self-understanding (Wadsworth & Santiago, 2008). In secondary coping, clients living in poverty are able to cope with painful realities and work toward cognitive restructuring or other advanced coping skills (Buckner, Mezzacappa, & Beardslee, 2003; Wadsworth & Santiago, 2008).

We empower clients when we help them acknowledge and understand how power has impacted their lives on multiple systems (Bienvenu & Ramsey, 2006). This development of awareness and insight must be followed by the utilization of positive coping and strength-based resources. In counseling for empowerment, we must first identify already existing resources, including wellness-related behaviors and social support networks (Myers & Gil, 2004). These may include community members, recreational activities, or religious participation. For many clients, family members can be a great untapped resource. Seccombe (2002) suggests that emphasis on family traditions, celebrations, and predictable routines can help individuals living in poverty to overcome crises. Positive and strong nuclear, extended, or chosen family members can be drawn into the counseling process to help clients meet specific treatment goals (Barnett, 2008).

For other clients, it is helpful to promote reclamation of a sense of self, meaning or purpose in life, and role in contributing positively to the lives of others (Perese, 2007). Creative therapies, including art, writing, or music, can be used to empower and motivate clients living in poverty (Smith, Chambers, & Bratini, 2009). Similarly, spirituality in its many forms can also serve as a profound strength for coping with poverty by promoting self-worth in spite of struggle and a spiritual connection to one's higher power (Aponte, 2009). These and other helpful aspects of empowerment can be identified and promoted through the use of

Myers and Sweeney's (2008) wellness model, which is an evidence-based counseling approach for promoting a variety of wellness dimensions through counseling.

Case Study 12.4

Marla is a clinical coordinator at a local child and family care agency. Marla primarily works with families living in poverty. Janet is biracial, being of African American and Italian American decent, and a mother of two who has presented for counseling due to "the daily stresses she experiences as a single parent." Marla notes signs of clinical depression. Janet is a bright, caring woman raising two elementary school children, 8 and 10 years old. She has been divorced for several years and doesn't rely on the infrequent child support payment for her family's financial survival. Janet explains that her children are blessed to be attending a local, not-for-profit, Christian school. Janet is having a difficult time caring for the children and attending the local community college. As well, she is trying to find time to spend with other adults and would like to pursue a long-term relationship. Sadly, the children are not comfortable with this person and act out when she brings him around. Her workload and parenting responsibilities are becoming overwhelming to her. "There are times when I need to take a time-out. I tell the children to give me 5 minutes to myself, just to clear my head," she states. Marla respects the fact that Janet practices healthy parenting and assists her in finding after-school care for her children. Whenever there is a resource that suits Janet's family needs, Marla presents these options. Janet is open to any assistance and graciously accepts the help.

FOLLOW-UP QUESTIONS

1. What assets could you identify within Janet? What assets might you find within her family or surrounding community?
2. What would you identify as treatment goals?
3. How can you help Janet negotiate the care of her children and self-care?
4. Using a wellness framework, evaluate Janet's level of wellness in various areas of her life.

IMPLICATIONS FOR FUTURE PRACTICE AND RESEARCH

As professional counselors, we must challenge ourselves to be more aware and sensitive to the needs of those living in poverty. Counseling is a value-laden enterprise, but counselors tend not to conceptualize their clinical work in these terms, especially in regard to those living in poverty (Foss et al., in press; Smith, Chambers, & Bratini, 2009). Though the work is hard, competent counseling involves a commitment to self-evaluation and exploration in regard to privilege, power, and best practices with diverse groups (Lee & Ramsey, 2006). This means taking responsibility for one's part in oppression and advocating for the needs of the poor. As an aspect of diversity, socioeconomic privilege is clearly linked to the literature on multicultural competence (Caldwell, 2009). Competence calls for the development of awareness, knowledge, and clinical skills in all aspects of client diversity, especially for those clients from marginalized or devalued groups (Sue, Arredondo, & McDavis, 1992). A competent counselor must be able to analyze power and privilege and understand how such resources impact the life of the client and society as a whole.

For those working with this population, maintenance of personal and professional stamina is critical. Seemingly insurmountable obstacles may cause a counselor to feel overwhelmed, insecure, and ineffective (Boyd-Franklin, 2003). However, self-care and a focus on one's own strengths can greatly assist with building professional resilience and avoiding burnout. The counselor may be helped by focusing on what can be changed through counseling interventions and advocacy in the short term, while simultaneously promoting social change for the long term. In this model, we provide tools for empowerment for clients. Similarly, we must empower ourselves as counselors, focusing not on deficits but rather on strengths and resources, rather than becoming mired in negativity and hopelessness. Engagement in personally rewarding recreation and social activities is particularly important, as is engagement with one's professional community, including active involvement with professional associations, colleagues, and continuing education (Meyer & Ponton, 2006). These strategies become particularly important when working with challenging populations such as those living in poverty. Without active pursuit of self and professional care, counselors seriously risk ineffectiveness and burnout.

Another aspect of quality provision of services involves constant evaluation of one's own performance as a professional counselor. The profession's emphasis on outcome assessment assists us in evaluating the efficacy of general approaches and interventions. Prilleltensky (2003) suggests that interventions with diverse peoples should be measured in the context of overcoming oppression and addressing political inequalities. For example, interventions should educate clients on the dynamics of oppression and facilitate alliances with others who are similarly oppressed. More importantly, the client should be directly involved in an outcome assessment process that he or she understands and finds meaningful.

CONCLUSION

In spite of the great needs of this underserved and underrepresented population, research on poverty and mental health is sparse (L. Smith, 2010). The research that has been conducted tends to ignore key systemic factors, especially those involved in patterns of poverty (Caldwell, 2009; Evans, 2004). It is especially important to address the relative silence around socioeconomic status and the invisibility of those living in poverty through research. In the accountability era of mental health practice we are increasingly called to use evidence-based practice, and yet there are few such resources in the professional literature or training community (Roy-Byrne et al., 2006). On an intuitive level, we know that systems theory and multicultural approaches may be superior to traditional therapy models. However, we are limited by what we do not know. It is critical that researchers and academics apply new theory, such as the CARE Model proposed in this chapter, for the purpose of developing specific interventions based on outcomes evidence.

13

The Role of Social Class in Assessment, Diagnosis, and Treatment Planning

CLARRICE A. RAPISARDA AND LOUISA L. FOSS

In this chapter we discuss the role of social class in the assessment, diagnosis, and treatment planning process. Case studies and items for consideration are offered to assist with fair and accurate progression through each of these processes. The manifestation of social class, be it through difficulty accessing resources, inconsistency with treatment, or access to top-of-the-line and abundant resources, undoubtedly impacts all aspects of assessment, diagnosis, and treatment planning.

Case Study 13.1

Nicole is a verbal, intelligent, insightful female client that you have been counseling for several sessions. Her treatment goals upon intake included reducing depression and learning coping skills to better manage anxiety. She just disclosed that she is facing foreclosure. You are aware that her income is limited to the short-term disability check she receives from her current place of employment. She has applied for long-term disability several times and is currently in the process of appeal. Several times Nicole has shared stories of how she has financially assisted friends over the last few months. You are confused by this in light of her pending foreclosure. She explains how she is able to help friends and yet not pay her mortgage. There is always someone worse off than herself, she tells you, and if she does not help them, who will? She adds that her income is not enough to fully pay all of her bills anyway, and at least with her friends she knows the money is being used for a good reason. She describes that she cannot begin to predict what will happen to her in the long term, so saving money seems inconsequential when she can see how it is needed and can bring someone relief right now. She states that her friends rely on her and know that she will help them however possible.

FOLLOW-UP QUESTIONS

1. What is your initial reaction to Nicole's story? What difference is there in your thoughts and feelings when you read her story from a counselor perspective versus your personal perspective?
2. What cultural factors may be operating for Nicole in this scenario?
3. What cultural factors are operating for you as you listen to Nicole share her story?
4. How does this information affect the treatment goals that were set for her at the start of counseling? How might you modify the goals in light of the information she discussed?
5. What other information would be helpful to know?

Counselors and other helping professionals must provide culturally sensitive and competent services when working with clients (ACA, 2005). This ethical code is a basic tenet learned by counselors early in their counseling career, and it applies to every aspect of counseling, from the initial intake assessment through to termination of the counseling relationship. This includes not only awareness and knowledge of the client's culture, but awareness and knowledge by counselors of their own cultures as well (Dana, 2005). In this chapter we are going to focus on one particular aspect of culture, that of the culture of social class. We acknowledge, however, that even when focusing on the culture of social class, it has many interactions with other cultural aspects (Acevedo-Polakovich et al., 2007; Jun, 2010).

For helping professionals, qualifications for administration of assessments may vary by state and license as well as by assessment; therefore, we are not going to attempt to list out specific instruments. What we will do is highlight key areas in this chapter that practitioners should be aware of in order to most effectively work with clients of all social classes in the assessment, diagnosis, and treatment planning processes. Under the assessment section, we will focus on the intake assessment, test bias, examiner bias, and test-taker factors. In the section on diagnosis we will focus on the diagnostic assessment and considerations when working with the *Diagnostic and Statistical Manual of Mental Disorders*, Fourth Edition, Text Revision (DSM-IV-TR; American Psychiatric Association, 2000). Finally, in the treatment planning section we will explore problem identification, establishment of goals and objectives, the development of interventions, and the importance of working with a flexible approach. Throughout the chapter, case studies and questions will be utilized to apply material discussed and encourage reflection and discussion.

It is helpful to review two multicultural concepts that form a foundation to the assessment process before we focus specifically on the impact of social class on assessment, diagnosis, and treatment planning. The terms *etic* and *emic* may be familiar to you from multicultural literature. They are often used to refer to a particular perspective from which a client or counselor may be viewing the world. In assessment, these terms are also used; however, they serve a different purpose. The etic perspective emphasizes universal qualities among human beings by comparing different cultures from a standpoint outside those cultures (Drummond & Jones, 2010). Assessments created from an etic perspective involve comparing clients from different cultures on a universal construct. For example, an assessment that focuses on the construct of self-esteem would be administered to a culturally diverse group of clients. One goal might be to find universal components of self-esteem that are experienced by clients from different cultures. Assessments from the etic perspective may include personality measures, psychopathology tests, and intelligence tests (Drummond & Jones, 2010).

The emic perspective is culture specific. It examines behavior from within a culture. Assessments following an emic perspective will utilize criteria that are specific to the culture of the client. To utilize assessments from an emic perspective, the therapist needs to have knowledge of the client's culture (Drummond & Jones, 2010). Assessments from the emic perspective may provide a description of the client's personality that reflects the culture of the client as well as the client data (Dana, 1993). Projective assessments are often from an emic perspective. These may include word association tests, sentence completion tests, drawing tests, picture story techniques, case studies, and behavioral observations (Drummond & Jones, 2010). It is important to take into account whether assessments are based on etic or emic perspectives. Helping professionals need to select the assessment from the perspective that best matches the client's goals for the assessment process.

We will now focus on the specific cultural factor of social class. Throughout previous chapters, you have learned information about social class at every level. We will continue that here by exploring factors that may be different for clients from different social classes. When focusing on work with clients with lower socioeconomic status (SES), Foss, Generali, and Kress (2011) stress the importance of understanding clients' cultural values and expectations. Taking the time to do this may facilitate clients' engagement in the therapeutic relationship. It has been noted that people in poverty routinely underutilize counseling services and may terminate early when they do start counseling (M. J. Gonzalez, 2005; Milner & O'Byrne, 2004). This is concerning, as studies have shown a connection between clients in poverty and an increased prevalence of reported mental health issues (Kessler et al., 2008; Paniagua, 2005). Some of the cultural aspects in which to take note are evident in the case of Nicole. Through her story, Nicole is focused on the present moment, which Foss et al. (2011) suggest is one of the cultural values of clients from lower social class status. Payne (1996) describes the valuing of personal relationships over material possessions. Nicole demonstrates this value as she describes the importance of helping her friends meet their needs, even at the cost of her own needs being met.

SOCIAL CLASS AND ASSESSMENT

Clinical assessment is used throughout the therapeutic relationship. With clinical assessment, information is collected in a variety of methods and from many sources (Drummond & Jones, 2010). Myers and Gill (2004) stress the importance of counselors being able to work as a team with a variety of providers as counselors gather information needed to help address the client's social/economic, family, and individual issues. Often clients do not self-refer to counseling. It is important for helping professionals to be familiar with the different sources clients may go to first because these sources will then issue the referral for the clients to come to counseling (Hays, 2001). Such sources may be a spiritual or religious figure, a medical professional, a case worker, or a friend. It can be helpful for practitioners to familiarize themselves with who clients may seek out for support and how this may vary, depending on the SES of the clients. It can be good policy to build connections with possible referral sources and discuss with them when it might be appropriate to suggest counseling to someone.

Once the referral has occurred, the assessment process of the client begins. It often starts with the initial intake assessment and diagnosis of the client during which a practitioner gathers relevant information from the client and then organizes and integrates it (Drummond & Jones, 2010). The practitioner then draws on clinical judgment to formulate a diagnosis and continues on with creating a treatment plan, developing interventions, monitoring client progress, and finally evaluating therapeutic outcomes (Drummond & Jones, 2010). Jun (2010) states an accurate assessment is the foundation for developing effective treatment for the client. It is especially critical for clients of diverse cultural backgrounds. In this section we will highlight key areas to be aware of within the assessment process. These areas are the intake assessment, test bias, examiner bias, and test-taker factors.

Intake Assessment

To facilitate an accurate initial assessment, Liu (2011) recommends utilizing a biopsychosocial approach. This allows the therapist to explore the impact of social class and social context on the client's life in addition to the biological and psychological history of the client. The client has an opportunity to share how societal factors may be impacting current life stressors. The therapist is able to gain a broader perspective, which facilitates conceptualization of the client's issues and helps in the formulation of potential strategies for addressing these issues. Because social class is often left out of intake assessments or addressed only minimally

(Paniagua, 2005), it is important that social class and classism be a part of the interview process. Often the therapist will already have factual socioeconomic data from the client (i.e., job, income); therefore, therapists are encouraged to explore the client's perceptions and subjective experiences of socioeconomic experiences and social class (Liu, 2011). Therapists are encouraged to pay attention to how social class may impact the development of a client's values and expectations, as these values and expectations may significantly influence how the client will view treatment in counseling and counseling interventions (Liu, 2011).

Test Bias

The initial intake assessment is often the first assessment that helping professionals will complete with their clients. It is, however, not the last. They may choose to administer additional assessments to clarify a diagnosis such as depression or attention deficit-hyperactivity disorder, to assess for severity of symptoms such as level of anxiety, or to further explore the client's personality. Because of this, practitioners need to know the reliability and validity of any assessment they use in order to select the most culturally appropriate assessment for the client. An additional cultural element to be aware of is the population on which the assessment was normed. Drummond and Jones (2010) state this is necessary in order to evaluate the assessment for potential test bias. Test bias occurs when individuals with the same abilities perform differently on the same assessment because of their affiliations with a particular group (Drummond & Jones, 2010); that is, SES, gender, or race. There are three areas of test bias that helping professionals should analyze before deciding if an assessment is a culturally appropriate fit for the client. The areas are (1) content bias, (2) bias in internal structure, and (3) selection bias (Drummond & Jones, 2010).

To assess for content bias, the practitioners will want to examine the material that is in the assessment. Is the content covered by the assessment general knowledge to a client from any cultural group? Does the content appear to be more familiar to one particular cultural group? Another area to investigate is the language used by the assessment to form the questions. What words are actually used in the questions? Is it possible for clients from different cultural groups to have multiple interpretations of the same question being asked? A third area would be to assess the clarity of the instructions. Are the instructions concrete and clear, or do they assume a certain level of knowledge that the client may or may not have? Finally, when evaluating for content bias, practitioners will also want to pay attention to the scoring procedures and assess them for clarity and fairness (Drummond & Jones, 2010).

Drummond and Jones (2010) describe bias in internal structure when there are underlying dimensions of an assessment that are inconsistent across groups. Bias in internal structure may be present in the following example. Three clients each have the same level of knowledge and ability but are from different social classes. They each take the same assessment and have similar scores in two sections of the assessment but have different scores on one section of the test. Selection bias occurs when there are variations in the predictive validity of an assessment across groups. An example of this would be a college entrance exam that showed variations in the predicted success of students in college based on the students' social class status.

Examiner Bias

Whereas test bias focuses on the actual elements of the assessments, examiner bias focuses on the beliefs and values held by those administering the assessments. Counselors and other helping professionals need to accurately assess for examiner bias. To do this it is critical for these professionals to be aware of their own personal biases and to understand how these biases may influence the interpretation of results from assessments given to clients (Drummond & Jones, 2010). In other words, even if a counselor has selected an appropriate and fair assessment for use with a client, the assessment process could still be affected from the examiner's own biases and values (Liu, 2011). This is why the importance is stressed that as helping professionals we know and are aware of our own beliefs and biases (Jun, 2010). Baruth and Manning (2007) describe different elements where examiner bias may occur, starting with a basic acknowledgment that bias may occur simply because the social class and cultural values between the helping professional and client are different. Another area for bias may occur when practitioners do not understand their own culture and beliefs. They may have faulty assumptions about a client's level of acculturation, leading to misunderstanding of the client's worldview. Client behaviors that vary from expected social norms may be diagnosed as mental health concerns when in reality these behaviors may be functional and necessary within the client's social context. To assist practitioners in addressing these potential areas of bias in relation to the cultural factor of social class, Jun (2010) encourages them to focus on their own history and experiences with classism. Increasing understanding of how they view classism within their own lives will better help counselors and other helping professionals to then be open to learning how classism impacts clients' lives.

SELF-REFLECTION OPPORTUNITY 13.1

How do you view classism in your own life? What messages did you receive growing up about the role of class and its influence on people? How do these messages influence your personal values and beliefs? Reflect on how this may be informing your interactions as a counselor when working with clients of different SES.

TEST-TAKER FACTORS

In addition to test bias and examiner bias, there may be factors unique to the client as the test taker that may impact the assessment process. Drummond and Jones (2010) highlight several key areas as factors of the test taker. Here we will discuss the test-taker factors of (1) language, (2) test wiseness, (3) motivation and anxiety, and (4) family and social influences.

Language

Drummond and Jones (2010) suggest that one test-taker factor to consider is the language—of both the client and the assessment being used. Counselors and other helping professionals may want to ask several questions about the language usage of the client. Is English the client's primary language? If no, what is the primary language? In which language would the client prefer to complete assessments? Practitioners should ask clients about their level of verbal and written proficiency as well as reading proficiency in each language. A client may be verbally proficient in English as a second language, for example, but may not be comfortable completing a written assessment in English. If clients prefer to complete assessments in their primary language, it is incumbent on the practitioners to first ascertain if a particular assessment has been translated into that language. Next, practitioners need to verify the validity and reliability of the translated assessment (Drummond & Jones, 2010). This is important because an assessment may have adequate validity and reliability in the English version but may not in the translated version, depending on what procedures were followed to create the translation of the assessment.

It behooves helping professionals to consider many of the factors discussed here even when English is the primary language of the client. A client may be a native English speaker and therefore may have verbal fluency but may have limited or no reading or writing fluency. Assessments should be consulted on an individual basis to find out if and how the assessment allows for the consideration of these different language factors in its administration.

Test Wiseness

Test wiseness refers to how familiar a client may be to the test or testing process (Drummond & Jones, 2010). During the first session with a client, prior to administering any assessments, the helping professional should determine if test wiseness is a factor for the client. For example, it would be important for a counselor to know if a client has an extensive mental health history, including multiple psychological batteries. In this case, the counselor will want to ensure that whichever assessments are selected are appropriate in light of potential past experience and exposure that client may have had to certain instruments. The client in this example may require little additional clarification of questions or the actual testing process. Another factor to be considered under test wiseness is the format of the assessment to be administered. Has the client only had experience with paper-and-pencil instruments and the current assessment is computerized? Social class can play a factor with test wiseness as well. Helping professionals should be careful not to assume levels of familiarity or access to computers of the clients based on their social class.

A final factor to consider regarding test wiseness is whether the client is familiar with the amount of time and attention different tests will require. It is possible for the results of an assessment to be not valid from the simple fact of a client not understanding just how much time and focus and attention an assessment may require. For example, a client may schedule the second session to come and complete the assessments without allowing adequate time. After one hour of taking the assessment the client sees it is only half complete. The client knows that in half an hour the child care that was arranged for the client's family ends. The client may now rush through the remainder of the assessment without the care and thought needed because of this pressure, thus invalidating the results for the second half of the assessment. A client may come in to take the assessments as scheduled but recently may have experienced a trauma or life crisis that could then impact the client's ability to focus on the material in the assessment and give it full attention. Again, this may impact the validity of the assessment, as the results may not be an accurate reflection of the client's levels of skills or abilities.

Motivation and Anxiety

The next factors that we are going to focus on that may impact the test taker are motivation and anxiety of the test taker. The motivation of the client to complete the assessments and whatever level of anxiety the client may be experiencing often are influenced by the client's family or social peers, which will be explored further under family and social influence. It is important for practitioners to explore with the client what expectations the client has of the assessment process. This discussion helps clarify and form the specific goals or questions that will guide the assessment process. The practitioners should discuss with the client how the results of the testing may impact the client. For example, is the client's ability to be able to continue to live independently dependent on the results from the cognitive assessment that will be administered? Knowing how significantly the results of the assessments may impact the client's life can give the therapist clues into the client's level of motivation. From this the therapist may also assess and understand the client's level of anxiety about completing the assessments as well as receiving the results. Motivation can play a role in whether the client wants to be successful or not successful with a particular assessment. For example, a 14-year-old client takes a placement test to qualify for honors courses the following year in ninth grade. For this client, there may be little motivation to succeed. Regardless of the client's social class, placing into honors courses may result in the client being separated from friends. The client may face added pressures from family to continue to achieve at a higher level.

Family and Social Influence

Counselors and other helping professionals should be listening for family and social influence as they assess the client's levels of motivation and anxiety related to the assessment process. If the client is a minor, the therapist may need to verify that what the parents are requesting matches what is in the best interests of the client. In our example of the 14-year-old, the parents may be requesting that the client complete the placement exam. As a continuation of our example, let's say the client took the assessment seriously and gave it full effort. The results show that the client may not have the cognitive skills to be successful at an honors level of work. As a good clinician, the therapist looks for additional information to verify the accuracy of these results. The therapist finds that the results are supported by the fact that the client is a C average student with grades in the client's current level of work in regular classes. The therapist may then be faced with a challenging conversation with the parents when discussing the results.

SOCIAL CLASS AND DIAGNOSIS

Case Study 13.2

Alan is a 24-year-old male. He was referred to counseling as part of his aftercare plan from being an inpatient at a psychiatric hospital. His primary issues are substance use, including alcohol and drugs, and psychotic symptoms, including auditory hallucinations and delusional thinking. Alan reports that he is currently homeless and has already started drinking again. When you question him about his choice to start using again he reports that the alcohol does a better job at drowning out the voices he hears than the medicine they gave him in the hospital. He reports that he is able to function just fine as long as the voices are not shouting. Upon further questioning, Alan reports a family history of mood disorders, including depression and bipolar disorder on the maternal side of his family. He also reports a substance use history on both the paternal and maternal sides of his family. Alan states that currently he has low energy, no appetite, and while he does not think he would kill himself at the moment, he does not know how much longer life is worth living. Alan's appearance is disheveled and unkempt, which could be due in part to his current living situation of being homeless. Alan clarifies that he is not really living on the street yet but is able to go between different buddies and crash at their places for a few nights at a time. Alan states that it works out fine to only stay at each place for a few nights because when he stays at any one place too long, he knows "they" are going to find him. The voices have told him this. He says several times he left a friend's place in the middle of the night because the voices woke him up and told him that "they" had found him and were coming. When you try to clarify who "they" are Alan becomes visibly agitated and anxious. He tells you he does not want to talk about "them" because that is one of the ways "they" use to find him. He says it works similar to how the Death Eaters trapped Harry Potter because he used Voldemort's name. Alan reports he first noticed the voices, infrequently, around his 20th birthday. He says that now, unless he drinks, the voices almost never stop. At the present time, Alan appears to have no current means of income and is not employed.

FOLLOW-UP QUESTIONS

1. What diagnosis would you give Alan based on the above information?
2. What would you like clarified about Alan's story?
3. How would your interpretation of Alan's story change if you knew that Alan was from a lower social class? From a higher social class? In what ways might his social class impact your assessment and diagnosis of him?
4. Discuss what role social class may play in how symptoms are interpreted during a diagnostic assessment.

DIAGNOSTIC ASSESSMENT

The initial client interview discussed earlier in the chapter serves as a fundamental component of clinical assessment. The initial interview may include formal components such as a survey or questionnaire and informal components such as observation of the client's facial appearance, overall physical appearance, and nonverbal gestures (Drummond & Jones, 2010). It is often during this first interview that helping professionals have to form their diagnostic impressions of a client and assign a diagnosis. The role of social class can have a definite influence over the diagnostic assessment. In this section we will explore this in relation to the five axes of the DSM-IV-TR. We will discuss different aspects professionals should consider when preparing to assign a diagnosis to a client.

Before assigning a diagnosis to a client, it is critical for the practitioner to thoroughly review the client history and information (Jun, 2010). As part of the review of information, the counselor or other helping professional may want to verify clinical impressions with other providers (Hays, 2001) upon receiving the appropriate client release of information. Once a client is given a diagnosis, the diagnosis becomes part of the client's record (Jun, 2010). Therefore, before assigning a diagnosis, the counselor may want to reflect on the impact that the diagnosis will have on the client, the client's life, and the client's possible access to services. Drummond and Jones (2010) caution counselors against diagnosing prematurely. As the counselor reviews the client story, it is important to remember that client experiences and symptoms that are considered to be culturally appropriate responses to life events should not be diagnosed as mental disorders, even when they may cause distress to the client (Neukrug & Fawcett, 2006).

When considering social class, counselors and other helping professionals will want to pay attention to symptoms that may vary from social norms, but may be functional for the client given the environmental setting (Drummond & Jones, 2010). An example of this is a client from a lower social class who frequently does not show for appointments. What could appear as client resistance to treatment may in fact be the results of having to rely on public transportation whose services were interrupted due to weather. Another cause for a missed appointment could be the client choosing to keep a doctor's appointment that just opened up last minute to treat medical concerns that were impairing the client's physical functioning. Both of these examples reflect the very concrete challenges facing clients of lower social class (Liu, 2011). Viewing these symptoms outside of the appropriate cultural frame of reference may lead the helping professional to see pathology where none is really present.

CONSIDERATIONS WITH THE DSM-IV-TR

We will now explore the impact of social class on the assignment of diagnoses. To do this we will look at the DSM-IV-TR (APA, 2000), the main manual for assigning mental health diagnoses, and highlight key areas for helping professionals to keep in mind as they work through determining a client's diagnosis. Jun (2010) offers a word of caution about the DSM-IV-TR, stating that it is based on the medical model and assumes categories and symptoms are universal. What is considered normal and abnormal for a client is located within the self, viewed in isolation from other cultural factors or influences (Jun, 2010). The DSM-IV-TR, however, does include an appendix on cultural considerations and culture-specific diagnoses. It is noted that helping professionals should take into account the client's ethnic and cultural context in the evaluation of each of the DSM-IV-TR axes (APA, 2000). In particular, it is suggested that the practitioner pay attention to the cultural identity of the client, cultural explanations of the client's symptoms, cultural elements of the relationship between the client and counselor, and cultural factors related to the client's psychosocial environment (APA, 2000). Regarding social class as a cultural factor, the DSM-IV-TR includes differences in the prevalence according to social class for some diagnoses. The practitioner should attend to all of this as a diagnosis is considered.

To review, a diagnosis based on the DSM-IV-TR (APA, 2000) follows five axes. Axis I is for clinical disorders. Axis II is for personality disorders and mental retardation. Axis III is for general medical conditions. Axis IV contains qualitative descriptions of the client's psychosocial and environmental factors. Axis V contains the Global Assessment of Functioning (GAF) score. We will now focus on several axes in light of social class considerations.

Counselors and other helping professionals typically work with clients dealing with issues related to diagnoses on Axis I. There are several factors to keep in mind regarding diagnoses clients may have in relation to their reported social class. Certain issues have been found to be present with clients in both upper and lower social classes. Liu (2011) reports children from both upper and lower social classes describe feeling a lack of attachment to their primary caregivers. This may be due to the amount of time the primary caregivers are at work and away from the home. The primary caregivers may then bring these children in with complaints of communication issues, defiance, or lack of respect.

For clients with lower social class standings, research has shown that children living in poverty are more likely to have an Axis I diagnosis (Costello, Compton, Keeler, & Angold, 2003). Waldegrave (2005) reports families living in poverty may often be viewed clinically as dysfunctional and their symptoms pathologized. Families reported fewer symptoms, such as depression, when they were no longer living in poverty, with that being the only major factor that was changed (Costello et al., 2003; Leventhal & Brooks-Gunn, 2003). When considering a diagnosis related to cognitive disorders, it is important for practitioners to pay attention to how social class may affect a client's degree of orientation. For example, a client may appear not oriented to place or time. The client may be unaware of the date or of recent occurrences in the local news. This could be a symptom of a possible cognitive deficit; however, if the client is from a lower social class, the client's focus may be on daily survival, and knowing the exact date or paying attention to events happening outside of his or her immediate needs may be irrelevant.

Research has been conducted on which diagnoses were prevalent with clients from the upper social class. Madeline Levine (2006) found that these clients often showed high levels of anxiety. This anxiety manifested itself in extreme perfectionism. Clients often showed limited coping skills for dealing with any criticism or negative feedback. This would result in diagnoses for clients in the anxiety spectrum of the DSM-IV-TR (APA, 2000). Levels of substance use were also noted in clients from the upper social class. Researchers theorized that clients were using substances as a form of self-medication to manage the symptoms (Luthar, 2003; Luthar & Sexton, 2005).

There are times when symptoms may appear to fit several different diagnostic criteria. It has been noted that when this occurs, one deciding factor in making the diagnosis is the client's social class. For example, a 9-year-old client may present with hyperactivity, hypervigilance, distractibility, and irritability. If this 9-year-old client is from an upper social class, the client is more likely to receive a diagnosis of attention deficit-hyperactivity disorder. If the client is from a lower social class, the same symptoms may be viewed as oppositional defiant disorder. It should be noted, however, that regardless of social class, the same symptoms could be the presence of posttraumatic stress disorder in response to a trauma the client had witnessed a few months ago. If the client was witness to a trauma and depending on the current environmental conditions in which the client is living, it is possible that the same symptoms may not actually be pathological but rather functional for the client's survival.

If we return to the case study of Alan that we read about at the beginning of this section, his social class may well have an influence on what diagnosis he receives. If Alan is from an upper social class, his symptoms of tiredness, lack of appetite, and family history of mood disorders may be seen as the primary focus, and the auditory hallucinations he is experiencing as secondary. This may lead to a diagnosis of major depression with psychotic features. The same counselor, however, may see Alan's auditory hallucinations as the primary focus, with the depressive symptoms as secondary if he is from a lower social class. Alan would then be assigned a diagnosis of paranoid schizophrenia.

In looking at Axis II, Hays (2001) encourages helping professionals to remember that personality is a social construction. Counselors and others tasked with diagnosis should therefore use caution before diagnosing a client with a personality disorder until cultural factors, such as social class, have been considered. In general with Axis III, counselors are working off of client self-report for any general medical conditions that may be present. It is important to consult with the client's other health care providers if the counselor is unsure of the origin of symptoms (Hays, 2001). Counselors should pay particular attention to this when clients report that they do not receive regular and routine physicals. Axis IV is important because it is the space for counselors to include the context or qualitative data from the client about the client's social class, environmental factors, social conditions, recent life changes, and any major stressors or traumas (Jun, 2010). The counselor is able to note on Axis IV what impact each of these areas has on the client's presenting symptoms. Finally, in Axis V the counselor assesses the client on the GAF Scale (APA, 2000). This is a subjective assessment on the part of the counselor. Jun (2010) encourages counselors to keep in mind the sociocultural context of the client. The counselor should determine if the GAF score is applicable in the context of the client's life based on a possible history of nondominant value orientation.

SOCIAL CLASS AND TREATMENT PLANNING

Following assessment and diagnosis, treatment planning is a critical next step in the therapeutic process. Treatment planning provides a plan for moving forward, achieving an end goal, and finding a destination. It is essentially based on the principle that if we do not know where we are going, we are likely never to arrive. Treatment plans also provide a level of accountability for the outcomes of counseling, a helpful and necessary aspect of work with third-party payers (Maruish, 2002; Seligman, 2004). Further, treatment planning is an effective way to empower clients with information and strategies for achieving their therapeutic goals (Adams & Grieder, 2005). This collaboration is particularly important when we take into account the varied and diverse backgrounds of our clients. This is no less true with socioeconomic diversity, and in fact more so given the profession's relative silence on the issue of socioeconomic status in the entire counseling process (Caldwell, 2009).

According to Maruish (2002), there are four common elements in the treatment planning process: identification of the problem, establishment of aims and goals of counseling, development of strategies and tactics, and an overall flexible approach. We will now apply the dynamics of socioeconomic diversity to each of these elements.

Problem Identification

The influence of social class in the context of diversity necessarily impacts the nature and type of problems experienced by clients (Foss et al., 2011). Class and socioeconomic status impact realities of daily life and provide a lens through which we view the world. A systemic approach to goal development helps practitioners address the client's current life context (Grimes & McElwain, 2008). For example, an individual living in poverty may struggle with issues of safe housing, overcrowded living environments, and food stability, in addition to challenges associated with a mental illness. Too often, clinicians are eager to identify problems in the context of middle class values and fail to address the daily struggles experienced by clients who live in poverty (Waldegrave, 2005). For those classified as working poor, rigid work schedules, safe child care, and financial worries may serve as a backdrop for pressing mental health issues (Dakin & Wampler, 2008). In some cases, these constant financial pressures may serve as primary treatment concerns, as they represent current living crises low on the Maslow (1943) hierarchy of needs. These crises may interfere significantly with active engagement in counseling. For example, coping with a possible eviction may obviously take precedence over attending a counseling session. Similarly, a tenuous employment arrangement may make it virtually impossible to take time off to attend a counseling session during typical counseling office hours.

In addition to these struggles and barriers, difficult living conditions may be related to particularly insidious experiences that may interact with mental health in complex ways. For example, those living in high-poverty areas tend to experience or observe crime at a far higher rate than those in middle class neighborhoods (Hsieh & Pugh, 1993). This may cause externalizing behavior problems among children, general anxiety, or posttraumatic symptoms (Ceballo, Dahl, Aretakis, & Ramirez, 2001). Further, there may exist an overarching "realm of trauma" whereby clients may report multiple layers of trauma and loss, as well as trauma associated with surviving in near-impossible circumstances (Altman, 1995).

Even if one possesses relative material resources, Western culture encourages a sense of being poor, with the possible result of problems with life satisfaction (Csikszentmihalyi, 1999). Indeed, stigma exists for those living in the middle class who attend high-status universities, with pressures for those from the middle class to present themselves as having the cultural knowledge of the more privileged, upper classes (Johnson, Richeson, & Finkel, 2011). Similarly, those in both the middle and upper-middle classes may struggle to meet performance expectations associated with the attempt toward even higher upward mobility. For example, parents may feel a burden to give one's children "an edge" in future vocational and career pursuits. They may feel the pressure of high academic or athletic achievement for their children, resulting in overcommitment to a vast array of taxing activities. The pressure may push a family to involve their child in every possible learning experience with the possibility of music lessons, sports activities, tutoring, and a myriad of other activities that may stress the family unit and possibly disrupt important family bonding (Luthar & Latendresse, 2005). Similar achievement pressures may exist for single persons or child-free families. Importantly, the client in the middle class may also worry over job stability or slippage into financial danger, a very real possibility given the new economic climate in the United States.

For those in the upper-middle and upper classes, the ever-present need to achieve may be particularly stressful (Luthar & Latendresse, 2005). Pressures to participate in prominent organizations or activities may present unique challenges. In order to maintain one's status in the community, one must attend to social relationships with community power brokers. The quest to achieve or maintain membership in particular social groups or community boards may produce unique stressors. Similar to the middle class, there may be a strong pressure for children to perform above standard career expectations. It may be more important for children to pursue higher education at only the most prestigious schools. Similarly, it may be critical for their children to attend selective private schools at the primary or secondary levels. It may be unthinkable that a child should pursue vocational or other nonprofessional careers. Similarly, child-free couples or single persons may feel obligated to the same types of stressors. Clients in these upper classes may also feel burdened with issues related to the management of one's finances and social relationships involved therein. So while it may to be true that those with additional financial resources have additional societal power and life options versus those in the middle and lower classes, membership in these upper classes comes with unique burdens that ought to be considered when identifying problems for the treatment planning process. These burdens may be linked to elevated incidences of depression, anxiety, and risky behavior among adolescents in particular (Racz, McMahon, & Luthar, 2011).

As indicated earlier in the chapter, certain socioeconomic groups may more commonly present with some diagnoses or symptom clusters versus other diagnoses. We must be attuned to inquire thoroughly about the symptoms common to each socioeconomic group while also resisting the natural inclination to stereotype. For if we fail to adequately identify the problem, we will struggle significantly in the counseling process, experiencing therapeutic blockages or client dropout. Further, inappropriate diagnosis or assessment and related problem identification is likely to subject the client to the repeating patterns of misunderstanding or classism that often hinder their growth and adjustment in daily life.

Case Study 13.3

Suzanne is a 38-year-old female living in a West Coast suburb. Eight years ago, Suzanne married Chin Ho. Chin Ho earned a respectable income as a stockbroker but has seen his earnings drastically cut by a financial downturn. Suzanne left her job as a commercial artist to work in the home raising their 6-year-old child, Hana. During the good times the couple purchased a home in an affluent area where they could enjoy a safe and quiet neighborhood surrounded by other professionals. However, now that money is tight, they have been struggling to maintain their lifestyle. Hana is enrolled in an expensive private school and attends myriad extra learning opportunities, including piano, dance, and theater lessons. Chin Ho enjoys golf outings and weekend trips to the city. Chin Ho has urged Suzanne to return to work, but Suzanne enjoys a supportive friends network of other full-time mothers who regularly meet at the local exercise club, dine out at lunch, and take shopping excursions together. Suzanne serves on two volunteer boards with the ladies and is active in the garden club. In spite of the financial problems, Suzanne and Chin Ho just went on a pricey vacation with their social group. Suzanne has always struggled with some mild anxiety. Since these stressors have increased, she now finds it difficult to get out of bed in the morning and has dramatically stepped up her use of the benzodiazepine prescribed by her general practitioner in addition to increasing her evening drinking. Suzanne is concerned that if they reveal their true financial status or if they begin to draw back on some of the expensive social activities they engage in, they will lose their friendship network. She reports fears that they may "lose it all."

FOLLOW-UP QUESTIONS

1. How does social class status impact Suzanne's symptom presentation?
2. If the couple were to reveal their financial concerns, what impact would that have on the following?

   a. Marital relationship
   b. Friendships
   c. Recreational outlets
   d. Community status
3. How might this situation be impacting the couple's daughter?
4. What kind of impact might the loss of their social circle have on their family relationships?
5. What are the potential impacts of the couple's Korean descent?
6. What kind of hidden resources might this family possess?
7. What would be important in a counseling relationship with Suzanne or the larger family system?
8. As the counselor, what is your reaction to listening to Suzanne's story? What difference is there in your thoughts and feelings when you hear her story from a counselor perspective versus your personal perspective?

Establishment of Goals and Objectives

A critical step in the therapeutic process is developing a shared definition of the problem. What does the client hope to achieve through the therapeutic process? For those categorized as poor or working class, it is important that helping professionals break out of middle class problem definitions and embrace the problems presented by clients living in a wide variety of socioeconomic circumstances. As with all clients, this may involve educating the client about the role and functions of the counselor and developing realistic expectations about the process. Importantly, it involves problem definitions that are core to the client's lived, daily experience, which often involves factors related to class and socioeconomic systems (Grimes & McElwain, 2008).

After a problem has been clearly identified, therapeutic goals may be defined as an overarching aim of treatment, an outcome that serves as an umbrella under which objectives may be located. According to the principle of parsimony, we should aim to conceptualize the client's concerns in as few goals as possible. This also makes the treatment process appear to be less daunting and more realizable. The objectives may be defined as subgoals, or segments of the goal that can be independently addressed in pursuit of the larger goal.

With socioeconomically diverse clients, it is again critical that these goals and objectives link back to problems that are important to the client and relevant to their situation. Failure to truly listen to the client can alienate the client, causing him or her to feel that counseling is irrelevant to his or her daily life, and resulting in disengagement or dropout (Ware, Tugenberg, & Dickey, 2004). For this reason, the goals and objectives must be presented in language that is easily understood by the client and tied to issues that may be specific to all aspects of the client's diversity, rather than reflective of middle class values alone. For example, a person living in poverty may be highly disinclined to ask for needed social services such as heat or food assistance due to family or cultural values that emphasize personal autonomy and responsibility. This may be especially true for individuals who have dropped from higher socioeconomic strata to working class or poverty status. Similarly, those who have relied heavily on public assistance may have had varied experiences with help seeking, some of which may be linked to overall distrust of the social services system. Thus it is critical to attend to multiple layers of individual differences and diversity, which often interplay with poverty in unique and sometimes challenging ways.

Case Study 13.4

Lionel is a 29-year-old Caucasian who lives in a rural community in the Northeast. Lionel works part-time at a bakery and tries to pick up construction work with a local roofer. Lionel comes to counseling explaining that he feels "stuck" and that he can never get ahead. Lionel's family has limited financial resources and community connections. His brother dropped out of high school and his sister works part-time cleaning houses. His mother is deceased. Lionel has a history of mental illness, including most significantly a major depressive episode shortly after he came out as homosexual at age 25. His siblings and friends at the time were highly judgmental of Lionel's orientation and were unsupportive through the process. During that time, Lionel was hospitalized for suicidal ideation. With the help of a supportive counselor, he was able to recover from the episode and move forward. However at this time, Lionel sleeps and eats excessively and experiences intensely low self-esteem. He has no friends through either of his places of employment, no identified recreational outlet, and limited contact with his family. Lionel is worried that things may never get better for him.

FOLLOW-UP QUESTIONS

1. Describe possible challenges Lionel faces in his day-to-day life.
2. How might his work environments make it especially difficult to be gay?
3. What kind of relationship might Lionel's socioeconomic difficulty have with his depressive symptoms?
4. How might Lionel's situation be different if he had financial resources?
5. What goals would a counselor identify as important for Lionel? What goals might Lionel readily identify? Which of these goals might you address first?

Development of Interventions

Interventions should be tailored around the diverse needs of the client. At this stage, it is important to assess the motivational level of the client. What is his or her willingness to engage in life-changing behaviors, and what pace might be appropriate for such changes? For those in upper-middle and upper classes, is there a willingness to continue to attend counseling in spite of embarrassment or concern for stigma, as well as the packed daily schedules that typically accompany privilege (Luthar & Latendresse, 2005)? Again, one must consider to what extent contextual pressures might help or hinder their participation in particular interventions both inside and outside of the counseling session. Failure to appreciate the client's unique daily living demands, pressures, or obligations could result in an irrelevant or unhelpful treatment plan that may serve to slow or stop counseling progress.

For those living in poverty, Wilton (2004) suggests that the domains of basic needs, family, social relations, self-esteem, and leisure should all be addressed during the counseling process. The involvement of family is important for all clients; however, family and social support may be particularly helpful for those living in poverty (Brown, 2002). Contrary to most clinical training, interventions that include money management and strategies for increasing income may also be pertinent to clients and therefore pertinent to fulfilling certain objectives (Ware & Goldfinger, 1997). In such situations, case management may also be a helpful adjunct to treatment.

Liu (2011) recommends considering interventions that will address both internal factors (i.e., resiliency, support) and external factors. Liu discusses the importance of talking with clients about the external factor of money and how it may impact their attendance at sessions. Counselors and other helping professionals may encourage clients to schedule appointments for the time of month when it will be less draining on the client's financial resources. Another practical intervention to help contribute to the success of treatment planning is for counselors to consider how they set up their appointment schedule. Milner and O'Byrne (2004) report that counselors need to have flexibility in their schedules. They suggest matching counseling schedules to coincide with public transportation schedules. It may be helpful to schedule in an open block of time where clients know they can drop in and be seen on a first come, first served basis. This can be helpful for clients who are dependent on others for transportation. It can be challenging for clients to set specific appointments of their own when they have to fit into someone else's schedule.

In treatment planning, we describe these interventions in observable, measurable, and behavioral goals. Frequently this involves the use of cognitive-behavioral language, which in many ways lends itself well to the needs of those in lower socioeconomic situations. Concrete interventions (Liu, 2011) may give those who are struggling with acute crises the tools to begin movement right away, rather than waiting for amorphous concepts such as insight to emerge. And yet, it is critical that all levels of client development be addressed, including existential or meaning-oriented issues that may motivate a client to overcome extremely challenging or painful circumstances (Grimes & McElwain, 2008; L. Smith, 2010). On the other hand, humanistic approaches involving higher degrees of self-exploration have been emphasized as an effective approach for those with higher levels of education and higher socioeconomic status (Day, 2008). The danger in promoting these alternate theoretical approaches is that we may engage in elitist thinking, assuming that the working poor are less capable of the advanced personal growth offered by the more introspective theoretical approaches. Each theoretical approach has its limitations in regard to diverse groups. Avoiding stereotypes and tailoring treatment in the client's social context is a must.

Case Study 13.5

Cesarina is a 55-year-old biracial woman living in an urban environment. She presents to counseling with concerns about her grandson. Cesarina's daughter and grandson, Tomas, have lived with her for the past year. Tomas is 15 years old and has begun to show some irritability and oppositional behavior at home. His grades have begun to slide and he is frequently withdrawn from family and friends. Cesarina wants to know how to help support Tomas while also doing what she can as the leader of her household. Cesarina lost her job 5 years ago when the factory she worked for went out of business. Cesarina's daughter has debilitating depression and has been unable to work for the past year. For years Cesarina has experienced generalized anxiety, especially since she was mugged in her neighborhood at about age 40. Lately she has also been experiencing panic attacks. These come on unexpectedly and occur in a variety of settings. She says there are a lot of worries in the home: Tomas, limited finances, and a new concern that the family may soon be evicted. She feels like she is unable to help Tomas get back on track and feels powerless about their financial situation.

FOLLOW-UP QUESTIONS

1. What are the most pressing issues for Cesarina?
2. What are some appropriate treatment goals?
3. Is there a particular theoretical orientation that might lend itself better to Cesarina's situation? Name some specific interventions that Cesarina might readily accept.
4. What adjunctive services might you suggest?
5. What strengths might you tap to empower Cesarina to move forward?

Flexible Approach

We use the term treatment *process* to emphasize that treatment planning is never static. We should assume that the client is in a constant state of transition, especially during mental health crises. Similarly, the assumption that change is always occurring can be helpful in moving counseling forward with all client populations (DeJong & Berg, 2002). In this way all aspects of the treatment plan should be reconsidered on a regular if not session-by-session basis, rather than the typical 90 days minimum as required by third-party payers and other stakeholders. The intervention needs of the client may change over time, and it is the job of the clincian to advocate for approaches that are tailored to each client's unique presentation.

CONCLUSION

In this chapter we have explored social class in the assessment, diagnosis, and treatment planning processes. We know that as counselors and other helping professionals we must provide culturally sensitive and competent services, including assessment, when working with clients (ACA, 2005). This includes not only awareness and knowledge of the client's culture, but awareness and knowledge by counselors of their own cultures as well (Dana, 2005). When considering social class in the assessment process it is important for counselors to remember some basic facts about assessment. Counselors work to give fair treatment to clients by using assessment procedures that are appropriate, fair, and useful in reporting the abilities and traits in diverse clients (Drummond & Jones, 2010; Jun, 2010; Liu, 2011). To do this, counselors may utilize assessments from both the etic perspective, in order to gain more universal information, and the emic perspective, to allow for more individualized information (Dana, 1993; Drummond & Jones, 2010).

In the first section we looked at social class in the assessment process. We reviewed the basic three-session assessment structure and then looked at the intake process. We examined test bias and considered how test bias could be present in the content, internal structure, and selection of assessments (Drummond & Jones, 2010). Next we shifted to exploring biases that could be present within counselors as examiner bias. The last thing we discussed in this first section was how the assessment process could be impacted by several specific test-taker factors, including the language, test wiseness, motivation, and anxiety levels of the test taker, and family and social influences on the test taker. The second section looked at social class and diagnosis, a specific form of assessment. We discussed general points to keep in mind during the diagnostic assessment. The focus then shifted to the impact of social class on the five axes of the DSM-IV-TR (APA, 2000). Each axis was reviewed with key information highlighted for counselors to pay attention to during the diagnostic assessment. In the final section, social class was considered in the treatment planning process. Four common elements in the treatment planning process were reviewed (Maruish, 2002). The four elements were the identification of the problem, establishment of aims and goals of counseling, development of strategies and tactics, and an overall flexible approach. Each of these areas was addressed with particular attention to the influence of social class.

In conclusion, we believe it is important to take time to accurately assess, diagnose, and complete a treatment plan with the client. The decisions that come from these processes directly impact current and future work with the client and become part of the client record. To do this in a culturally sensitive manner may require counselors to use holistic thinking as they critically examine the client information from a multidimensional perspective (Jun, 2010).

14

Advocacy Competency: The Helping Professional's Role in Addressing Issues of Social Class

Donna M. Gibson and Tanesha Jones

In this book, social class is explored in relationship to how individuals perceive and experience it in their lives, as well as how helping professionals conceptualize mental health and provide services utilizing this framework. This chapter will offer a framework for helping professionals as they embrace the role of advocate in order to effect positive change for individuals, systems, and social/political policy.

SELF-REFLECTION OPPORTUNITY 14.1

Throughout this book, the different contributors have offered the most recent literature and evidence that indicates how social class, classism, middle class, poor, wealthy, and privileged are perceived and experienced in the United States. To be effective as a helping professional who attends to issues related to social class, an awareness of your own perceptions and experiences related to social class needs development. Reflect on the following questions to begin this process or to re-reflect as you may have a change in perspective that can inform your practice:

1. What does social class mean to you now? Has it had the same meaning for you during your entire life? If not, what were your previous definitions? What made it change?
2. Do you believe that others see you differently because of your social or economic status? Why or why not?

SELF-REFLECTION OPPORTUNITY 14.1 *(Continued)*

3. Have you been marginalized based on your economic or social class? What is your most vivid memory of this occurrence? What were your thoughts at that time? What were your feelings at that time? Did you form a "plan of action" to change how you were treated? If so, what was it and did you act on it? What were the results?
4. Do you believe that people are responsible for their own behavior, or do our social and economic systems provide specific options to different groups of people that affect the decisions that people make about their own behavior?
5. Have you treated anyone differently because of their economic or social class? What is your most vivid memory of this occurrence? What were your thoughts at that time? What was the rationale for your behavior? What were your feelings at that time? Would you interact with this person differently now? Why or why not?

In the helping professional fields, there has been a stronger emphasis on social justice advocacy (Kiselica & Robinson, 2001; Ratts & Hutchins, 2009; Toporek, Gerstein, Fouad, Roysircar, & Israel, 2006). This form of advocacy is focused on "issues related to power, privilege, allocation of resources, and various forms of prejudicial discrimination and violence toward underrepresented individuals or groups" (Smith, Reynolds, & Rovnak, 2009, p. 483). Hence, power structures that enable these privileges and discriminatory behaviors are targeted for change.

In terms of social class, classism acts as the discriminatory and prejudicial function (Liu, Soleck, Hopps, Dunston, & Pickett, 2004). However, social class cannot be fully understood without the context of other oppressions, such as racism and sexism (Harley, Jolivette, McCormick, & Tice, 2002). Therefore, a comprehensive perspective of issues related to social class is multilayered and makes determining a plan of advocacy a complex process.

In order to provide a structure to the creation of an advocacy plan, the American Counseling Association (2003) counseling advocacy competencies will be presented to illustrate the meaning and application of each of the competency domains. In Figure 14.1, the advocacy competency domains are identified as client/student, school/community, and public arena. As noted in the model, the columns represent the different levels of advocacy activities, with microlevel activities represented in the far left column with progression to macrolevel activities represented in the far right column. For example, the microlevel activities would involve clients or students with a progression to macrolevel activities that involve different community systems and possibly public policy and politics.

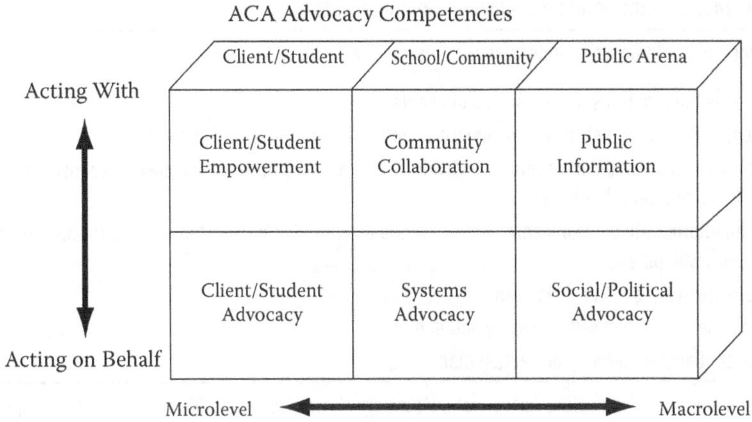

Figure 14.1 American Counseling Association advocacy competency domains. (Reprinted from Lewis, J.A., Arnold, M.S., House, R., and Toporek, R.L., *ACA Competency Domains*, 2002. Copyright © 2002 by the American Counseling Association. Further reproduction is prohibited without written permission of the American Counseling Association.)

In Figure 14.1, rows represent how professionals are working as advocates, whether it is acting *with* individuals and groups or acting on *behalf* of those individuals and groups. Based on the advocacy plan, helping professionals may need to empower the individual or group to advocate for themselves in a situation, or they may need to act on behalf of the individual or group in order to gain access to resources that will aid in advocacy activities (Gibson, 2010).

Using this model, the advocacy process for helping professionals working with individuals and systems on issues of social class is outlined throughout this chapter. Helping professionals will learn when to empower their clients and when to advocate on behalf of them. Case studies are included to illustrate these advocacy domains, and exercises are provided for helping professionals to process their own advocacy skills development.

DOMAIN ONE: CLIENT/STUDENT EMPOWERMENT

In domain one, first-level (client/student empowerment) empowerment strategies are incorporated in the work of the helping professional with the client (ACA, 2003). Although these strategies are applicable equally in working with students, the focus in this domain and subsequent domains will be on advocacy with and on behalf of clients. Within the model, specific advocacy counselor competencies are provided at each level of the three domains. Table 14.1 is a list of the empowerment counselor competencies as direct counseling interventions (ACA, 2003). In addition, understanding empowerment theory will be helpful in working with both clients and students.

Table 14.1 Empowerment Counselor Competencies

In direct interventions, the professional counselor is able to:

1. Identify the strengths and resources of clients
2. Identify the social, political, economic, and cultural factors that affect the client
3. Recognize signs indicating that an individual's behaviors and concerns reflect responses to systemic or internalized oppression
4. At an appropriate developmental level, help the individual identify external barriers that affect his or her development
5. Train clients in self-advocacy skills
6. Help clients develop self-advocacy action plans
7. Assist clients in carrying out action plans

Source: American Counseling Association, *Advocacy Competencies*, 2003. Retrieved from http://www.counseling.org/Resources/

Empowerment theory is founded in Paulo Freire's educational theory, in which he emphasized the humanity of the oppressed and their needs as learners (Freire, 1970). Freire was successful in empowering the oppressed due to his empathy with the oppressed and his ability to transform their "oppressors through reflection and action" (Demmitt & Oldenski, 1999, p. 234). Similar to the process in Self-Reflection 14.1 in this chapter, the client should develop a critical consciousness and positive identity in order to take social action (Carr, 2003; Gutierrez, 1995).

In developing a critical consciousness, helping professionals can help clients gain an understanding of their current sociopolitical context that is linked to clients' membership in specific social class communities (Hipilito-Delgado & Lee, 2007). Helping professionals can have clients explore how their membership in these specific communities influences their daily lives, political representation, and opportunities for advancement in American society. Although this process is typically prescribed for those clients who have experienced oppression, some helping professionals may believe that clients from wealthy and privileged social class communities do not experience oppression. However, there are many forms of classism that are explored in this book that argue that all individuals experience some type of oppression based on social class, including the wealthy and privileged. For example, *upward classism* is "prejudice and discrimination directed toward individuals who are perceived to be of a higher social class" (Liu, Soleck, et al., 2004, p. 108). Essentially, the behaviors of those perceived to be of a higher social class are belittled. Another example is *lateral classism*, which is discriminatory practices to keep people in a specific social class or reinforce the economic values of the specific social class community. If an individual within a community displays behaviors or attitudes incongruent with a specific social class, he or she may experience marginalization.

Because a large part of this process is for clients to gain knowledge and awareness, communicating with clients and developing an empathic understanding of them and the impact of their sociopolitical context is necessary for the development of the relationship between the client and the helping professional (Gibson, 2010). In this relationship, helping professionals can not only empathize with clients but also reflect the contextual experiences shared by clients and offer information about the systematic social class barriers that acted as oppressive agents in their lives (Gutierrez, 1995; Hanna, Talley, & Guindon, 2000). Learning to recognize these barriers and the roles they have played in their lives, clients can begin to connect those experiences to the overt and covert messages about their social class. Rejecting the negative and oppressive messages is one part of self-advocacy.

As clients learn more about their sociopolitical contexts, they are also in the process of learning about their identity. With any client who has experienced oppression due to social class, there is a process of humanization where the client comes to appreciate his or her own experiences as part of a specific social class (Duran & Duran, 1995; Freire, 1970). Developing this positive self-identity empowers clients, validates their experiences, and inspires them to advocate for themselves and others as a form of social action to improve their "sociopolitical circumstances" (Hipilito-Delgado & Lee, 2007). Case Study 14.1 is an application of empowerment counselor competences in domain one.

Case Study 14.1

Nadia presented in counseling with a history of anxiety and panic attacks. She reported that she is currently working as a case manager and educational consultant for preschool-aged children with developmental disabilities. In this role, she provides educational therapies to children in the home environment as well as consultation services to their families. Nadia reported that she "hates" her job and feels the most anxiety when talking with the parents of the children. When asked specifically about the context of this anxiety, she reported that the families whom she works with do not have good language and have reported to her supervisor that they believe Nadia acts "better than them" on her visits. Nadia disclosed that she grew up in an "upper class" community in a large Southern city, attended private schools and colleges, and has friends with similar backgrounds. However, she admits to feeling less connected to this "community" since finishing college and working in this job. Additionally, Nadia reported that she "wishes that she could say how she really feels to family and friends" but does not do this because of her own anxiety.

FOLLOW-UP QUESTIONS

1. What helps you understand Nadia's sociopolitical context in her own life? What about the people she serves at work?
2. What are some types of classism that are represented in this case? How would you reflect this to Nadia?
3. In what ways does Nadia need to develop a positive self-identity in relationship to her social class? How is her anxiety related to social class issues? How do you see this as helping her self-advocate? What should be the goal of her self-advocacy?

DOMAIN ONE: CLIENT/STUDENT ADVOCACY

The majority of helping professionals that provide some form of counseling to clients have been trained to understand human development and multicultural development, to provide consultation, and to conduct research (House & Sears, 2002; Kiselica & Robinson, 2001; Ratts & Hutchins, 2009). Consequently, helping professionals are in the optimal position of advocating on behalf of their clients. Often, this comes in the form of consultation (Dinkmeyer & Carlson, 2006).

In order to determine when helping professionals advocate on behalf of their clients, a problem assessment has to be conducted (Gibson, 2010). In the first step of problem assessment, the etiology of the problem is identified. Subsequently, a determination is made if the client has the skills, resources, or sense of empowerment in order to advocate. If not, then the helping professional and client engages in a co-construction of an advocacy plan. In Table 14.2, client advocacy counselor competencies are outlined interventions that can be acted on on behalf of clients by helping professionals and can be part of the advocacy plan.

However, a larger statement inherent to privilege is being made in this stage of advocacy. Yes, there is privilege in the position of helping professional! For example, advocating in the role of professional counselor meets the definition of "privilege" very well in that it is a special advantage, it is granted (based on the educational degree associated with it), and it is a right that is related to a preferred

Table 14.2 Client Advocacy Counselor Competencies

In environmental interventions on behalf of clients, the counselor is able to:
1. Negotiate relevant services on behalf of clients
2. Help clients gain access to needed resources
3. Identify barriers to the well-being of individuals and vulnerable groups
4. Develop an initial plan of action of confronting these barriers
5. Identify potential allies for confronting the barriers
6. Carry out the plan of action

status (Black & Stone, 2005; Robinson & Howard-Hamilton, 2000). Because professional counselors and many helping professionals possess advanced graduate degrees, this level of education can be depicted as a social class privilege. However, due to professional ethics and standards (ACA, 2005; National Association of Social Workers (NASW), 2001, 2008), it is imperative to acknowledge privilege and advocate for those who are oppressed by the societal structures that marginalize different groups. Hence, helping professionals use this privilege of education and professional status to help others. Self-Reflection 14.2 is provided to enable helping professionals to examine this privilege and how to examine its usefulness in advocating on behalf of clients.

SELF-REFLECTION OPPORTUNITY 14.2

When assessing the need to advocate on behalf of clients, what privileges and powers do you possess that will allow you to be effective? Why will you do this? To benefit the client? Will it benefit you in any way? If you use your privilege as a professional, will you be marginalizing others? If so, how? How can you advocate using your privilege without oppressing others but to the benefit of your client?

Although helping professionals need to have a good understanding of their clients' needs prior to advocating on behalf of them, they also need to possess a good understanding of the different systems, such as agencies and other professionals, they will be interacting with in their effort to advocate (Gibson, 2010). Helping professionals need to be aware of their own personalities and impact of their personalities on others; hence, flexibility, persuasiveness, and ability to compromise are important skills to utilize in advocating. Finally, co-constructing realistic goals with clients and systems will be predictive of a more successful advocacy effort. Case Study 14.2 illustrates the application of client advocacy counselor competencies.

Case Study 14.2

Sheena is a 45-year-old White female who has been in counseling for approximately 1 year. For the majority of her life, she has identified with a lower-middle class economic level. As a high school graduate, she is employed as a child care worker and lives as a single mother with her two young daughters. During the past year, her older, adult son has committed illegal acts that have left him imprisoned. Since his prison sentencing, Sheena has been unable to sleep, to the point she has become physically exhausted. After her employer points out her exhaustion and encourages her to receive medical attention, Sheena visits a doctor and receives medication to help her sleep. However, this medication is not effective. Although Sheena reports that a change in medication may be warranted, she reports feeling uncomfortable discussing this with the physician (as she is typically uncomfortable talking with doctors). After discussing her concerns, the counselor and Sheena decide that the counselor should contact the doctor to advocate for a change of medication.

FOLLOW-UP QUESTIONS

1. What are Sheena's resources, skills, and abilities?
2. Why do you think there is a need to advocate for Sheena in this situation?
3. Identify the social class issues that may be affecting Sheena's ability to self-advocate.

DOMAIN TWO: COMMUNITY COLLABORATION

In ACA's (2003) advocacy competency domains model, there is a progression from the microlevels of advocacy that include client/student empowerment and advocacy to the school/community collaboration and systems advocacy. Similar to how helping professionals can work with clients to develop a critical consciousness and positive self-identity related to social class issues, helping professionals can also identify social class issues among their clients and collaborate with community groups in an effort to effect positive change in regard to those identified social class issues. Table 14.3 is a list of the community collaboration counselor competencies offered by ACA (2003).

Helping professionals work in a variety of settings and have interactions and knowledge of different community organizations, such as public and private schools, colleges, mental health providers, medical providers, businesses,

Table 14.3 Community Collaboration Counselor Competencies

In support of groups working toward systemic change at the community level, the advocacy-oriented counselor is able to:

1. Identify environmental factors that impinge upon clients' development
2. Alert community groups with common concerns related to the issue
3. Develop alliances with groups working with change
4. Use effective listening skills to gain understanding of the group's goals
5. Identify strengths and resources that the group members bring to the process of systemic change
6. Communicate recognition of and respect for these strengths and resources
7. Identify and offer skills that the professional counselor can bring to the collaboration
8. Assess the effect of the counselor's interaction with the community

and nonprofit organizations. In addition to being responsible for client needs, helping professionals are aware of the needs within the community. For helping professionals, this awareness is often discovered in the themes among their clients' stories and experiences in counseling. This role is often similar to the one of researcher, collecting qualitative data to code for subcategories, categories, and eventually themes within the data (stories/experiences) collected. In this case, the themes are related to social class and privileges associated or not associated with social class status. The social class issues that resonate with communities include lack of access to quality education, adequate medical care, and employment at a living wage (Black & Stone, 2005). Complete Self-Reflection 14.3 to explore social class "themes" associated with your own community.

SELF-REFLECTION OPPORTUNITY 14.3

What are some of the themes or problem situations that are connected to issues of social class and marginalization due to social class within your own community? How can/do these themes affect your clients?

Based on the skills set of helping professionals, assessment, research, consultation, and interpersonal communication services can be offered to community groups in an effort to make change happen (Gibson, 2010). One place to begin is to assess the problem, which has begun with the identification of themes "heard" via the helping professionals' clients. However, this assessment continues with groups who are either experiencing or reacting to these same issues. The helping professional learns about the community groups' experiences with these issues and aligns with them to problem solve. Identifying the groups' strengths and resources will help to facilitate the construction of an effective advocacy plan. Case Study 14.3 illustrates community collaboration for advocacy.

Case Study 14.3

Taylor is a helping professional who has recently provided mental health services for several clients in the past 6 months who cannot afford a yearly physical evaluation. Each of these clients does not qualify for public assistance, and their jobs do not provide medical benefits. She is concerned because each of these clients may have a medical condition that may be affecting their mental health and could be easily remedied through inexpensive medications, so Taylor decided to ask different organizations at the next community mental and physical health consortium if this was also a concern for them. During the meeting, Taylor asked and discovered that approximately 30% of the adults in the community were not receiving medical care based on the same criteria—ineligible for public assistance and no medical insurance. During the meeting Taylor facilitated a brainstorming session of the resources and strengths that each community group offered as well as assessed what interventions had been attempted. After several meetings, the community groups formed a medical resource for individuals to receive limited medical services if they were not eligible for public assistance and had no medical insurance.

FOLLOW-UP QUESTIONS

1. What social class issue is related to the primary theme in this case?
2. What skills did the helping professional utilize to advocate?
3. What other skills and resources should be considered?

DOMAIN TWO: SYSTEMS ADVOCACY

Kiselica and Robinson (2001) remind helping professionals they need to know how systems work before they can advocate for them. In this domain, systems are both small and large. For example, small school systems refer to teachers, administrators, parents, and students, and large school systems refer to communities, school districts, and state departments of education (Gibson, 2010). Once barriers to the development of clients are identified, the environment or system may need to be changed through an advocacy process because of the presence of these barriers in the system (House & Hayes, 2002).

Table 14.4 is a list of competencies for systems advocacy counselors. In this list, collecting, analyzing, and interpreting data indicates that research is a requirement in this phase of advocacy. In prior types of advocacy discussed in this chapter, research and use of data is encouraged but not required as part of the assessment process. However, evidence for the need to change a system has

Table 14.4 Systems Advocacy Counselor Competencies

In exerting systems change leadership at the community level, the advocacy-related counselor is able to:

1. Identify environmental factors impinging on clients' development
2. Provide and interpret data to show the urgency for change
3. In collaboration with other stakeholders, develop a vision to guide change
4. Analyze the sources of political power and social influence within the system
5. Develop a step-by-step plan for implementing the change process
6. Develop a plan for dealing with probable responses to change
7. Recognize and deal with resistance
8. Assess the effect of counselor's advocacy efforts on the system and constituents

to be required in order to provide a rationale for change (Gibson, 2010). There is an assumption that an assessment has been conducted during this level of advocacy to indicate a problem is *present*, but data collection is warranted to determine *how* it is a problem systemically. This type of research may include program evaluation, applied research methodology, or action research. Review Self-Reflection 14.4 to assess your readiness for this level of advocacy.

SELF-REFLECTION OPPORTUNITY 14.4

How would you begin to assess how clients and community systems are affected by social class issues? What research skills do you possess now and what do you need to learn? How will you obtain the research skills and knowledge you will need to obtain data that are helpful for this level of advocacy?

At this level of advocacy, helping professionals and community groups continue their collaborative efforts to effect change based on the identified theme issues that were discussed earlier in regard to community collaboration. However, it is expanded to the creation of a "bigger picture" or a vision for change that includes analyzing the sources of political power and social influence within the system. Lopez-Baez and Paylo (2009) compared this to force field analysis (Lewin, 1948), where there is an assessment of how different factors/forces are influencing a social situation, positively (helping) and negatively (hindering). Often, the helping professional is taking the lead in facilitating the collaborative efforts of the community groups, conducting the required research, and advocating directly to the system for change to occur (Toporek, Lewis, & Crethar, 2009). Part of leading involves co-constructing an action plan that outlines specific goals for implementing the necessary changes that need to occur, in addition to how available resources will be used effectively in this process (Trusty & Brown, 2005). Finally, anticipated difficulties should be discussed, including resistance, as to how they will be handled (Gibson, 2010). Case Study 14.4 provides an illustration of social class issues addressed by systems advocacy.

Case Study 14.4

In a Southern rural county, a professional school counselor worked at one of the two elementary schools in the county. This county had only one school district, with four schools: two elementary schools, one middle school, and one high school. The majority of the students were White, lower middle class, and children of farming families. However, the school counselor had noted an increased amount of bullying occurring at her school within the past year.

She met with the school counselors in the other district schools who concurred that bullying had also increased at their schools. Based on this information, they decided they needed to evaluate why this had increased and how it was affecting the students. One observation made by all of the school counselors was that some of the children had been bullied about their lack of new clothes, which may have resulted from the recent economic recession. They surveyed the students, staff, administrators, parents, and community on several factors that may influence the bullying behavior. After collecting and analyzing the data, they created a detailed plan to decrease the bullying utilizing the resources available through their schools and communities.

FOLLOW-UP QUESTIONS

1. What factors would you assess in this situation?
2. How would you identify the community groups to survey?
3. Who would you present this information to? What informs you of this?
4. How would you present this information?
5. How would you evaluate the effectiveness of the program created to address the bullying causes and effects?

DOMAIN THREE: PUBLIC INFORMATION

At this macrosystemic level of advocacy, the focus for helping professionals is to collaborate with professionals across disciplines and settings to create, research, and disseminate information that not only creates dialogues about social class issues that act as barriers to healthy human development and growth, but also creates change in the existence of these barriers (Gibson, 2010). Table 14.5 provides a list of competencies for helping professionals to utilize in this effort.

Table 14.5 Public Information Counselor Competencies

In informing the public about the role of environmental factors in human development, the advocacy-oriented counselor is able to:

1. Recognize the impact of oppression and other barriers to healthy development
2. Identify environmental factors that are protective of healthy development
3. Prepare written and multimedia materials that provide clear expectations of the role of specific environmental factors in human development
4. Communicate information in ways that are ethical and appropriate for the target population
5. Disseminate information through various media
6. Identify and collaborate with other professionals who are involved in disseminating public information
7. Assess the influence of public information efforts undertaken by the counselor

Specifically, this level of advocacy involves informing the general public about social class issues that affect groups of people negatively, most often those who are being marginalized and discriminated against due to these issues (Ratts et al., 2007). One significant way that helping professionals can contribute at this level of advocacy is to contribute to the research. Unfortunately, social class has not received much attention in the research (Liu, Ali, et al., 2004), although it is one of the most meaningful cultural dimensions in people's lives (Fouad & Brown, 2000) and associated with many human experiences (Brown, Fukunaga, Umemoto, & Wicker, 1996; Frable, 1997). Additionally, a criticism of the existing research available is that it is "inconsistent and may be confusing" (Liu, Ali, et al., 2004, p. 16). Therefore, it may not be effective in advocacy efforts and is an indication that more focused research efforts should be directed on issues of social class. O'Connor (2000) encourages a focus away from "poverty research" that emphasizes the characteristics and failings of poor people toward a more directed research agenda of examining the influence of "mainstream political economy and culture that relegates so many people to economic insecurity and social marginality" (p. 557).

Based within a culture in the United States emphasizing individualism versus collectivism, individualistic attributions for poverty (e.g., laziness, lack of motivation) are emphasized more in public information than structural explanations for poverty (e.g., low wages) (Bullock & Lott, 2001). In essence, this is how the victim is blamed in public systems and environments. Social class issues that need further research include beliefs about income inequality or wealth; beliefs that support capitalism, class hierarchy, and social dominance; classist attitudes that promote the devaluing of the poor while supporting privilege for the nonpoor; and an examination of public support for child care, living wages, housing legislation, health care, as well as policies that affect middle and upper SES groups (i.e., tax breaks) (Bullock & Lott, 2001).

In addition to the focus of social class research changing, the type of research methodologies utilized in this research should be more inclusive. Typically, previous social class research has included survey data about general beliefs about poverty or experimental research on classist stereotypes (Lott & Saxon, 2002). To be more inclusive, helping professionals are encouraged to conduct qualitative research that focuses on grounded theory methodology, phenomenology, and participatory methods that will offer insight into the experiences of individuals affected by social class barriers that limits their development (Bullock & Lott, 2001).

Once research is conducted and collected, it needs to be disseminated, which is also part of the role of advocate for the helping professional. Although research can be published in the form of journal articles, books, presentations, and reports, the most efficient method of disseminating information is often through public media forums. The American Counseling Association has offered several guidelines for how to prepare materials to be used in the media for public information

Table 14.6 ACA Guidelines for Preparation of Public Information for the Media

1. Examine ongoing issues that are important to members of the helping professional's schools, institutions, or communities. Determine if these same issues are appearing in local newspapers and other media.
2. Determine if helping professionals' skills and expertise can be used to address these issues.
3. Assess and determine the resources available to implement the public information activities (e.g., human, monetary, services).
4. Determine how much time the helping professional can devote to these activities.

Source: ACA, *Public Awareness Ideas and Strategies for Professional Counselors*, Alexandria, VA, 1995.

(see Table 14.6). Use Self-Reflection 14.5 to examine your advocacy skills utilizing public information.

SELF-REFLECTION OPPORTUNITY 14.5

What would you choose as a focus in social class research? What methodology would you utilize? Why? How would you choose to disseminate your social class research results to the public? How would you determine this (what factors are important to examine)? Who are some other professionals that you could involve in this process? Why? What resources do you need and what are available to you? How will you assess your efforts to advocate utilizing public information?

DOMAIN THREE: SOCIAL/POLITICAL ADVOCACY

In this final area of advocacy, helping professionals have an opportunity to advocate on behalf of those affected by social class issues in the largest arena available in the United States—social and political groups that create policy (Gibson, 2010). At this level of advocacy, the helping professional has assessed that social class issues experienced by clients or communities need to be addressed positively at a policy or legislative level (Toporek et al., 2009). Furthermore, a pattern of systemic injustice, mistreatment, or neglect due to issues of social class has been identified and needs intervention to effect change. Ethically, helping professionals "must be willing to assume an advocacy role that is focused on affecting public opinion, public policy, and legislation" (Lee & Rodgers, 2009, p. 284). In doing so, they are acting on behalf of constituent groups, which requires continuous open communication with those groups (i.e., clients and communities) to ensure their advocacy efforts are consistent with the groups' needs (see Table 14.7 for social/political advocacy counselor competencies).

Table 14.7 Social/Political Advocacy Counselor Competencies

In influencing public policy in a large, public arena, the advocacy-oriented counselor is able to:

1. Distinguish problems that can best be resolved through social/political action
2. Identify appropriate mechanisms and avenues for addressing these problems
3. Seek out and join with potential allies
4. Support existing alliances for change
5. With allies, prepare convincing data and rationales for change
6. With allies, lobby legislators and other policy makers
7. Maintain open dialogue with communities and clients to ensure that the social/political advocacy is consistent with the initial goals

Although helping professionals may have a responsibility to advocate, creating a change in policy cannot be accomplished alone. Therefore, they are encouraged to seek and take advantage of opportunities to build relationships with key stakeholders who will share responsibility for the outcome of the advocacy effort (Lee & Rodgers, 2009). Stakeholders could include counselors, social workers, psychologists, health care professionals, educational professionals, child welfare officials, and religious/spiritual leaders. Helping professionals should look for stakeholders that can contribute to the goals of advocacy through their "social influence, political credibility, financial influence, leadership abilities, technical competence, authority, or diversity" (Lee & Rodgers, 2009, p. 285). Consequently, helping professionals may find themselves working with local, state, and federal political lobbyists or legislators as part of the action plan. Lee and Rodgers (2009) suggest that helping professionals that form a coalition with lobbyists demonstrate a united front and clear picture of the issue that is evidence based when presenting the issue to legislators and policy makers.

In order to advocate at this level, helping professionals assume leadership positions in their community on issues of social class (Lee & Rodgers, 2009). Inherent to effective leadership is the ability to create a vision for change and then a plan to make the change occur. Not surprisingly, the plan for change includes a research plan, for without evidence to support the change, change will not occur. Finally, helping professionals need to understand that there may be personal and professional risks in advocating for change. Hence, they must have courage. This courage comes from a place of self-awareness (hint: remember Self-Reflection 14.1) and remembering the goal of advocating for the elimination of barriers based on social class. Examine your courage in the context of the following scenario.

Case Study 14.5

In the spring of 2011, Osama bin Laden was captured and killed by the U.S. military. In the United States, there is an understanding that this man and his followers were responsible for the deaths of thousands on September 11, 2001. However, these actions instigated the U.S. military commitments in Iraq and Afghanistan, which are still continuing as this is written. What does this mean for helping professionals? In 2008, the RAND Center for Military Health Policy Research released a report that 20% (approximately 300,000) of U.S. military veterans who served in Iraq and Afghanistan suffered from post-traumatic stress disorder (PTSD) or major depression (Karney, Ramchand, Osilla, Caldarone, & Burns, 2008). The U.S. Department of Veterans Affairs (VA, 2009) estimates that nearly 13,000 of Iraq and Afghanistan veterans have a dependence on alcohol. These statistics do not account for the mental health needs of the families and friends of these veterans as they deal with separation due to deployment, grief due to loss, and anxiety/adjustment due to the physical and rehabilitation needs of an injured veteran. Over the past decade, it became evident that veterans need additional mental health care, but based on their insurance (Tricare), counselors and marriage and family therapists were not eligible to provide this according to the insurance regulations. In response to the need, the National Board of Certified Counselors (NBCC), American Counseling Association (ACA), American Mental Health Counseling Association (AMHCA), and other interested groups began to work with lobbyists to change Tricare to include licensed professional counselors (LPCs) and licensed marriage and family therapists (LMFTs) as providers of mental health services. In 2006, President George W. Bush signed into law that mental health counselors be added to the list of mental health professionals eligible to be employed by the Veterans Administration. In 2009, the VA announced the creation of a new occupational category that included LPCs and LMFTs as new occupational categories (so they could be hired by the VA). The creation of standards for these categories has been conducted by NBCC, ACA, AMHCA, and the VA and was finalized in 2010. However, the total acceptance for Tricare has not occurred. These groups are still working with the Department of Defense to finalize this process; however, they have not stopped advocating.

FOLLOW-UP QUESTIONS

1. What do you believe was the evidence for the policy changes?
2. Is the time worth the effort? Are the results worth the effort?
3. What are the social class issues embedded in this "real" scenario?

CONCLUSION

Social class issues affect all individuals, no matter what race, ethnicity, gender, SES, sexual orientation, or disability; however, they are rarely addressed in graduate programs, specialized trainings, or policy. As helping professionals, the imperative is to act "with" and on "behalf of" clients and communities that are marginalized due to the barriers that social class issues create. Although it is an ethical responsibility to advocate, there are moral undertones to allowing social injustice to continue occurring.

Although the structure of the chapter was based on ACA's advocacy competencies, many other disciplines have addressed the need to advocate on issues of social class. The profession of social work evolved as an interclass profession with an emphasis on social justice being found in interclass cooperation (Addams, as cited in Strier, 2009). Additionally, the American Psychological Association has focused more efforts on issues related to social class in research.

However, there is room for more advocacy. Helping professionals are conducting action and participatory research but need to disseminate their findings. Gaining technical skills to conduct research and publicize it is part of the professional development process. Becoming aware of the inner leader and trusting the self to take risks at systemic and political levels of advocacy are goals to achieve. As a helping professional, the courage is to advocate for clients and communities but also to eliminate any internalized class biases that may still exist within yourself.

RESOURCES

The following books and articles are highly recommended reading on this topic:

Bullock, H.E., & Lott, B. (2001). Building a research and advocacy agenda on issues of economic justice. *Analyses of Social Issues and Public Policy, 1*, 147–162.

Harley, D.A., Jolivette, K., McCormick, K., & Tice, K. (2002). Race, class, and gender: A constellation of positionalities with implications for counseling. *Journal of Multicultural Counseling and Development, 30*, 216–238.

Lee, C.C., & Rodgers, R.A. (2009). Counselor advocacy: Affecting systemic change in the public arena. *Journal of Counseling and Development, 87*, 284–287.

O'Connor, A. (2000). Poverty research and policy for the post-welfare era. *Annual Review of Sociology, 26*, 547–562.

Smith, S.D., Reynolds, C.A., & Rovnak, A. (2009). A critical analysis of the social advocacy movement in counseling. *Journal of Counseling and Development, 87*, 483–491.

Strier, R. (2009). Class-competent social work: A preliminary definition. *International Journal of Social Welfare, 18*, 237–242. doi: 10.1111/j.1468-2397.2008.00588.x

Toporek, R., Gerstein, L., Fouad, N., Roysircar, G., & Israel, T. (Eds.). (2006). *Handbook for social justice in counseling psychology: Leadership, vision, and action*. Thousand Oaks, CA: Sage.

Epilogue

One of the hopes we had throughout the process of bringing this book to you was that it would serve as a professional guide as well as a personal journey. Before we conceptualized the book as a whole, we discussed our own awareness and experiences with social class. We discovered that although we had some similar experiences, we also recognized some of the differences. These differences are recognized as the textured fabric of social class in our country, and we knew that each author we invited to write in this book would weave more interesting aspects of social class into our awareness.

Based on our own exercise of sharing our stories with each other, we invited each of our contributing writers to journal their experience examining social class and found that several things happened. First, everyone felt that the topic of social class has not been given sufficient attention in our field, and they were excited about expanding the discussion. But with that opportunity came the acknowledgment that each would also need to take a close look at his or her own experience with class, and it may be a little uncomfortable; as Chanta reported, "I have to be honest enough to say that the topic makes me a little nervous. I am not nervous about the particulars of poverty but in what I have to expose about myself to truly understand the topic." In effect, the writing assignment became a self-examination and self-assessment process. Although a process such as this is typical in the world of helping, it can catch people unaware when disguised in an "academic" pursuit such as writing a book chapter. Early in the book, we discussed the notion that as you deconstruct your own experiences with social class and gain an awareness of how you have internalized social class, you begin the process of constructing new narratives of social class, not only in your own life but in the lives of your clients. For all of the writers in this book, we interacted with the research in ways that were uniquely personal. In fact, some of our experiences even seemed contrary at times. For example, one of our writers shared that even through her pursuit of education, she never felt that the playing field became level. Yet another writer shared the feeling that her pursuit of education and commitment to academia led her to believe education is the great equalizer. For some of us, the time spent reflecting on social class experiences through childhood was a painful reminder of the long-standing effects of internalized classism, especially revealing in this author's reflection on the opportunities provided by his father working several jobs: "I always felt different and sometimes did not believe I fit in with that group. They [other kids] would tease me about being so smart and about making good grades in school, but it was all in fun and I took it in stride." However, other authors found a new sense of pride or understanding after looking at that experience in a new light.

Gaining a new understanding of our own experiences was not a benefit we had foreseen, but it was one that paralleled our decision to end the book with a chapter on advocacy. Unsurprisingly, advocacy and social justice emerged from many of the self-reflections of the authors. Once we looked inside and spent time with the discomfort, each of us felt compelled to take some form of personal and professional action, as evident in this reflection:

"Writing this chapter and editing this book reminds me that I have a professional and personal responsibility to do more in advocating in regard to social class issues. Sometimes issues of race and gender divide us, professionally and personally, but there is often a common thread in social class. I realized in this process that I need to weave it more purposefully in my life." Many realized a need to advocate within the profession, to broaden the discourse on social class, to present at conferences, and to bring it into our classrooms. For one author, she realized her awareness of social class issues in her own life can be a beneficial process to share with others: "I wonder why I felt so anxious about writing about social class after all. It feels liberating to talk about class and to invite others to do the same. Not only can I write about it, finally, I can also *feel* it."

In the end, we experienced an affirmation of something we believed all along: class *matters*. It matters to our profession as we seek to understand the worldview and life experiences that impact the stories of our clients, as we work to become culturally competent practitioners, and as we arm ourselves to tackle some of the difficult systemic issues perpetuating classism. And it matters personally. While class influences our view of self as we consider our hopes, dreams, vocation, family, and direction, it is equally tied to our past and woven into the personal texture of our identity. Oftentimes society pushes us to hide our story or any evidence of the places from which we came. Terms like *rising above* or *getting out* perpetuate a belief that upward mobility—through education, income, or employment—is a triumph over something *lesser*. We hope that you are able to look at your own family's social class experience with pride and an awareness that class is not about *upper* or *lower*. Treasure your story and seek to understand the stories of those you meet.

Finally, we wanted to share this piece written by Amy M. Sifford, one of our contributing writers, with a sincere hope that you will continue to challenge your thoughts, feelings, and beliefs about class and see the richness around you.

You correct my grammar,
snicker behind my back,
call me ignorant,
hillbilly,
white trash.
I see
the arrogance in your eyes.
I hear
the contempt in your voice.
I know
the great lengths you go through
to forget where you came from.
Your grandparents
had the same lint in their hair
as did mine.
Our parents slept like cordwood
in crowded beds
with the dozen or so siblings
our grandmothers bore.
Large feisty women that they were
dipping snuff
and holding court
sitting high on their aluminum and plastic thrones
in swept dirt yards
demanding that their children
and grandchildren
never get above their raising.
Our parents,
yours and mine,
became slaves to the grind
just to prove that their children,
you and me,
were just as good
as the children that lived in neighborhoods
with grand names,
manicured lawns,
and patios.
They hoped sometimes against hope
that their children,
you and me,
would one day live in
houses with more than one

bathroom,
air conditioning,
and basements.
They hoped sometimes against hope
that their grandchildren
would have no memories
of powdered egg breakfasts,
fat back biscuit lunches,
hand me down clothes,
and lint covered furniture.
Our parents succeeded
in climbing up and over the
mill hill
but the price they paid
was to create
children who learned to call their own history
ignorant,
hillbilly,
and white trash.
To have children unable to appreciate
the raw passion displayed at tent revivals,
camp meetings,
and home comings.
To have children with no memories
of sweet snuff stained kisses,
the loving touch of mother-spit baths,
or the silky feeling of green grass
when running barefoot through
lightning bug summers.
It is these memories that
compel me to intentionally butcher the English language,
walk around my yard in pajamas,
wear my bedroom slippers to the grocery store,
play hillbilly music, loud
and claim fat back as a delicacy.
It is with pride that I
curse like a lost child of God
and talk too loud in upscale restaurants.
It is with pride that I remember where I came from
because where I came from
is not
ignorant,

hillbilly,
or white trash.
Where we came from is
true grit
so embrace it,
celebrate it,
and never allow anyone
to call us
ignorant,
hillbilly,
white trash.

References

Acevedo-Polakovich, I.D., Reynaga-Abiko, G., Garriot, P.O., Derefinko, K.J., Wimsatt, M.K., & Gudonis, L.C., (2007). Beyond instrument selection: Cultural considerations in the psychological assessment of U.S. Latinas/os. *Professional Psychology: Research and Practice, 38*(4), 375–384.

Ackerman, S.J., & Hilsenroth, M.J. (2003). A review of therapist characteristics and techniques positively impacting the therapeutic alliance. *Clinical Psychology Review, 23*(1), 1–33.

Adams, M., Bell, L. B., & Griffin, P. (2007). *Teaching for diversity and social justice.* (2nd ed). New York: Routledge/Taylor & Francis.

Adams, N., & Grieder, D.M. (2005). *Treatment planning for person-centered care: The road to mental health and addiction recovery.* Burlington, MA: Elsevier.

Adelman, C. (1999). *Answers in the tool box: Academic intensity, attendance patterns, and bachelor's degree attainment.* Washington, DC: U.S. Department of Education.

Adelman, C. (2006). *The tool box revisited: Paths to degree completion from high school through college.* Washington, DC: U.S. Department of Education.

Ægisdóttir, S., & Gerstein, L.H. (2005). Reaching out: Mental health delivery outside the box. *Journal of Mental Health Counseling, 27,* 221–224.

Allport, G.W. (1954). *The nature of prejudice.* New York: Doubleday.

Allport, G.W. (1979). *The nature of prejudice.* Cambridge, MA: Addison-Wesley.

Altman, N. (1995). *The analyst in the inner city.* Hillsdale, NJ: Analytic Press.

Alvarez, L., & Kolker, A. (Producers and Directors). (2001). *People like us: Social class in America* [Television documentary, move] United States: CNAM & WETA.

Alves, J. (2006, October 13). Class struggles. *The Chronicle of Higher Education, 53*(8), p. B5.

Amatea, E., & West-Olatunji, C. (2007). Joining the conversation about educating our poorest children: Emerging leadership roles for school counselors in high-poverty schools. *Professional School Counseling, 11*(2), 81–89.

American Counseling Association (ACA). (2003). *Advocacy competencies.* Retrieved June 7, 2011, from http://www.counseling.org/Resources/

American Counseling Association (ACA). (2005). *ACA code of ethics.* Alexandria, VA: Author.

American Psychiatric Association. (2000). *Diagnostic and statistical manual of mental disorders* (rev. 4th ed.). Washington, DC: Author.

American School Counselor Association. (2003). *The ASCA national model: A framework for school counseling programs.* Alexandria, VA: Author.

Annual Social and Economic Supplement. (2008). *Current population survey of the census for the Bureau of Labor Statistics.* Washington, DC: Bureau of the Census. Retrieved on June 8, 2010, from http://www.census.gov/apsd/techdoc/cps/cpsmar08.pdf

Aponte, H.J. (2009). The stresses of poverty and the comfort of spirituality. In F. Walsh (Ed.), *Spiritual resources in family therapy* (2nd ed., pp. 125–140). New York: Guilford Press.

Aronowitz, S. (2003). *How class works: Power and social movement*. New Haven, CT: Yale University Press.

Arredondo, P. (1999). Multicultural counseling competencies as tools to address oppression and racism. *Journal of Counseling and Development, 77*, 102–108.

Arredondo, P., Toporek, R., Brown, S.P., Sanchez, J., Locke, D.C., Jones, J., et al. (1996). Operationalization of the multicultural counseling competencies. *Journal of Multicultural Counseling and Development, 24*, 42–78.

Association for Lesbian, Gay, Bisexual, Transgender Issues in Counseling. (2010). *Competencies for counseling gay, lesbian, bisexual and transgendered (LGBT) clients*. Retrieved from http://www.algbtic.org/competencies.html

Attewell, P., Lavin, D., Domina, T., & Levey, T. (2004). The black middle class: Progress, prospect, and puzzles. *Journal of African American Studies, 8*, 6–19.

Ballinger, L., & Wright, J. (2007). "Does class count?" Social class and counselling. *Counselling and Psychotherapy Research, 7*, 157–163.

Balmforth, J. (2009). "The weight of class": Clients' experiences of how perceived differences in social class between counselor and client affect the therapeutic relationship. *British Journal of Guidance and Counselling, 37*(3), 375–386.

Barnett, M.A. (2008). Economic disadvantage in complex family systems: Expansion of family stress models. *Clinical Child and Family Psychology Review, 11*(3), 145–161.

Barratt, W. (2007). Talking about social class on campus. *NASPA NetResults*. Retrieved March 15, 2011, from wbarratt.indstate.edu/documents/talking_about_social_class.htm

Baruth, L.G., & Manning, M.L. (2007). *Multicultural counseling and psychotherapy: A lifespan perspective* (4th ed.). Upper Saddle River, NJ: Pearson.

Bassuk, E., Dawson, R., & Huntington, N. (2006). Intimate partner violence in extremely poor women: Longitudinal patterns and risk markers. *Journal of Family Violence, 21*(6), 387–399.

Bean, J.A., & Mattingly, M.J. (2011). More than one in ten American households relies on supplemental nutrition assistance program benefits. The Carsey Institute Issue Brief No. 20. Durham, NH.

Belgrave, F.Z., & Allison, K.W. (2006). *African American psychology: From Africa to America*. Thousand Oaks, CA: Sage Publications.

Belle, D., & Doucet, J. (2003). Poverty, inequality, and discrimination as sources of depression among U.S. women. *Psychology of Women Quarterly, 27*(2), 101–113.

Bemak, F., & Chung, R.C.Y. (2005). Advocacy as a critical role for urban school counselors: Working toward equity and social justice. *Professional School Counseling, 8*, 196–203.

Berger, B. (2000). Prisoners of liberation: A psychoanalytic perspective on disenchantment and burnout among career women lawyers. *Journal of Clinical Psychology, 56*, 665–673.

Bienvenu, C., & Ramsey, C.J. (2006). The culture of socioeconomic disadvantage: Practical approaches to counseling. In C.C. Lee (Ed.), Multicultural issues in counseling (pp. 345–353). Alexandria, VA: American Counseling Association.

Black, L.L., & Stone, D. (2005). Expanding the definition of privilege: The concept of social privilege. *Journal of Multicultural Counseling and Development, 33*, 243–255.

Black, M.M., & Krishnakumar, A. (1998). Children in low-income, urban settings: Interventions to promote mental health and well-being. *American Psychologist, 53*, 635–646.

Blackwell, D., Lee, E.B., & Brooks, G. (1990). Friends in low places [Recorded by G. Brooks]. On *No fences* [CD]. Nashville, TN: Capitol Records.

Bohn, A. (2007). A framework for understanding Ruby Payne. *Rethinking Schools, 21*(2), 13–15.

Borg, M., Sells, D., Topor, A., Mezzina, R., Marin, I., & Davidson, L. (2005). What makes a house a home: The role of material resources in recovery from severe mental illness. *American Journal of Psychiatric Rehabilitation, 8*, 243–256.

Bourdieu, P., & Passeron, J.C. (1977). *Reproduction in education, society and culture* (R. Nice, Trans.). London: Sage Publications. (Original work published 1970.)

Bowman, N.A., Kitayama, S., & Nisbett, R.E. (2009). Social class differences in self, attribution, and attention: Socially expansive individualism of middle-class Americans. *Personality and Social Psychology Bulletin, 35*, 880–893.

Boyd-Franklin, N. (2003). Race, class, and poverty. In F. Walsh (Ed.), *Normal family processes: Growing diversity and complexity* (3rd ed., pp. 260–279). New York: Guilford Press.

Boysen, G.A. (2010). Integrating implicit bias into counselor education. *Counselor Education and Supervision, 49*, 210–227.

Bradley, C., & Holcomb-McCoy, C. (2002). Current status of ethnic minority counselor educators in the United States. *International Journal for the Advancement of Counselling, 24*(3), 183–192. Retrieved from http://www.springer.com/psychology/psychotherapy+%26+counseling/journal/10447

Bradshaw, T.K. (2006). *Theories of poverty and anti-poverty programs in community development*. Corvallis, OR: Rural Poverty Research Center.

Brody, G.H., Ge, X., Conger, R., Gibbons, F.X., Murry, V.M., Gerrard, M., et al. (2001). The influence of neighborhood disadvantage, collective socialization, and parenting on African American children's affiliation with deviant peers. *Child Development, 72*(4), 1231–1246.

Brooks, D. (2000). *Bobos in paradise: The new upper class and how they got there*. New York: Simon & Schuster.

Brown, M.T., Fukunaga, C., Umemoto, D., & Wicker, L. (1996). Annual review, 1990–1996: Social class, work, and retirement behavior. *Journal of Vocational Behavior, 49*, 150–189.

Brown, S.L. (2002). We are, therefore I am: A multisystems approach with families in poverty. *The Family Journal: Counseling and Therapy for Couples and Families, 10*(4), 405–409.

Bruce, M.L., Takeuchi, D.T., & Leaf, P.J. (1991). Poverty and psychiatric status: Longitudinal evidence from the New Haven Epidemiologic Catchment Area Study. *Archives of General Psychiatry, 48*(5), 470–474.

Buckner, J.C., Mezzacappa, E., & Beardslee, W.R. (2003). Characteristics of resilient youths living in poverty: The role of self-regulatory processes. *Development and Psychopathology, 15*(1), 139–162.

Bullock, H.E., & Limbert, W.M. (2003). Scaling the socioeconomic ladder: Low-income women's perceptions of class status and opportunity. *Journal of Social Issues, 59*, 693–709.

Bullock, H.E., & Lott, B. (2001). Building a research and advocacy agenda on issues of economic justice. *Analyses of Social Issues and Public Policy, 1*, 147–162.

Burgess-Proctor, A. (2006). Intersections of race, class, gender, and crime: Future directions for feminist criminology. *Feminist Criminology, 1*(1), 27–47. doi: 10.1177/1557085282899

Burney, V., & Beilke, J.R. (2008). The constraints of poverty on high achievement. *Journal for the Education of the Gifted, 31*(3), 295–321.

Busacca, L.A., Beebe, R.S., & Toman, S.M. (2010). Life and work values of counselor trainees: A national survey. *Career Development Quarterly, 59*, 2–18.

Caldwell, L.D. (2009). Counseling with the poor, underserved, and underrepresented. In C.M. Ellis & J. Carlson (Eds.), *Cross cultural awareness and social justice in counseling* (pp. 283–300). New York: Routledge.

Camayd-Freixas, Y. (2006). A Latino middle class emerges from the diaspora: The case of New Hampshire. Paper presented at the annual meeting of the American Anthropological Association, Santa Fe, NM. Retrieved from http://home.comcast.net/~drcamayd/Publications/LMCNH.pdf

Campbell, C., Richie, S.D., & Hargrove, D.S. (2003). Poverty and rural mental health. In B.H. Stamm (Ed.), *Rural behavioral health care: An interdisciplinary guide* (pp. 41–51). Washington, DC: American Psychological Association.

Carr, E.S. (2003). Rethinking empowerment theory using a feminist lens: The importance of process. *Affilia, 18*, 8–20.

Carter Andrews, D.J. (2009). The construction of black high-achiever identities in a predominantly white high school. *Anthropology and Education Quarterly, 40*(3), 297–313. doi: 10.1111/j.1548–1492.2009.01046.x

Cass, V.C. (1979). Homosexual identity formation: A theoretical model. *Journal of Homosexuality, 4*(3), 219–235.

Caughy, M.O., O'Campo, P.J., & Muntaner, C. (2003). When being alone might be better: Neighborhood poverty, social capital, and child mental health. *Social Science and Medicine, 57*, 227–237.

Ceballo, R. (2004). From barrios to Yale: The role of parenting strategies in Latino families. *Hispanic Journal of Behavioral Sciences, 26*, 171–186.

Ceballo, R., Dahl, T.A., Aretakis, M.T., & Ramirez, C. (2001). Inner-city children's exposure to community violence: How much do parents know? *Journal of Marriage and Family, 63*, 927–940.

Centers for Disease Control and Prevention. (2009). Prevalence of autism spectrum disorders—Autism and Developmental Disabilities Monitoring Network, United States, 2006. *Morbidity and Mortality Weekly Report, 58*, 1–20.

Cheatle, L., Fischler, S., Sucher, J., & Toub, M. D. (Producers). (2001, February 1). Swastika to Jim Crow [Television broadcast]. Arlington: PBS.

Chen, E.S., & Tyler, T.R. (2001). Cloaking power: Legitimizing myths and the psychology of the advantaged. In A.Y. -LeeChai & J.A. Bargh (Eds.), *The use and abuse of power: Multiple perspectives on the cause of corruption* (pp. 241–261). Philadelphia: Psychology Press.

Children's Defense Fund. (2007). *America's Cradle to Prison Pipeline report.* Washington, DC: Author.

Chodoff, P. (1991). Effects of the new economic climate on psychotherapeutic practice. In S. Klebanow & E.L. Lowenkopf (Eds.), *Money and mind* (pp. 253–263). New York: Plenum Press.

Churilla, A. (2008, Summer). *Urban and rural children experience similar rates of low-income and poverty* (Issue Brief No. 2). Retrieved November 23, 2011, from http://www.carseyinstitute.unh.edu/IB_UrbanRuralChildren08.pdf

Clawson, R.A., & Trice, R. (2000). Poverty as we know it: Media portrayals of the poor. *The Public Opinion Quarterly, 64*, (1), 53–64.

Cochran, J.L., & Cochran, N.H. (2006). *The heart of counseling: A guide to developing therapeutic relationships.* Belmont, CA: Thomson Education.

Cohen, P. (2010, October 17). "Culture of poverty" makes a comeback. *The New York Times.* Retrieved from http://www.nytimes.com/2010/10/18/us/18poverty.html

Cohen, S., Kaplan, G.A., & Salonen, J.T. (1999). The role of psychological characteristics in the relation between socioeconomic status and perceived health. *Journal of Applied Social Psychology, 29*, 445–468.

Coiro, M.J. (2001). Depressive symptoms among women receiving welfare. *Women and Health, 32*(1–2), 1–23.

Cole, E.R., & Omari, S.R. (2003). Race, class and the dilemmas of upward mobility for African Americans. *Journal of Social Issues, 59*, 785–802.

Collard, P., Anvy, N., & Boniwell, I. (2008). Teaching mindfulness based cognitive therapy (MBCT) to students: The effects of MBCT on the levels of mindfulness and subjective well-being. *Counseling Psychology Quarterly, 21*, 323–336. doi: 10.1080/09515070802602112

Collins, C., & Yeskel, F. (2005). *Economic apartheid in America*. New York: New Press.

Collins, P.H. (1993). Toward a new vision: Race, class, and gender as categories of analysis and connection. *Race, Sex, and Class, 1*, 25–45.

Condrasky, M., & Marsh, J. (2005). Food stamps and dietary intake of low-income women in the rural south in the time of welfare reform. *Topics in Clinical Nutrition, 20*, 366–374.

Constantine, M.G. (2001). Addressing racial, ethnic, gender, and social class issues in counselor training and practice. In D.B. Pope-Davis & H.L.K. Coleman (Eds.), *The intersection of race, class, and gender in multicultural counseling* (pp. 341–350). Thousand Oaks, CA: Sage.

Constantine, M.G. (2002). The intersection of race, ethnicity, gender, and social class in counseling: Examining selves in cultural contexts. *Journal of Multicultural Counseling and Development, 30*, 210–215.

Corey, G. (2009). *Theory and practice of counseling and psychotherapy*. Belmont, CA: Brooks/Cole Publishing.

Costello, E.J., Compton, S.N., Keeler, G., & Angold, A. (2003). Relationship between poverty and psychopathology: A natural experiment. *Journal of the American Medical Association, 290*(15), 2023–2029.

Coulton, C., Crampton, D., Irwin, M., Spilsbury, J., & Korbin, J. (2007). How neighborhoods influence child maltreatment: A review of the literature and alternative pathways. *Child Abuse and Neglect, 32*(11–12), 1117–1142.

Cox, A.A., & Lee, C.C. (2007). Challenging educational inequities: School counselors as agents of social justice. In C.C. Lee (Ed.), *Counseling for social justice* (2nd ed., pp. 3–14). Alexandria, VA: American Counseling Association.

Cox, J.W. (1990). Social class, mental illness, and social mobility: The social selection drift hypothesis for serious mental illness. *Journal of Health and Social Behavior, 31*(4), 344–353.

Cozzarelli, C., Wilkinson, A.V., & Tagler, M.J. (2001). Attitudes toward the poor and attributions for poverty. *Journal of Social Issues, 57*, 207–227.

Cross, W.E. (1971). The negro-to-black conversion experience: Towards a psychology of black liberation. *Black World, 20*, 13–27.

Cross, W.E. (1995). The psychology of Nigresence: Revising the Cross model. In J.G. Ponterotto, J.M. Casas, L.A. Suzuki, & C.M. Alexander (Eds.), *Handbook of multicultural counseling* (pp. 93–122). Thousand Oaks, CA: Sage.

Csikszentmihalyi, M. (1999). If we are so rich, why aren't we happy? *American Psychologist, 54*, 821–827.

Cullen, J. (2003). *The American dream: A short history of an idea that shaped a nation*. New York: Oxford University Press.

Dakin, J., & Wampler, R. (2008). Money doesn't buy happiness, but it helps: Marital satisfaction, psychological distress, and demographic differences between low- and middle-income clinic couples. *American Journal of Family Therapy, 36*, 300–311.

Damaske, S. (2009). Brown suits need not apply: The intersection of race, gender, and class in institutional network building. *Sociological Forum, 24*(2), 402–424. doi: 10.1111/j.1573-7861.2009.01105.x

Dana, R.H. (1993). *Multicultural assessment perspectives for professional psychology.* Boston: Allyn & Bacon.

Dana, R.H. (2005). *Multicultural assessment: Principles, applications and examples.* Mahwah, NJ: Lawrence Erlbaum Associates.

Davenport, R.F., Tolbert, M., Myers-Oliver, D., Brissett, J.M., & Roland, A.J. (2007). Hope out of poverty. *Principal Leadership, 7*(7), 36–39.

Day, S.X. (2008). *Theory and design in counseling and psychotherapy* (2nd ed.). Boston: Lahaska Press.

DeJong, P., & Berg, I.K. (2002). *Interviewing for solutions* (2nd ed.). Pacific Grove, CA: Brooks/Cole.

Delgado, R., & Stephancic, J. (2001). *Critical race theory: An introduction.* New York: New York University Press.

Delpit, L. (1995). *Other people's children: Cultural conflict in the classroom.* New York: The New Press.

Demmitt, A., & Oldenski, T. (1999). The diagnostic process from a Freirean perspective. *Journal of Humanistic Counseling, Education, and Development, 37,* 232–239.

Diener, E. (2000). Subjective well-being: The science of happiness and a proposal for a national index. *American Psychologist, 55,* 34–43.

Diener, E., & Biswas-Diener, R. (2002). Will money increase subjective well-being? *Social Indicators Research, 57,* 119–169.

Dinkmeyer, D., Jr., & Carlson, J. (2006). *Consultation: Creating school-based interventions* (3rd ed.). New York: Taylor & Francis.

Dire Straits. (1998). Money for nothing. *Sultans of swing: The very best of Dire Straits.* Retrieved January 12, 2011, from http://www.metrolyrics.com/dire-straits-albumslist.html

Dittmar, L. (1995). All that Hollywood allows: Film and the working class. *Radical Teacher, 46,* 38–45.

Domhoff, G.W. (2009). *Who rules America? Challenges to corporate and class dominance.* New York: McGraw Hill.

Downing, N.E., & Roush, K.L. (1985). From passive acceptance to active commitment: A model of feminist identity development for women. *The Counseling Psychologist, 13,* 695–709.

Drellich, M.G. (1991). Money and countertransference. In S. Klebanow & E.L. Lowenkopf (Eds.), *Money and mind* (pp. 155–162). New York: Plenum Press.

Drummond, R.J., & Jones, K.D. (2010). *Assessment procedures for counselors and helping professionals* (7th ed.). Upper Saddle River, NJ: Pearson.

Duran, E., & Duran, B. (1995). *Native American postcolonial psychology.* Albany: State University of New York Press.

Earle, J. (1990). Counselor/advocates: Changing the system. *Public Welfare, 48*(3), 16–24.

Eaton, W.W., Muntaner, C., Bovasso, G., & Smith, C. (2001). Socioeconomic status and depressive syndrome: The role of inter- and intra-generational mobility, government assistance and work environment. *Journal of Health and Social Behavior, 42,* 277–294.

Economic Opportunity Act of 1964. Pub.L. 88-452, § 2701, 78 Stat. 508, 42 U.S.C.

Education Trust. (2005). *Achievement in America: 2005.* Washington, DC: Author.

Elementary Teachers Federations of Ontario. (2009). *Building understanding about classism.* Retrieved June 9, 2011, from http://www.etfo.ca/Resources/ForTeachers/Documents/Building%20Understanding%20About%20Classism.pdf

Erickson, D., Reid, C., Nelson, L., O'Shaughnessy, A., & Berube, A. (Eds.) (2008). *The enduring challenge of concentrated poverty in America: Case studies from communities across the U.S.* Washington, DC: Federal Reserve System.

Erickson, F. (2005). Culture in society and in educational practices. In J.A. Banks & C.A. McGee Banks (Eds.), *Multicultural education: Issues and perspectives* (5th ed., pp. 31–60). Hoboken, NJ: Wiley.

Erikson, E. (1968). *Identity Youth and crisis*. New York: Norton and Company.

Erikson, E.H. (1963). *Childhood and society*. New York: W.W. Norton & Company.

Evans, G.W. (2004). The environment of childhood poverty. *American Psychologist*, *59*(2), 77–92.

Evans, G.W., & Kantrowitz, E. (2002). Socioeconomic status and health: The potential role of environmental risk exposure. *Annual Review of Public Health*, *23*, 303–331. doi:10.1146/annurev.publhealth.23.112001.112349

Farkas, G. (2003). Racial disparities and discrimination in education: What do we know, how do we know it, and what do we need to know? *Teachers College Record*, *105*(6), 1119–1146.

Feagin, J.R. (1972). Poverty: We still believe that God helps those who help themselves. *Psychology Today*, *6*, 101–110.

Feinstein, A., & Holloway, F. (2002). Evaluating the use of a psychiatric intensive care unit: Is ethnicity a risk factor for admission? *International Journal of Social Psychiatry*, *48*(1), 38–46. doi: 10.1177/002076402128783073

Fitzsimons, S., & Fuller, R. (2002). Empowerment and its implications for clinical practice in mental health: A review. *Journal of Mental Health*, *11*(5), 481–499.

Ford, T., Goodman, R., & Meltzer, H. (2004). The relative importance of child, family, school, and neighbourhood correlates of childhood psychiatric disorder. *Social Psychiatry and Psychiatric Epidemiology*, *39*(6), 487–496.

Fortney, J.C., Xu, S., & Dong, F. (2009). Community-level correlates of hospitalizations for persons with schizophrenia. *Psychiatric Services*, *60*(6), 772–778.

Foss, L.L., Generali, M.M., & Kress, V.E. (2011). Counseling people living in poverty: The CARE model. *Journal of Humanistic Counseling*, *50*(2), 161–171.

Fouad, N.A., & Brown, M.T. (2000). Role of race and social class in development: Implications for counseling psychology. In S.D. Brown & R.W. Lent (Eds.), *Handbook of counseling psychology* (3rd ed., pp. 379–408). New York: Wiley.

Fouad, N.A., Chen, Y.L., Guillen, A., Henry, C., Kantamneni, N., Novakovic, A., et al. (2007). Role induction in career counseling. *Career Development Quarterly*, *56*(1), 19–33. Retrieved from http://www.associationdatabase.com/aws/NCDA/pt/sp/cdquarterly

Fox, M. (1994). *The reinvention of work: A new vision of livelihood for our time*. San Francisco: Harper.

Fox, S. (2011, February). *Profiles of health information seekers: Who gathers health information online?* Retrieved on June 21, 2011, from http://www.pewinternet.org/Reports/2011/HealthTopics/Part-2.aspx?view=all

Frable, D.E.S. (1997). Gender, racial, ethnic, sexual, and class identities. *Annual Review Psychology*, *48*, 139–162.

Frank, J.D., & Frank, J.B. (1991). *Persuasion and healing: A comparative study of psychotherapy* (3rd ed.). Baltimore: Johns Hopkins University Press.

Freeman, J., Ferrer, R.L., & Greiner, K. A. (2007). Viewpoint: Developing a physician workforce for America's disadvantaged. *Academic Medicine*, *82*(2), 133–138.

Freire, E.S., Koller, S.H., Piason, A., & Silva, R.B. (2005). Person-centered therapy with impoverished, maltreated, and neglected children and adolescents in Brazil. *Journal of Mental Health Counseling*, *27*, 225–237.

Freire, P. (1970). *Pedagogy of the oppressed*. New York: Seabury Press.

Fukuyama, M., & Ferguson, A.D. (2000). Lesbian, gay, and bisexual people of color: Understanding cultural complexity and multiple oppressions. In R.M. Perez, K.A. DeBord, & K.J. Bieschke (Eds.), *Handbook of counseling and psychotherapy with lesbian, gay, and bisexual clients* (pp. 107–131). Washington, DC: American Psychological Association.

Gafford, F.D. (2010). Rebuilding the park: The impact of Hurricane Katrina on a black middle-class neighborhood. *Journal of Black Studies, 41*(2), 385–404.

Galassi, J.P., & Akos, P. (2004). Developmental advocacy: Twenty-first century school counseling. *Journal of Counseling and Development, 82*(2), 146–157.

Galassi, J.P., & Akos, P. (2007). *Strengths-based school counseling: Promoting student development and achievement.* Mahwah, NJ: Lawrence Erlbaum Associates.

Gallo, L.C., Bogart, L.M., Vranceanu, A.-M., & Matthews, K.A. (2005). Socioeconomic status, resources, psychological experiences, and emotional responses: A test of the reserve capacity model. *Journal of Personality and Social Psychology, 88*, 386–399.

Gallo, L.C., & Matthews, K.A. (2003). Understanding the association between socioeconomic status and physical health: Do negative emotions play a role? *Psychological Bulletin, 129*, 10–51.

Gans, H.J. (1995). *The war against the poor.* New York: Basic Books.

Gardner, W.L., Gabriel, S., & Hochschild, L. (2002). When you and I are "we," you are not threatening: The role of self-expansion in social comparison. *Journal of Personality and Social Psychology, 82*, 239–251.

Garland, A.F., Lau, A.S., Yeh, M., McCabe, K.M., Hough, R.L., & Landsverk, J.A. (2005). Racial and ethnic differences in utilization of mental health services among high-risk youths. *American Journal of Psychiatry, 162*, 1336–1343.

Geiger, H. J. (2003). Racial and ethnic disparities in diagnosis and treatment: A review of the evidence and a consideration of causes. In B.D. Smedley, A.Y. Stith, & A.R. Nelson (Eds.), *Unequal treatment: Confronting racial and ethnic disparities in health care* (pp. 417–454). Washington, DC: The National Academies Press.

Gerstein, L., & Ægisdóttir, S. (2005). A trip around the world: A counseling travelogue. *Journal of Mental Health Counseling, 27*, 95–103.

Gerstein, L.H., & Ægisdóttir, S. (2007). Training international social change agents: Transcending a U.S. counseling paradigm. *Counselor Education and Supervision, 47*, 123–139.

Gerstein, L.H., Rountree, C., & Ordonez, M.A. (2007). An anthropological perspective on multicultural counselling. *Counselling Psychology Quarterly, 20*, 375–400.

Gibbons, M.M., & Borders, L.D. (2010). Prospective first-generation college students: A social-cognitive perspective. *Career Development Quarterly, 58*, 194–208. Retrieved from http://www.associationdatabase.com/aws/NCDA/pt/sp/cdquarterly

Gibson, D.M. (2010). Advocacy counseling: Being an effective agent of change for clients. In B.T. Erford (Ed.), *Orientation to the counseling profession: Advocacy, ethics, and essential professional foundations* (pp. 340–358). Upper Saddle River, NJ: Pearson Education.

Gilens, M. (1995). Racial attitudes and oppositions to welfare. *Journal of Politics, 57*(4), 994–1014.

Glosoff, H.L., & Durham, J.C. (2010). Using supervision to prepare social justice counseling advocates. *Counselor Education and Supervision, 50*(2), 116–129.

Goldberg, E.M., & Morrison, S.L. (1963). Schizophrenia and social class. *British Journal of Psychiatry, 109*, 785–803.

Gonzalez, G. (2005). Acculturation and identity: Intra-ethnic distinctions among Mexican Americans. In S.K. Anderson & V.A. Middleton (Eds.), *Explorations in privilege, oppression, and diversity* (2nd ed., pp. 181–193). Belmont, CA: Brooks/Cole.

Gonzalez, M.J. (2005). Access to mental health services: The struggle of poverty affected urban children of color. *Child and Adolescent Social Work Journal, 22*(3–4), 245–256.

Good, B.J. (1996). Culture and DSM-IV: Diagnosis, knowledge and power. *Culture, Medicine and Psychiatry, 20*(2), 127–132. doi: 10.1007/BF00115857

Goodman, R.D., & West-Olatunji, C.A. (2009). Traumatic stress, systemic oppression, and resilience in post-Katrina New Orleans. *Spaces for Difference: An Interdisciplinary Journal, 1,* 51–68. http://repositories.cdlib.org/ucsb_ed/spaces/vol1/iss2/art5

Gordon, E.W. (2006). Establishing a system of public education in which all children achieve at high levels and reach their full potential. In T. Smiley (Ed.), *The covenant with black America* (pp. 23–45). Chicago: Third World Press.

Gorski, P. (2007). The question of class. *Education Digest, 73*(2), 30–33.

Gorski, P. (2008). The myth of the "culture of poverty." *Educational Leadership, 65*(7), 32–36.

Gorski, P.C. (2010). *Critical multicultural pavilion.* Retrieved June 9, 2011, from http://www.edchange.org/multicultural/activityarch.html

Greenberg, D., Mandell, M., and Onstott, M. (2000). The dissemination and utilization of welfare-to-work experiments in state policymaking. *Journal of Policy Analysis and Management, 19*(3), 367–382.

Greenberg, D.H., & Robins, P.K. (2010). *Have welfare-to-work programs improved over time in putting welfare recipients to work?* Madison, WI: Institute for Research on Poverty.

Grimes, M.E., & McElwain, A.D. (2008). Marriage and family therapy with low-income clients: Professional, ethical, and clinical issues. *Contemporary Family Therapy, 30,* 220–232.

Grossman, P., Neimann, L., Schmidt, S., & Walach, H. (2004). Mindfulness-based stress reduction and health benefits: A meta-analysis. *Journal of Psychosomatic Research, 57,* 35–43. doi: 10.1016/S0022-3999(03)00573-7

Gudrais, E. (2008, July–August). Unequal America: Causes and consequences of the wide—and growing—gap between rich and poor. *Harvard Magazine.* Retrieved from http://harvardmagazine.com/2008/07/unequal-america-html?page=0,2

Gutierrez, L.M. (1995). Understanding the empowerment process: Does consciousness make a difference? *Social Work Research, 19,* 229–237.

Hagan, M. (2004). Acculturation and an ESL program: A service learning project. *Journal of Multicultural Counseling and Development, 32,* 443–448.

Hahn, T. N. (1991). *Peace is every step: The path of mindfulness in everday life.* New York: Bantam.

Halperin, D.M., Weitzman, M.L., & Otto, M.W. (2010). Therapeutic alliance and common factors in treatment. In M.W. Otto & S.G. Hofmann (Eds.), *Avoiding treatment failures in the anxiety disorders* (pp. 51–66). New York: Springer.

Hanna, F.J., Talley, W.B., & Guindon, M.H. (2000). The power of perception: Toward a model of cultural oppression and liberation. *Journal of Counseling and Development, 78,* 430–441.

Hanson, S.L., & Zogby, J. (2010). The polls—Trends: Attitudes about the American dream. *Public Opinion Quarterly, 74*(3), 570–584. doi: 10.1093/poq/nfq010

Harley, D.A. (2009). Multicultural counseling as a process of empowerment. In C.C. Lee, D.A. Burnhill, A.L. Butler, C.P. Hipolito-Delgado, M. Humphrey, O. Munoz, et al. (Eds.), *Elements of culture in counseling* (pp. 127–147). Columbus, OH: Pearson.

Harley, D.A., Jolivette, K., McCormick, K., & Tice, K. (2002). Race, class, and gender: A constellation of positionalities with implications for counseling. *Journal of Multicultural Counseling and Development, 30,* 216–238.

Harris, A.H.S., Thoresen, C.E., & Lopez, S.J. (2007). Integrating positive psychology into counseling: Why and (when appropriate) how. *Journal of Counseling and Development, 85*, 3–13.

Harris, E. (2005). *Key strategies to improve schools: How to apply them contextually.* Lanham, MD: Scarecrow Press.

Harry, B., & Klingner, J. (2007). Discarding the deficit model. *Educational Leadership, 64*(5), 16–21.

Hay, C., Fortson, E.N., Hollist, D.R., Altheimer, I., & Schaible, L M. (2007). Compounded risk: The implications for delinquency of coming from a poor family that lives in a poor community. *Journal of Youth and Adolescence, 36*, 593–605.

Hays, P.A. (2001). *Addressing cultural complexities in practice.* Washington, DC: American Psychological Association.

Helms, J.E. (Ed.). (1990). *Black and white racial identity: Theory, research, and practice.* Westport, CT: Greenwood.

Helms, J.E., & Cook, D.A. (1999). *Using race and culture in counseling and psychotherapy: Theory and process.* Boston: Allyn and Bacon.

Herrnstein, R., & Murray, C. (1994). *The bell curve.* New York: Free Press.

Hidalgo, N. (1993). Multicultural teacher introspection. In T. Perry & J. Fraser (Eds.), *Freedom's plow: Teaching in the multicultural classroom* (pp. 99–106). New York: Routledge.

Hines, P.L., & Fields, T.H. (2004). School counseling and academic achievement. In R. Perusse & G.E. Goodnough (Eds.), *Leadership, advocacy, and direct service strategies for professional school counselors* (pp. 3–33). Belmont, CA: Brooks/Cole.

Hipilito-Delgado, C.P., & Lee, C.C. (2007). Empowerment theory for the professional school counselor: A manifesto for what really matters. *Professional School Counseling, 10*, 327–332.

Hirshberg, M., & Ford, G. (2001). Justice, work, poverty and welfare: The psychological connections. *Journal of Poverty, 5*(3), 65–86.

Holcomb-McCoy, C. (2007). *School counseling to close the achievement gap: A social justice framework for success.* Thousand Oaks, CA: Corwin Press.

Holvino, E. (2008). Intersections: The simultaneity of race, gender and class in organization studies. *Gender, Work and Organization, 17*(3), 248–277. doi: 10.1111/j1468-0432.2008.00400.x

hooks, b. (2000). *Where we stand: Class matters.* New York: Routledge.

Hopps, J., & Liu, W.M. (2006). Working for social justice from within the health care system: The role of social class in psychology. In R.L. Toporek, L.H. Gerstein, N.A., Fouad, G. Roysircar, & T. Israel (Eds.), *Handbook for social justice in counseling psychology: Leadership, vision, and action* (pp. 318–337). Thousand Oaks, CA: Sage.

Horner, A.J. (1991). Money issues and analytic neutrality. In S. Klebanow & E.L. Lowenkopf (Eds.), *Money and mind* (pp. 175–181). New York: Plenum Press.

House, R., & Sears, S.J. (2002). Preparing school counselors to be leaders and advocates: A critical need in the new millennium. *Theory Into Practice, 41*, 154–163.

House, R.M., & Hayes, R.L. (2002). School counselors: Becoming key players in school reform. *Professional School Counseling, 5*, 249–256.

Hout, M. (2008). How class works: Objective and subjective aspects of class since the 1970s. In A. Lareau & D. Conley (Eds.), *Social class: How does it work?* (pp. 25–64). New York: Russell Sage Foundation.

Hsieh, C., & Pugh, M.D. (1993). Poverty, income inequality, and violent crime: A meta-analysis of recent aggregate data studies. *Criminal Justice Review, 18*(2), 182–202.

Hunt, M.O. (1996). The individual, society, or both? A comparison of Black, Latino, and White beliefs about the causes of poverty. *Social Forces, 75*, 293–322.

Hutchison, B. (2011). The influence of perceived poverty and academic achievement on school counselor conceptualization. *Equity and Excellence in Education, 44*(2), 203–220.

Irizarry, J. (2009). *Cultural deficit model.* Retrieved June 9, 2001, from http://www.education.com/reference/article/cultural-deficit-model/

Isaacson, L.E., & Brown, D. (2000). *Career information, career counseling, and career development* (7th ed.). Needham Heights, MA: Allyn & Bacon/Pearson.

Jacobs, S., & Blustein, D.L. (2008). Mindfulness as a coping mechanism for employment uncertainty. *Career Development Quarterly, 57*(2), 174–180. Retrieved from http://www.associationdatabase.com/aws/NCDA/pt/sp/cdquarterly

Javier, R.A., & Herron, W.G. (2002). Psychoanalysis and the disenfranchised: Countertransference issues. *Psychoanalytic Psychology, 19*(1), 149–166.

Jenkins, R., Bhugra, D., Bebbington, P., Brugha, T., Farrell, M., Coid, J., et al. (2008). Debt, income and mental disorder in the general population. *Psychological Medicine: A Journal of Research in Psychiatry and the Allied Sciences, 38*(10), 1485–1493.

Jennings, J. (1994). *Understanding the nature of urban poverty in America.* Westport, CT: Praeger Publishers.

Jensen, L. (2006). At the razor's edge: Building hope for American's rural poor. *Rural Realities, 1*(1).

Johnson, S.E., Richeson, J.A., & Finkel, E.J. (2011). Middle class and marginal? Socioeconomic status, stigma, and self-regulation at an elite university. *Journal of Personality and Social Psychology, 100*, 838–852. doi: 10.1037/a0021956

Johnson, W., & Krueger, R.F. (2006). How money buys happiness: Genetic and environmental processes linking finances and life satisfaction. *Journal of Personality and Social Psychology, 90*, 680–691.

Jordan, G. (2004, Spring). The causes of poverty—cultural vs. structural: Can there be a synthesis? *Perspectives in Public Affairs, 1*, 18–34.

Jun, H. (2010). *Social justice, multicultural counseling, and practice: Beyond a conventional approach.* Los Angeles: Sage.

Kagan, R., & Schlosberg, S. (1989). *Families in perpetual crisis.* New York: W.M. Norton & Company.

Kaplan, G.A., & Keil, J.E. (1993). Socioeconomic factors and cardiovascular disease: A review of the literature. *Circulation, 88*, 1973–1998.

Kaplan, L., & Girard, J.L. (1994). *Strengthening high-risk families: A handbook for practitioners.* New York: Lexington Books.

Kareholt, I. (2001). The relationship between heart problems and mortality in different social classes. *Social Science and Medicine, 52*, 1391–1402.

Karney, B.R., Ramchand, R., Osilla, K.C., Caldarone, L.B., & Burns, R.M. (2008, April). *Invisible wounds: Predicting the immediate and long-term consequences of mental health problems in veterans of Operation Enduring Freedom and Operation Iraqi Freedom.* RAND Working Paper WR546. Retrieved from www.rand.org/pubs/working_papers/WR546.html

Kasser, T., Ryan, R.M., Zax, M., & Sameroff, A.J. (1995). The relations of maternal and social environments to late adolescents' materialistic and prosocial values. *Developmental Psychology, 31*, 907–914.

Kazdin, A.E., & Wassell, G. (2000). Predictors of barriers to treatment and therapeutic change in outpatient therapy for antisocial children and their families. *Mental Health Services Research, 2*, 27–40.

Keene, S.E. (2008, November/December). Higher education and the American dream: Why the status quo won't get us there. *Change, 40*(6), 65–68. Retrieved from http://www.changemag.org/Archives/Back%20Issues/November-December%202008/full-listening-to-students.html

Kessler, R.C., Heeringa, S., Lakoma, M., Petukhova, A.E., Rupp, A.E., Schoenbaum, M., et al. (2008). Individual and societal effects of mental disorders on earnings in the United States: Results from the national comorbidity survey replication. *American Journal of Psychiatry, 165*(6), 703–711.

Kiselica, M.S., & Robinson, M. (2001). Bringing advocacy counseling to life: The history, issues and human dramas of social justice work in counseling. *Journal of Counseling and Development, 79*, 387–398.

Kissman, K., & Allen, J. (1993). *Single-parent families*. London: Sage Publications.

Kliman, J. (1998). Social class as a relationship: Implications for family therapy. In M. McGoldrick (Ed.), *Re-visioning family therapy: Race, culture, and gender in clinical practice* (50–61). New York: Guilford Press.

Klose, M., & Jacobi, E. (2004). Can gender differences in the prevalence of mental disorders be explained by socioeconomic factors? *Archives of Women's Mental Health, 7*, 133–148.

Kluegel, J.R., & Smith, E.R. (1986). *Beliefs about inequality*. New York: Aldine de Gruyter.

Kohn, M. (1989). *Class and conformity: A study in values*. Chicago: University of Chicago Press.

Koplewicz, H.S., Gurian, A., & Williams, K. (2009). The era of affluence and its discontents. *Journal of the American Academy of Child and Adolescent Psychiatry, 48*(11), 1053–1055.

Kraus, M.W., Cote, S., & Keltner, D. (2010). Social class, contextualism, and empathic accuracy. *Psychological Science, 21*(11), 1716–1723.

Kraus, M.W., Piff., P.K., & Keltner, D. (2009). Social class, sense of control, and social explanation. *Journal of Personality and Social Psychology, 97*, 992–1004.

Lachman, M.E., & Weaver, S.L. (1998). The sense of control as a moderator of social class differences in health and well-being. *Journal of Personality and Social Psychology, 74*, 763–773.

Ladd, E.C. (Ed). (1993). Public opinion and demographic report: Reforming welfare. *Public Perspective, 4*(6), 86–87.

Lane, R.E. (1962). *Political ideology*. London: MacMillan.

Lapour, A.S., & Heppner, M.J. (2009). Social class privilege and adolescent women's perceived career options. *Journal of Counseling Psychology, 56*, 477–494.

Lareau, A. (2003). *Unequal childhoods: Class, race, and family life*. Los Angeles: University of California Press.

Lareau, A., & Conley, D. (Eds.). (2008). *Social class: How does it work?* New York: Russell Sage Foundation.

Larew, J. (1991). Why are droves of unqualified, unprepared kids getting into our top colleges? Because their dads are alumni. *Washington Monthly, 23*, 10–14. Retrieved from http://findarticles.com/p/articles/mi_m1316/is_n6_v23/ai_10844045/

Lauret, M. (2011). How to read Michelle Obama. *Patterns of Prejudice, 45*(1–2), 95–117.

Lazarus, E. (n.d.). New Colossus. Retrieved January 11, 2011, from http://www.howtallisthestatueofliberty.org/what-is-the-quote-on-the-statue-of-liberty/

Lee, C.C. (2001). Culturally responsive school counselors and programs: Addressing the needs of all students. *Professional School Counseling, 4*, 257–261.

Lee, C.C., & Ramsey, C.J. (2006). Multicultural counseling: A new paradigm for a new century. In C.C. Lee (Ed.), *Multicultural issues in counseling: New approaches to diversity* (3rd ed., pp. 3–12). Alexandria, VA: American Counseling Association.

Lee, C.C., & Rodgers, R.A. (2009). Counselor advocacy: Affecting systemic change in the public arena. *Journal of Counseling and Development, 87*, 284–287.

Lee, H. (1960). *To kill a mockingbird*. New York: Grand Central Publishing.

Lehmann, W. (2009). Becoming middle class: How working-class university students draw and transgress moral class boundaries. *Sociology, 43*, 631–647.

Lerner, J.A. (1991). Money, ethics, and the psychoanalyst. In S. Klebanow & E.L. Lowenkopf (Eds.), *Money and mind* (pp. 223–234). New York: Plenum Press.

Leventhal, T., & Brooks-Gunn, J. (2003). Moving to opportunity: An experimental study of neighborhood effects on mental health. *American Journal of Public Health, 93*(9), 1576–1582.

Levine, M. (2006). *The price of privilege: How parental pressure and material advantage are creating a generation of disconnected and unhappy kids*. New York: Harper Collins.

Levine, R. (Ed.). (2006). *Social class and stratification: Classic statements and theoretical debates* (2nd ed.). Lanham, MD: Rowman & Littlefield.

Levine-Rasky, C. (2011). Intersectionality theory applied to whiteness and middle classness. *Social Identities, 17*(2), 239–253.

Lewin, K. (1948). *Resolving social conflicts*. New York: Harper.

Lewis, J. A., Arnold, M. S., House, R., & Toporek, R. L. (2002). *ACA advocacy competencies*. Retrieved November 29, 2011, from http://www.counseling.org/Resources/

Lewis, J.A., & Elder, J. (2010). Substance abuse counseling and social justice advocacy. In M.J. Ratts, R.L. Toporek, & J.A. Lewis (Eds.), *ACA advocacy competencies: A social justice framework for counselors* (pp. 161–172). Alexandria, VA: American Counseling Association.

Lewis, M. (1978). *The culture of inequality*. Amherst, MA: University of Massachusetts Press.

Lewis, O. (1959). *Five families: Mexican case studies in the culture of poverty*. New York: Basic Books.

Lewis, O. (1961). *The children of Sanchez: Autobiography of a Mexican family*. New York: Random House.

Lin, N., Ao, D., & Song, L.J. (2009). Production and returns of social capital: Evidence from urban China. In R.M. Hsung, N. Lin, & R.L. Breiger (Eds.), *Contexts of social capital: Social networks in markets, communities, and families* (pp. 163–192). New York: Routledge.

Lindsey, R.B., Roberts, L.M., & CampbellJones, F. (2005). *The culturally proficient school: An implementation guide for school leaders*. Thousand Oaks, CA: Corwin Press.

Link, B.G., & Phelan, J.C. (2001). Conceptualizing stigma. *Annual Review of Sociology, 27*, 363–385.

Litchfield, M., & Watson, J.C. (2009). Clinical mental health counseling. In American Counseling Association (Ed.), *The ACA encyclopedia of counseling* (pp. 101–103). Alexandria, VA: American Counseling Association.

Liu, W.M. (2002). The social class–related experiences of men: Integrating theory and practice. *Professional Psychology: Research and Practice, 33*, 355–360.

Liu, W.M. (2011). *Social class and classism in the helping professions: Research, theory and practice*. Thousand Oaks: Sage.

Liu, W.M., & Ali, S.R. (2005). Addressing social class and classism in vocational theory and practice: Extending the emancipatory communitarian approach. *Counseling Psychologist, 33*, 189–196.

Liu, W.M., Ali, S.R., Soleck, G., Hopps, J., Dunston, K., & Pickett, T. (2004). Using social class in counseling psychology research. *Journal of Counseling Psychology, 51*, 3–18.

Liu, W.M., & Arguello, J.L. (2006). Using social class and classism in counseling. *Counseling and Human Development, 39*(3), 1–10.

Liu, W.M., & Estrada-Hernandez, N. (2010). Counseling and advocacy for individuals living in poverty. In M.J. Ratts, R.L. Toporek, & J.A. Lewis (Eds.), *ACA advocacy competencies: A social justice framework for counselors* (pp. 43–53). Alexandria, VA: American Counseling Association.

Liu, W.M., Hernandez, J., Mahmood, A., & Stinson, R. (2006). Linking poverty, classism, and racism in mental health. In D.W. Sue & M.G. Constantine (Eds.), *Addressing racism: Facilitating cultural competence in mental health and educational settings* (pp. 65–86). New York: Wiley.

Liu, W.M., Pickett, T., & Ivey, A.E. (2007). White middle-class privilege: Social class bias and implications for training and practice. *Journal of Multicultural Counseling and Development, 35,* 194–206.

Liu, W.M., & Pope-Davis, D.B. (2004). Understanding classism to effect personal change. In T.B. Smith (Ed.), *Practicing multiculturalism: Affirming diversity in counseling and psychology* (pp. 294–310). Boston: Pearson.

Liu, W.M., Soleck, G., Hopps, J., Dunston, K., & Pickett, T. (2004). A new framework to understand social class in counseling: The social class worldview model and modern classism theory. *Journal of Multicultural Counseling and Development, 32,* 95–132.

Lopez-Baez, S.I., & Paylo, M.J. (2009). Social justice advocacy: Community collaboration and systems advocacy. *Journal of Counseling and Development, 87,* 276–283.

Lorde, A. (1984). *Sister outsider.* Trumansburg, NY: The Crossing Press.

Lott, B. (2002). Cognitive and behavioral distancing from the poor. *American Psychologist, 57,* 100–110.

Lott, B., & Saxon, S. (2002). The influence of ethnicity, social class, and context on judgments about U.S. women. *The Journal of Social Psychology, 142,* 481–499. doi: 10.1080/00224540209603913

Lustig, D.C., & Strauser, D.R. (2007). Causal relationships between poverty and disability. *Rehabilitation Counseling Bulletin, 50*(4), 194–202.

Luthar, S.S. (2003). The culture of affluence: Psychological costs of material wealth. *Child Development, 73,* 1593–1610.

Luthar, S.S., & Becker, B.E. (2002). Privileged but pressured? A study of affluent youth. *Child Development, 74,* 1581–1593.

Luthar, S.S., & D'Avanzo, K. (1999). Contextual factors in substance use: A student of suburban and inner-city adolescents. *Development and Psychopathology, 11,* 845–867.

Luthar, S.S., & Latendresse, S.J. (2005). Children of the affluent: Challenges to well being. *Current Directions in Psychological Science, 14*(1), 49–53.

Luthar, S.S., & Sexton, C. (2005). The high price of affluence. In R.V. Kail (Ed.), *Advances in child development* (vol. 32, pp. 126–162). San Diego, CA: Academic Press.

Luthar, S.S., Shoum, K.A., & Brown, P.J. (2006). Extracurricular involvement among affluent youth: A scapegoat for ubiquitous achievement pressures? *Developmental Psychology, 42,* 583–597.

Manis, A.A., Brown, S.L., & Paylo, M.J. (2009). The helping professional as an advocate. In C.M. Ellis & J. Carlson (Eds.), *Cross cultural awareness and social justice in counseling* (pp. 23–44). New York: Routledge.

Manning, M., & Baruth, L. (2004). *Multicultural education of children and adolescents* (4th ed.). Boston: Pearson Education.

Markus, H., & Nurius, P. (1986). Possible selves. *American Psychologist, 41,* 954–969. doi: 10.1037/0003-066X.41.9.954

Maruish, M.E. (2002). *Essentials of treatment planning.* New York: Wiley.

Marx, K., & Engels, F. (2011). *The communist manifesto.* New York: Tribeca Books. (Original work published 1848.)

Maslow, A.H. (1943). A theory of human motivation. *Psychological Review, 50*(4), 370–396.

Mason, J., & Sullivan, A. (2011). *Factbox: What is "middle class" in the United States?* Reuters. Retrieved April 11, 2011, from http://www.reuters.com/article/2010/09/14/us-usa-taxes-middleclass-idUSTRE68D3QD20100914

Masucci, M., & Renner, A. (2000). Reading the lives of others: The Winton Homes Library Project—A cultural studies analysis of critical service learning for education. *High School Journal, 84*, 36–47.

Matthews, K.A., Räikkönen, K., Everson, S.A., Flory, J.D., Marco, C.A., Owens, J.F., et al. (2000). Do the daily experiences of healthy men and women vary according to occupational prestige and work strain? *Psychosomatic Medicine, 62*, 346–353.

Mattek, R.J., Jorgenson, E.T., & Fox, R.A. (2010). Home-based therapy for young children in low-income families: A student training program. *The Family Journal, 18*(2), 189–194.

Mattingly, M.J., & Bean, J.A. (2010). *The unequal distribution of child poverty: Highest rates among young blacks and children of single mothers in rural America.* Durham, NH: The Carsey Institute.

Mattingly, M.J., & Turcotte-Seabury, C. (2010). *Understanding very high rates of young child poverty in the South.* Durham, NH: Carsey Institute.

McAuliffe, G. (2008). *Culturally alert counseling: A comprehensive introduction.* Thousand Oaks, CA: Sage Publications.

McCarn, S.R., & Fassinger, R.E. (1996). Revisioning sexual minority identity formation. *The Counseling Psychologist, 24*, 508–534.

McConnell, S., & Ohls, J. (2002). Food stamps in rural America: Special issues and common themes. In B.A. Weber, G.J. Duncan, & L.A. Whitener (Eds.), *Rural dimensions of welfare reform* (pp. 413–432). Kalamazoo, MI: Upjohn Institute.

McGoldrick, M., & Giordano, J. (1996). Overview: Ethnicity and family therapy. In M. McGoldrick, J.Giordano, & J. Pearce (Eds.), *Ethnicity and family therapy* (2nd ed., pp. 1–27). New York: Guilford Press.

McIntosh, P. (1988). White privilege: Unpacking the invisible knapsack. Retrieved May 30, 2011, from http://www.nymbp.org/reference/WhitePrivilege.pdf

McIntosh, P. (2003). White privilege: Unpacking the invisible knapsack. In S. Plous (Ed.), *Understanding prejudice and discrimination* (pp. 191–196). New York: McGraw-Hill.

McKamy, E.H. (1976). Social work with the wealthy. In. F.J. Turner (Ed.), *Differential diagnosis and treatment in social work* (pp. 1109–1114). New York: The Free Press.

McLuhan, M. (1994). *Understanding media: The extensions of man.* Cambridge, MA: MIT.

McMahon, T.J., & Luthar, S.S. (2006). Patterns and correlates of substance use among affluent, suburban high school students. *Journal of Clinical Child and Adolescent Psychology, 35*, 72–89.

McNamee, S.J., & Miller, R.K., Jr. (2009). *The meritocracy myth* (2nd ed.). Lanham, MD: Rowman & Littlefield.

Melki, I.S., Beydoun, H.A., Khogali, M., Tamim, H., & Yunis, K.A. (2004). Household crowding index: A correlate of socioeconomic status and interpregnancy spacing in an urban setting. *Journal of Epidemiology and Community Health, 58*, 476–480.

Menacker, J. (1976). Toward a theory of activist guidance. *Personnel and Guidance Journal, 54*, 318–321.

Mendez, J.L., Carpenter, J.L., LaForett, D.R., & Cohen, J.S. (2009). Parental engagement and barriers to participation in a community-based preventive intervention. *American Journal of Community Psychology, 44*, 1–14.

Merriam-Webster collegiate dictionary (10th ed.). (1999). Springfield, MA: Merriam Webster.

Merriam-Webster collegiate dictionary (11th ed.). (2005). Springfield, MA: Merriam Webster.

Merwin, E., Hinton, I., Dembling, B., & Stern, S. (2003). Shortages of rural mental health professionals. *Archives of Psychiatric Nursing, 17*, 42–51.

Merwin, E., Snyder, A., & Katz, E. (2006). Differential access to quality rural healthcare: Professional and policy challenges. *Family and Community Health, 29*, 186–194.

Meyer, D., & Ponton, R. (2006). The healthy tree: A metaphorical perspective of counselor well-being. *Journal of Mental Health Counseling, 28*(3), 189–201.

Mickelson, K.D., & Williams, S.L. (2008). Perceived stigma of poverty and depression: Examination of interpersonal and intrapersonal mediators. *Journal of Social and Clinical Psychology, 27*(9), 903–930.

Miller, K.K., Crandall, M.S., & Weber, B.A. (2002). *Persistent poverty and place: How do persistent poverty and poverty demographics vary across the rural-urban continuum.* Washington, DC: Economic Research Service.

Milner, J., & O'Byrne, P. (2004). *Assessment in counseling: Theory, process, and decision-making.* New York: Palgrave.

Mississippi State Board of Examiners for Licensed Professional Counselors. (2011). *Rules and regulations*. Retrieved June 19, 2011, from http://www.lpc.state.ms.us/t3/rulesandregs.htm

Monk, G., Winslade, J., & Sinclair, S. (2008). *New horizons in multicultural counseling*. Los Angeles: Sage.

Muennig, P., Fiscella, K., Tancredi, D., & Franks, P. (2010). The relative health burden of selected social and behavioral risk factors in the United States: Implications for policy. *American Journal of Public Health, 100*(9), 1758–1764. doi:10.2105/AJPH.2009.165019

Muntaner, C., Borrell, C., & Chung, H. (2007). Class relations, economic inequality and mental health. In W.R. Avison, J.D. McLeod, & B.A. Pescosolido (Eds.), *Mental health, social mirror* (pp. 127–141). New York: Springer Science + Business Media.

Murali, V., & Oyebode, F. (2004). Poverty, social inequality and mental health. *Advances in Psychiatric Treatment, 10*, 216–224.

Myers, J.E., & Gill, C.S. (2004). Poor, rural, and female: Under-studied, under-counseled, more at-risk. *Journal of Mental Health Counseling, 26*(3), 225–242.

Myers, J.E., & Sweeney, T.J. (2008). Wellness counseling: The evidence base for practice. *Journal of Counseling and Development, 86*, 482–493.

Narcisse, D. (2010). Disconnected, disenfranchised, and poor: Addressing digital inequality in America. *Working-Class Perspectives: Commentary from the Center for Working Class Studies.* Retrieved June 21, 2011, from http://workingclassstudies.wordpress.com/category/issues/class-and-education/

National Association of Social Workers. (2001). *Standards for cultural competence in social work practice.* Retrieved June 8, 2011, from http://www.socialworkers.org/practice/

National Association of Social Work. (2008). *Code of ethics.* Retrieved June 8, 2011, from http://www.socialworkers.org/pubs/code/code.asp

National Center for Education Statistics. (2011). The Condition of Education 2010. Retrieved November 21, 2011 from http://nces.ed.gov

Nelson, M.L., Englar-Carson, M., Tierney, S.C., & Hau, J.M. (2006). Class jumping into academia: Multiple identities for counseling academics. *Journal of Counseling Psychology, 53*, 1–14.

Neukrug, E.S., & Fawcett, R.C. (2006). *Essentials of testing and assessment: A practical guide for counselors, social workers, and psychologists*. Belmont, CA: Thomson/Brooks Cole.

Newton, K.S. (2010). Social class and classism. In D.G. Hays & B.T. Erford (Eds.), *Developing multicultural counseling competence: A systems approach* (pp. 142–165). Boston: Pearson.

No Child Left Behind (NCLB). Act, 20 U.S.C. § 16301 et seq.

Nyman, S.J., Nafziger, M.A., & Smith, T.B. (2010). Client outcomes across counselor training level within a multi-tiered supervision model. *Journal of Counseling and Development, 88*, 204–209.
O'Connor, A. (2000). Poverty research and policy for the post-welfare era. *Annual Review of Sociology, 26*, 547–562.
O'Connor, A. (2001). *Poverty knowledge*. Princeton, NJ: Princeton University Press.
Ostrove, J., & Long, S. (2007). Social class and belonging: Implications for college adjustment. *The Review of Higher Education, 30*(4), 363–387.
Paisley, P.O., & Hayes, R.L. (2002). Transformations in school counselor preparation and practice. *Counseling and Human Development, 35*(3), 1–10.
Paniagua, F.A. (2005). *Assessing and treating culturally diverse clients*. Thousand Oaks, CA: Sage.
Pattillo-McCoy, M. (1999). *Black picket fences: Privilege and peril among the black middle class*. Chicago: University of Chicago Press.
Patton, W., & McIlveen, P. (2009). Practice and research in career counseling and development—2008. *Career Development Quarterly, 58*(2), 118–161. Retrieved from http://www.associationdatabase.com/aws/NCDA/pt/sp/cdquarterly
Payne, R. (2005). *A framework for understanding poverty*. (4th ed.) Highlands, TX: aha! Process.
Payne, R. (2008, April). Nine powerful practices: Nine strategies help raise the achievement of students living in poverty. *Educational Leadership, 65*, 48–52.
Payne, R.K. (1996). *A framework for understanding poverty*. Highlands, TX: aha! Process.
Pedersen, P.B. (2003). Culturally biased assumptions in counseling psychology. *The Counseling Psychologist, 31*, 396–403.
Perese, E.F. (2007). Stigma, poverty, and victimization: Roadblocks to recovery for individuals with severe mental illness. Journal of the *American Psychiatric Nurses Association, 13*(5), 285–296.
Perrucci, R., & Wysong, E. (2008). *The new class society: Goodbye American dream?* (3rd ed.). Lanham, MD: Rowman & Littlefield.
Perry, J.C., & Vance, K.S. (2010). Possible selves among urban youth of color: An exploration of peer beliefs and gender differences. *Career Development Quarterly, 58*, 257–269. Retrieved from http://www.associationdatabase.com/aws/NCDA/pt/sp/cdquarterly
Petterson, S., Williams, I.C., Hauenstein, E.J., Rovnyak, V., & Merwin, E. (2009). Race and ethnicity and rural mental health treatment. *Journal of Health Care for the Poor and Underserved, 20*(3), 662–677.
Piff, P.K., Kraus, M.W., Côté, S., Cheng, B.H., & Keltner, D. (2010). Having less, giving more: The influence of social class on prosocial behavior. *Journal of Personality and Social Psychology, 99*, 771–784.
Pittman, F.S. (1985). Children of the rich. *Family Process, 24*, 461–472.
Portal, E., Suck, A., & Hinkle, J. (2010). Counseling in Mexico: History, current identity, and future trends. *Journal of Counseling and Development, 88*(1), 33–37.
Poster, W.R., & Wilson, G. (2008). Introduction: Race, class, and gender in transnational labor inequality. *American Behavioral Scientist, 52*(3), 295–306. doi: 10.1177/0002764208323508
Prilleltensky, I. (2003). Understanding, resisting, and overcoming oppression: Toward psychopolitical validity. *American Journal of Community Psychology, 31*(1-2), 195–201.
Prilleltensky, I. (2010). Child wellness and social inclusion: Values for action. *Journal of Community Psychology, 46*(1–2), 238–249.
Racz, S., McMahon, R., & Luthar, S. (2011). Risky behavior in affluent youth: Examining the co-occurrence and consequences of multiple problem behaviors. *Journal of Child and Family Studies, 20*(1), 120–128.
Rank, M.R., & Hirschl, T.A. (1999). The likelihood of poverty across the American adult life span. *Social Work, 44*, 201–216.

Ratts, M. (2006). Social justice counseling: A study of social justice counselor training in CACREP-accredited counselor preparation programs (doctoral dissertation, Oregon State University, 2006). *Dissertation Abstracts International, 67*, 1234.

Ratts, M.J., DeKruyf, L., & Chen-Hayes, S.F. (2007). The ACA advocacy competencies: A social justice advocacy framework for professional school counselors. *Professional School Counseling, 11*, 90–97.

Ratts, M.J., & Hutchins, A.M. (2009). ACA advocacy competencies: Social justice advocacy at the client/student level. *Journal of Counseling and Development, 87*, 269–275.

Reece, J., & Gambhir, S. (2008). *The geography of opportunity: Review of opportunity mapping research initiatives.* Retrieved from the Kirwan Institute for the Study of Race and Ethnicity website: http://4909e99d35cada63e7f757471b7243be73e53e14.gripelements.com/pdfs/Opportunity_Mapping_Research_Initiatives.pdf

Remley, T.P., & Herlihy, B. (2010). *Ethical, legal, and professional issues in counseling* (3rd ed.). Upper Saddle River, NJ: Pearson Education.

Robbins, V., Dollard, N., Armstrong, B.J., Kutash, K., & Vergon, K.S. (2008). Mental health needs of poor suburban and rural children and their families. *Journal of Loss and Trauma, 13*, 94–122.

Robinson, T.L., & Howard-Hamilton, M.F. (2000). *The convergence of race, ethnicity and gender: Multiple identities in counseling.* Upper Saddle River, NJ: Merrill.

Rogalsky, J. (2009). Mythbusters: Dispelling the culture of poverty myth in the urban classroom. *Journal of Geography, 108*, 198–209.

Roosa, M.W., Morgan-Lopez, A., Cree, W., & Specter, M. (2002). Ethnic culture, poverty, and context: Sources of influence on Latino families and children. In J. Contreras, A. Neal-Barnett, & K. Kerns (Eds.), *Latino children and families in the United States: Current research and future directions* (pp. 27–44). Westport, CT: Praeger.

Rosenfeld, A., & Wise, N. (2001). *The overscheduled child: Avoiding the hyper parenting trap.* New York: St. Martin's Griffin.

Schmidt, P. (2010). In push for diversity, colleges pay attention to socioeconomic class. *The Chronicle of Higher Education.* Retrieved September 21, 2010, from http://chronicle.com/In-Push-For-Diversity/124446

Schnitzer, P.K. (1996). "They don't come in!" Stories told, lessons taught about poor families in therapy. *American Journal of Orthopsychiatry, 66*(4), 572–582.

Schure, M.B., Christopher, J., & Christopher, S. (2008). Mind-body medicine and the art of self-care: Teaching mindfulness to counseling students through yoga, meditation, and qigong. *Journal of Counseling and Development, 86*, 47–56.

Schwartz, B. (2000). Self-determination: The tyranny of freedom. *American Psychologist, 55*, 79–88.

Scott, D. (2010). Working within and between organisations. In F. Arney & D. Scott (Eds.), *Working with vulnerable families: A partnership approach* (pp. 71–89). New York: Cambridge University Press.

Scott, J. (2005). Life at the top in America isn't just better, it's longer. In *The New York Times* (Ed.), *Class Matters* (pp. 27–50). New York: Henry Holt.

Seccombe, K. (2002). "Beating the odds" versus "changing the odds": Poverty, resilience, and family policy. *Journal of Marriage and Family, 64*, 384–394.

Sedlak, A.J., Mettenburg, J., Basena, M., Petta, I., McPerson, K., Greene, A., et al. (2010). *Fourth National Incidence Study of Child Abuse and Neglect (NIS-4): Report to Congress.* Retrieved from U.S. Department of Health and Human Services Administration for Children, Youth, and Families website: http://www.acf.hhs.gov/programs/opre/abuse_neglect/natl_incid/index.html

Seligman, L. (2004). *Diagnosis and treatment planning in counseling* (3rd ed.). New York: Kluwer Academic/Plenum Publishers.

Sennett, R., & Cobb, J. (1972). *The hidden injuries of class*. New York: Knopf.

Shafran, R.B. (1992). Children of affluent parents. In J.D. O'Brien, D.J. Pilowsky, & O.W. Lewis (Eds.), *Psychotherapies with children and adolescents: Adapting the psychodynamic process* (pp. 269–288). Washington, DC: American Psychiatric Press.

Shainess, N. (1991). Countertransference problems with money. In S. Klebanow & E.L. Lowenkopf (Eds.), *Money and mind* (pp. 163–173). New York: Plenum Press.

Shapiro, T.M. (2004). *The hidden cost of being African American: How wealth perpetuates inequality*. New York: Oxford University Press.

Shipler, D.K. (2004). *The working poor: Invisible in America*. New York: Vintage Books.

Sidel, R. (1996). *Keeping women and children last*. New York: Penguin Books.

Singleton-Bowie, S.M. (1995). The effect of mental health practitioners' racial sensitivity on African Americans' perceptions of service. *Social Work Research, 19*(4), 238–244.

Slesnick, N., & Prestopnik, J.L. (2004). Office versus home-based family therapy for runaway, alcohol abusing adolescents: Examination of factors associated with treatment attendance. *Alcoholism Treatment Quarterly, 22*(2), 3–19.

Smith, E. (1989). Black racial identity development: Issues and concerns. *The Counseling Psychologist, 17*(2), 277–288.

Smith, L. (2005). Psychotherapy, classism, and the poor: Conspicuous by their absence. *American Psychologist, 60*(7), 687–696.

Smith, L. (2009). Enhancing training and practice in the context of poverty. *Training and Education in Professional Psychology, 3*(2), 84–93.

Smith, L. (2010). *Psychology, poverty, and the end of social exclusion: Putting our practice to work*. New York: Teachers College Press.

Smith, L., Chambers, D., & Bratini, L. (2009). When oppression is the pathogen: The participatory development of socially just mental health practice. *American Journal of Orthopsychiatry, 79*(2), 159–168.

Smith, L., Foley, P.F., &. Chaney, M.P. (2008). Addressing classism, ableism, and heterosexism in counselor education. *Journal of Counseling and Development, 86*, 303–309.

Smith, L.C., and Shin, R.Q. (2008). Social privilege, social justice, and group counseling: An inquiry. *Journal for Specialists in Group Work, 33*, 351–366.

Smith, S.D., Reynolds, C.A., & Rovnak, A. (2009). A critical analysis of the social advocacy movement in counseling. *Journal of Counseling and Development, 87*, 483–491.

Sokoloff, N.J., & Dupont, I. (2005). Domestic violence at the intersections of race, class, and gender. *Violence Against Women, 11*, 38–64.

Srole, L., & Langner, T.S. (1962a). Socioeconomic status groups: Their mental health comparison. In L. Srole, T.S. Langner, S.T. Michael, M.K. Opler, & T.A. Rennie (Eds.), *Mental health in the metropolis* (pp. 210–239). New York: McGraw-Hill.

Srole, L., & Langner, T.S. (1962b). Socioeconomic status groups: Their psychiatric patient. In L. Srole, T.S. Langner, S.T. Michael, M.K. Opler, & T.A. Rennie (Eds.), *Mental health in the metropolis* (pp. 240–252). New York: McGraw-Hill.

Srole, L., Langner, T.S., Michael, S.T., Opler, M.K., & Rennie, T.A. (1962). *Mental health in the metropolis*. New York: McGraw-Hill.

Stacey, B.G., & Singer, M.S. (1985). The perception of poverty and wealth among teenagers. *Journal of Adolescence, 8*, 231–241.

Stanley, T.J., & Danko, W.D. (1996). *The millionaire next door: The surprising secrets of America's wealthy*. Lanham, MD: Taylor Trade Publishing.

Staton, A.R. (2009). Socioeconomic status/socioeconomic class. In American Counseling Association (Ed.), *American Counseling Association encyclopedia of counseling* (pp. 508–510). Alexandria, VA: ACA.

Steele, C.M., & Aronson, J. (1995). Stereotype threat and the intellectual test performance of African-Americans. *Journal of Personality and Social Psychology, 69*, 797–811.

Stevens, J., Kelleher, K.J., Ward-Estes, J., & Hayes, J. (2006). Perceived barriers to treatment and psychotherapy attendance in child community mental health centers. *Community Mental Health Journal, 42*(5), 449–458.

Strier, R. (2009). Class-competent social work: A preliminary definition. *International Journal of Social Welfare, 18*, 237–242. doi: 10.1111/j.1468-2397.2008.00588.x

Strolovitch, D.Z. (2006). Do interest groups represent the disadvantaged? Advocacy at the intersections of race, class, and gender. *Journal of Politics, 68*, 894–910. doi: 10.1111/j.1468–2508.2006.00488.x

Sue, D.W., Arredondo, P., & McDavis, R.J. (1992). Multicultural counseling competencies and standards: A call to the profession. *Journal of Counseling and Development, 70*, 477–486.

Sue, D.W., Capodilupo, C.M., Torino, G.C., Bucceri, J.M., Holder, A.M.B., Nadal, K.L., et al. (2007). Racial microaggressions in everyday life: Implications for clinical practice. *American Psychologist, 62*(4), 271–286. doi: 10.1073/00003-066X.62.4.271

Sue, D.W., & Sue, D. (2008). *Counseling the culturally diverse: Theory and practice*. Hoboken, NJ: Wiley.

Sue, S. (1999). Science, ethnicity, and bias. Where have we gone wrong? *American Psychologist, 54*, 1070–1077.

Super, D., Savickas, M., & Super, C.M. (1996). The life-span, life-space approach to careers. In D. Brown, L. Brooks, & Associates (Eds.), *Career choice and development* (3rd ed., pp. 121–178). San Francisco: Jossey-Bass.

Thompson, M.F. (2009). Earnings of a lifetime: Comparing women and men with college and graduate degrees. *In Context, 10*(2), Retrieved April 1, 2011, from http://www.incontext.indiana.edu/2009/mar-apr/article1.asp

Thorne, D., Tickamyer, A., & Thorne, M. (2004). Poverty and income in Appalachia. *Journal of Appalachian Studies 10*(3), 341–357.

Tickamyer, A.J., White, J., Tadlock, B., Tadlock, & Henderson, D. (2007). Spatial politics of public policy. In L. Lobao, G. Hooks, & A. Tickamyer (Eds.), *The sociology of spatial inequalities* (pp. 113–139). Albany: SUNY Press.

Tomlinson-Clarke, S.M., & Clarke, D. (2010). Culturally focused community-centered service learning: An international cultural immersion experience. *Journal of Multicultural Counseling and Development, 38*, 166–175.

Toporek, R., Gerstein, L., Fouad, N., Roysircar, G., & Israel, T. (Eds.). (2006). *Handbook for social justice in counseling psychology: Leadership, vision, and action*. Thousand Oaks, CA: Sage.

Toporek, R.L., Lewis, J.A., & Crethar, H C. (2009). Promoting systemic change through the ACA advocacy competencies. *Journal of Counseling and Development, 87*, 260–268.

Toporek, R.L., & Liu, W.M. (2001). Advocacy in counseling: Addressing race, class, and gender oppression. In D.B. Pope-Davis & H.L.K. Coleman (Eds.), *The intersection of race, class, and gender in multicultural counseling* (pp. 385–416). Thousand Oaks, CA: Sage.

Toporek, R.L., & Pope-Davis, D.B. (2005). Exploring the relationships between multicultural training, racial attitudes, and attributions of poverty among graduate counseling trainees. *Cultural Diversity and Ethnic Minority Psychology, 11*(3), 259–271.

Tough, P. (2007, June 10). The class-consciousness raiser. *The New York Times*. Retrieved from http://www.nytimes.com/2007/06/10/magazine/10payne-t.html?scp=1&sq=the+class-consciousnessraiser&st=nyt

Trusty, J., & Brown, D. (2005). Advocacy competencies for professional school counselors. *Professional School Counseling, 8*, 259–265.

Tse, T.M., (2011). Buffett slams tax system disparities. *The Washington Post*, June 27, 2007. Retrieved February 6, 2011, from http://www.washingtonpost.com/wp-dyn/content/article/2007/06/27/AR2007062700097.html

United for a Fair Economy. (March 17, 2011). Schakowsky introduces bill to tax millionaires & billionaires. In Pressroom. Retrieved November 30, 2011, from http://faireconomy.org/press_room/2011/rep_schakowskys_bill_to_tax_millionaires_billionaires

U.S. Census Bureau. (2010, September). *Poverty: 2008 and 2009 American community survey briefs*. Retrieved March 28, 2011, from http://www.census.gov/prod/2010pubs/acsbr09-1.pdf

U.S. Department of Education. (2001). *1999–2000 schools and staffing survey analysis*. Washington, DC: Author.

U.S. Department of Veterans Affairs. (2009, September). VA, NIH to fund $7 million in substance abuse studies: Effort to focus on troops, veterans of operations Enduring Freedom and Iraqi Freedom. *VA Research Currents: Research News from the U.S. Dept. of Veterans Affairs* (p. 6). Retrieved June 9, 2011, from www.research.va.gov/resources/pubs/docs/va_research_currents_sept_09.pdf

Van de Werfhorst, H.G. (2002). A detailed examination of the role of education in intergenerational social class mobility. *Social Science Information, 41*(3), 407–438.

Vandiver, B.J., Fhagen-Smith, P.E., Cokley, K.O., Cross, W.E., Jr., & Worrell, F.C. (2001). Cross's Nigrescence model: From theory to scale to theory. *Journal of Multicultural Counseling and Development, 29*, 174–200.

Van Dorn, R.A., Kosterman, R., Williams, J.H., Chandler, K., Young, M.S., Catalano, R.F., et al. (2010). The relationship between outpatient mental health treatment and subsequent mental health symptoms and disorders in young adults. *Administration and Policy in Mental Health, 37*(6), 484–496.

Vasquez, M.J.T. (2007). Cultural difference and the therapeutic alliance: An evidence based analysis. *American Psychologist, 62*(8), 878–885.

Vick, B., Jones, K., & Mitra, S. (2010). *Poverty and psychiatric diagnosis in the U.S.: Evidence from the medical expenditure panel survey*. Fordham University Department of Economics Discussion Paper Series. Retrieved March 28, 2011, from http://www.fordham.edu/images/academics/graduate_schools/gsas/economics/dp2010_11_vick_jones_mitra.pdf

Vigeland, T. (2008). What is the middle class? *Marketplace Money*. Retrieved from http://marketplace.publicradio.org/display/web/2008/01/11/what_is_the_middle_class

Vona-Davis, L., & Rose, D.P. (2009). The influence of socioeconomic disparities on breast cancer tumor biology and prognosis: A review. *Journal of Women's Health, 18*(6), 883–893.

von Bertalanffy, L. (1950). An outline of general system theory. *British Journal for the Philosophy of Science, 1*, 134–165.

Wadsworth, M.E., & Santiago, C.D. (2008). Risk and resiliency processes in ethnically diverse families in poverty. *Journal of Family Psychology, 22*(3), 399–410.

Waldegrave, C. (2005). "Just therapy" with families on low incomes. *Child Welfare League of America, 2*, 265–276.

Ware, N.C., & Goldfinger, S.M. (1997). Poverty and rehabilitation in severe psychiatric disorders. *Psychiatric Rehabilitation Journal, 21*(1), 3–9.

Ware, N.C., Tugenberg, T., & Dickey, B. (2004). Practitioner relationships and quality of care for low-income persons with serious mental illness. *Psychiatric Services, 55*(5), 555–559.

Warner, S.L. (1991). Psychoanalytic understanding and treatment of the very rich. In S. Klebanow & E.L. Lowenkopf (Eds.), *Money and mind* (pp. 183–195). New York: Plenum Press.

Warner, W.L., Meeker, M., & Eels, K. (1960). What social class is in America. In *Social class in America* (pp. 3–33). New York: Harper & Row.

Watts, R.J. (1994). Paradigms of diversity. In E.J. Trickett, R.J. Watts, & D. Birman (Eds.), *Human diversity: Perspectives on people in context* (pp. 49–80). San Francisco: Jossey-Bass.

Waughray, A. (2010). Caste discrimination and minority rights: Case of India's Dalits. *International Journal on Minority and Group Rights, 17*, 327–353.

Weber, L. (1998). A conceptual framework for understanding race, class, gender, and sexuality. *Psychology of Women Quarterly, 22*, 13–32.

Weber, M. (1978). Economy and society: An outline of interpretive sociology. In G. Roth & C. Wittich, (Eds.), *Economic sociology* (pp. 100–103). Berkeley: University of California Press.

Weissberg, J. (1991). The fiscal blindspot in therapy. In S. Klebanow & E.L. Lowenkopf (Eds.), *Money and mind* (pp. 245–251). New York: Plenum Press.

Westefeld, J.S., & Heckman-Stone, C. (2003). The integrated problem-solving model of crisis intervention: Overview and application. *The Counseling Psychologist, 31*(2), 221–239.

West-Olatunji, C. (2008). Culture-centered case conceptualization: The case of "Joseph." In C. Lee, D. Burnhill, A. Butler, C.P. Hipolito-Delgado, M. Humphrey, O. Munoz, et al. (Eds.), *Elements of culture in counseling.* (pp. 163–176). Upper Saddle River, NJ: Pearson.

West-Olatunji, C. (2010a). ACA advocacy competencies with culturally diverse clients. In M.J. Ratts, R.L. Toporek, & J.R. Lewis, *ACA advocacy competencies: A social justice framework* (pp. 55–64). Alexandria, VA: American Counseling Association.

West-Olatunji, C. (2010b). Book review of *Psychology, poverty, and the end of social exclusion: Putting our practice to work. Teachers College Record*, ID 16222. Retrieved November 4, 2010, from http://www.tcrecord.org

Whittaker, V.A., & Neville, H.A. (2010). Examining the relation between racial identity attitude clusters and psychological health outcomes in African American college students. *Journal of Black Psychology, 36*(4), 383–409.

Williams, D.R. (1995). African American mental health: Persisting questions and paradoxal findings. *African American Research Perspectives, 2*(1), 8–16.

Williams, W.R. (2009). Struggling with poverty: Implications for theory and policy of increasing research on social class-based stigma. *Analyses of Social Issues and Public Policy, 9*(1), 37–56.

Wilton, R. (2004). Putting policy into practice? Poverty and people with serious mental illness. *Social Science and Medicine, 58*(1), 25–39.

Wittchen, H. (2010). Women-specific mental disorders in DSM-V: Are we failing again? *Archives of Women's Mental Health, 13*(1), 51–55. doi: 10.1007/s00737-009-0138-6

Wolfe, J.L., & Fodor, I.G. (1996). The poverty of privilege: Therapy with women of the "upper classes." *Women and Therapy, 18*, 73–89.

Women's Theological Center. (1997). *The invisibility of upper class privilege.* Retrieved June 9, 2011, from http://www.thewtc.org/Invisibility_of_Class_Privilege.pdf

World Health Organization. (2011). *Gender and women's mental health.* Retrieved March 28, 2011, from http://www.who.int/mental_health/prevention/genderwomen/en/

Wright, L.S.H. (2009). The death of the American dream. *Virginia Quarterly Review, 85*(4), 196–199.

Yates, T.M., Tracy, A.J., & Luthar, S.S. (2008). Nonsuicidal self-injury among "privileged" youths: Longitudinal and cross-sectional approaches to developmental process. *Journal of Counseling and Clinical Psychology, 76*, 52–62.

Yoshino, I.R., & Murakoshi, S. (1977). *The invisible visible minority*. Osaka, Japan: Buraku Kaiho Kenkyusho Press.

Young, A.M.W., Meryn, S., & Treadwell, H.M. (2008). Poverty and men's health. *Journal of Men's Health, 5*, 184–188.

Zakaria, F. (2010, November). Restoring the American dream. *Time, 176*(18), 30–35.

Index

B

C

D

E

F

G

H

I

L

M

N

O

P

For Product Safety Concerns and Information please contact our EU representative GPSR@taylorandfrancis.com Taylor & Francis Verlag GmbH, Kaufingerstraße 24, 80331 München, Germany